茶文化‖学英语

张丽霞　朱法荣　主编

中国出版集团
世界图书出版公司
西安　北京　上海　广州

图书在版编目（CIP）数据

茶文化学英语/张丽霞，朱法荣主编. —西安：世界图书出版西安有限公司，2015.9（2024.7重印）
ISBN 978-7-5100-8493-5

Ⅰ. ①茶… Ⅱ. ①张…②朱… Ⅲ. ①茶叶—文化—英语—教材 Ⅳ. ①H31

中国版本图书馆CIP数据核字（2015）第236203号

茶文化学英语

主　　编	张丽霞　朱法荣
责任编辑	李江彬
出版发行	世界图书出版西安有限公司
地　　址	西安市雁塔区曲江新区汇新路355号
邮　　编	710061
电　　话	029-87233647(市场营销部)
	029-87234767(总编室)
传　　真	029-87279675
经　　销	全国各地新华书店
印　　刷	陕西龙山海天艺术印务有限公司
开　　本	185mm×260mm　1/16
印　　张	15.25
字　　数	300千
版　　次	2015年9月第1版
印　　次	2024年7月第7次印刷
书　　号	ISBN 978-7-5100-8493-5
定　　价	40.00元

☆如有印装错误,请寄回本公司更换☆

前 言
Foreword

随着我国经济腾飞和国际影响力的增强,进一步提高我国文化软实力,实现中华民族的伟大复兴,是近年来我国政府的一项重要举措,而源远流长的茶文化正是中华传统文化中最靓丽的名片之一。

我国是茶的原产地和茶文化的发源地,是世界上最早发现和利用茶树的国家。我国不仅有着世界上最丰富的茶树种质资源、多姿多彩的茶叶产品和精湛的茶叶加工技艺,而且有着源远流长和独具东方特色的茶文化。在历史的悠悠长河中,中华茶文化通过多种途径不断向外传播,使茶成为风靡世界的三大无酒精饮料之一,目前世界上有160多个国家和地区的近30亿人口在饮茶。然而,对于中国人而言,茶绝非一杯普通的饮料,人们已不仅仅局限于解渴饮茶、保健饮茶,而是将饮茶上升为品茶,使之与情感交流、生活情趣和修身养性相结合,逐渐成为调节现代社会的一种慢生活方式。人们在品茶之间,感受自然和艺术之美,体验一叶一菩提的禅境之美,感悟中国哲人的人生智慧。

近年来,国际茶文化活动频繁,极大地促进了世界对中国茶文化的了解,但我们同时也感觉到,要使中国茶文化更好地走向世界，需要有一大批真正懂茶并了解中国传统文化、英语沟通能力强的人才致力于传播中国茶文化，才能跨越文化和语言的鸿沟，以茶为媒搭建起一座中西方文化交流的桥梁。目前高校茶学本科课程中开设有《茶学专业英语》，但缺乏正式出版的教材，讲授内容通常较偏重科技方面，而现有的几本英文专著多为外国人所编撰，内容上不能系统全面地反映中国茶文化特色，且年代较为久远，资料比较陈旧，不适宜作为教材。故而，出版一本由中国人自己编写的中英文对照版《茶文化学英语》教材很有必要，这将有利于促进中国茶文化的传播，促进世界茶文化的交流。

为了实现上述目标，本教材在编写时着重考虑了以下几个方面：

第一，英语与专业相结合，注重培养学生的跨文化交际能力和国际视野。本书两位主编分别为茶学和英语专业资深教授，具有丰富的教学、科研和实践经验；所选课文既有我国传统茶文化的描述，也有其他国家的茶文化介绍，有些课文来自英文资料选编，有些资料译自中文经典著作，使学习者既能享受到原汁原味的英文，也能学习到如何将中文经典翻译为英文。

第二，既重人文也重科学，文化现象和科学研究相得益彰。本教材不仅提供了有关茶的起源、饮茶习俗和茶的精神等人文知识，还介绍了茶的种植、制作和品评等相关科学知识，为学生提供了一定的茶学专业知识和文化表达方式。

第三，科学安排，主辅结合。本教材共有8个单元，31篇课文，一些课文后附有相关内容的扩展阅读，可供学生自学。

第四，适用性和可操作性较强，课文难易程度适中。每篇主课课文后都跟有词汇解释、难点注释和汉语译文，可以帮助教师和学生尽快扫清语言障碍，节省课堂时间，使学生有更多时间和信心参与课堂讨论，提高英文口语表达能力。

世界图书出版西安有限公司的编辑为本教材的出版付出了辛勤的劳动。从2013年起，历经三年时间的反复校对，从内容编排、词汇标注、汉语译文到每个单元的图片编辑，责任编辑都做了非常细致的审核和校对工作，对此，我们表示衷心地感谢。

虽然，本书主编和责任编辑都做了最大努力，但是不足之处在所难免，欢迎各位专家学者和读者批评指正，我们一定认真听取意见，使本教材在语言和专业水平上都能日臻完善。此外，课文材料来源除所附列参考文献之外，还有部分来自网络，因无法与作者取得联系，如有不妥之处，请与编者联系。

张丽霞　朱汉荣

2015年9月

目 录
Contents

Unit 1　General Description of Tea

Lesson 1　Origin of Tea in China ································ 2
Lesson 2　Chinese Tea Books ···································· 10
Lesson 3　Spread of Tea to Other Countries ····················· 20

Unit 2　Custom of Tea Drinking

Lesson 4　Tea in Chinese Daily Life ····························· 26
Lesson 5　Chinese Minorities and Tea ···························· 37
Lesson 6　English Time for Tea ·································· 46

Unit 3　Tea Tree and Its Cultivation

Lesson 7　Botanical Characters of Tea Plant ······················ 56
Lesson 8　Optimal Environment of Growth of Tea Tree ············ 66
Lesson 9　Tea Cultivars and Propagation ························· 74
Lesson 10　Tea Cultivation and Plucking ························· 82

Unit 4　Tea Processing and Storage

Lesson 11　Tea and Its Processing ································ 88
Lesson 12　The Category of Tea ·································· 95

Lesson 13	Green Tea Processing	106
Lesson 14	Black Tea Processing	110
Lesson 15	Oolong Tea Processing	115
Lesson 16	Dark Tea Processing	122
Lesson 17	Processing of Other Teas	127
Lesson 18	Storage of Tea	133

Unit 5   Evaluation of Tea Quality

Lesson 19	Sensory Evaluation of Tea Quality	140
Lesson 20	Description of Tea Quality	146
Lesson 21	How to Estimate the Quality of Black Tea	156

Unit 6   Benefits of Tea Drinking

Lesson 22	Tea and Health Care	164
Lesson 23	A Cup of Tea a Day Keeps the Doctor Away	170
Lesson 24	Drink Tea Correctly	174

Unit 7   Essentials in Tea Drinking

Lesson 25	Chinese Teahouse	180
Lesson 26	Tea Wares	187
Lesson 27	How to Make a Good Cup of Tea	193

Unit 8   Tea Ceremony

Lesson 28	Chinese Tea Art	202
Lesson 29	Japanese Tea Ceremony	214
Lesson 30	Etiquette in Tea Ceremony	221
Lesson 31	The Spirit of Tea	228
参考文献		235
后记		236

Unit 1
General Descrition of Tea

Lesson 1
Origin of Tea in China

The discovery and origin of tea and tea drinking are generally **ascribed** to China. Its legendary history dates back to the year 2737 BC. In the account of the *Herbal Canon of Shen Nong*, the Chinese Emperor Shen Nong claimed that tea was able to **detoxify** 72 kinds of poisons. It is stated in an ancient Chinese document published in 347 AD, that people living in southwest of China used tea for paying **tribute** to Chinese emperors as early as 1066 BC. *The Book of Songs*: *Er Ya*, which was published in 130 BC, described the ecology of tea trees and tea drinking. In this era, tea was used as medicine as well as for entertaining guests. The **antiquity** of tea is also evident in the essay *Tong Yue*, published in 59 BC, in which there is evidence of the making and sale of tea, as well as the establishment of schools during the second century to instruct people on how to grow and drink tea. The existence of tea market in 130 BC is also documented in the recent publications. Obviourly, China had been enjoyed a flourishing tea industry centuries before the Christian era. **Excavated** Western Han Tombs of the second century BC, which is situated in the Hunan Province of China, revealed that tea was one of the items included in the list of burial objects.

Records indicate that tea production and tea drinking were restricted to southwest of China until about the fifth century BC. At about that time, China entered its "Warring States Period", and this led to a steady movement of populations across the country. As a result of the migration, tea was spread to other regions of China. During the third century BC, the custom of tea drinking was introduced to northwest of China and Mongolia. By the beginning of the Tang Dynasty(618 AD—907 AD), tea had become one of the principal goods of trade in the Turpan Depression. The use of tea increased because the spread of Buddhism in China and by the edict of the Imperial Court that tea should replace the use of wine. As a result, tea became a staple **commodity**, second only to salt. In 780 AD, Lu Yu published the book *The classic of Tea*, in which he gave a comprehensive introduction of the origin, variety, cultivation, processing and storage of the tea, as well as the tea drinking customs, described the ecology of tea trees, and extolled the virtues of tea drinking.

By the time of the Song Dynasty(960 AD—1271 AD), the major tea plantations in China extended to the southeast of China, and people offered tea as tribute in place of grain and money. During the Ming Dynasty(1368 AD—1644 AD), harsh laws even death penalty, were imposed on illegal business practices in the sale of tea. In 1397 AD, Ouyang Lun, the son-in-law of the first emperor(Zhu Yuanzhang) of the Ming Dynasty, was sentenced to death for demanding high prices for the sale of his illegal hoard of tea. It was in this era that the tea-horse trade became popular because fine horses required by the army were not available at that time. It was reported that in the year 1,398 AD, 250,000 kilograms of tea were **bartered** for 13,584 horses. This tea-horse trade had **prevailed** for several generations and was **instrumental** in spreading the popularity of the tea. After the Ming Dynasty, tea became the national drink in China. In fact, tea became a necessity of life, equal to fuel, rice, cooking oil and salt. Chinese minorities would go without rice for three days but would not go without tea for a single day.

New words and expressions
生词和短语

ascribe [əˈskraɪb] v. 将……归因于	detoxify [diːˈtɒksɪfaɪ] v. 解毒
tribute [ˈtrɪbjuːt] n. 礼物；贡品	antiquity [ænˈtɪkwɪtɪ] n. 古物
excavate [ˈekskəveɪt] v. 挖掘	barter [ˈbɑːtə] n. 货物交换；易货；贸易
commodity [kəˈmɒdɪtɪ] n. 货物；日用品	
prevail [prɪˈveɪl] v. 盛行；流行	
instrumental [ˌɪnstrʊˈmentl] adj. 有帮助的	

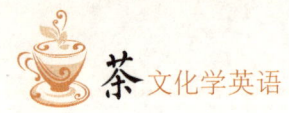

Comprehension

Give answers to the following questions in your own words and complete sentences as far as possible.

1. In what classics did the tea firstly come into appearance in ancient China?
2. What caused the break of the restriction of tea production and tea drinking?
3. Due to what factors the use of tea increased in Tang Dynasty?
4. What made the tea-horse trade popular in Ming Dynasty?
5. When was the tea used as the tribute to ancient emperors in China?

Translation

茶叶在中国的起源

通常认为：中国是茶叶及饮茶的发源地，这一传奇般的历史可以追溯到公元前2737年。根据《神农本草经》，炎帝神农认为茶可以解72种毒。公元347年的一本中国古代文献中记载，早在公元前1066年，中国西南部的人们就用茶进贡。公元前130年的《诗经·尔雅》中就有关于茶树的生态特性和饮茶风俗的描述。在这一时期，茶除了用于招待宾客，还可做药用。对茶较早的描写同样也可见于公元前59年的散文《僮约》，文中记载了茶叶的制作和交易，同时也记载了公元2世纪成立专门用于指导人们种茶及品茶的学校。最近的出版物中同样记载了公元前130年出现的茶叶交易市场。显而易见，中国茶业早在公元前就已繁荣了几个世纪。从湖南省出土的公元前2世纪西汉古墓中的茶叶是当时的陪葬物品之一。

有记载表明：公元前5世纪之前，仅在中国西南部产茶及饮茶。大约那时，中国进入战国时期，发生了持续性的全国范围内的人口迁徙，这把茶叶带到了全国其他地区。公元前3世纪，饮茶的风俗传入了中国西北部和蒙古。唐朝（公元618至907年）初期，茶叶已成为吐鲁番盆地的重要交易物品。随着佛教在中国的传播以及以茶代酒皇令的颁布，茶叶在中国得到普及，成为仅次于盐的第

4

二大商品。公元 780 年，陆羽的《茶经》问世。书中全面介绍了茶的起源、品种、栽培、加工、储存以及品茶习俗，同时还介绍了茶树的生态特征和饮茶的益处。

在宋代（公元 960 至 1271 年），中国东南部开始大规模种植茶树，而茶叶也取代了谷物与银两，成为当地的贡品。到了明代（公元 1368 至 1644 年），非法买卖茶叶会受判严刑，甚至是死刑。公元 1397 年，明开国皇帝朱元璋的驸马欧阳伦就因过分抬高其非法囤积的茶叶价格而被处斩。也是在这一时期，由于明朝军用良马供应不足，茶马贸易开始盛行。据记载：公元 1398 年，共计 25 万公斤的茶叶换回 13 584 匹马。这种茶马贸易持续了好几代，对茶叶的普及起到了重要作用。明朝后，茶叶成了中国的国饮。事实上，茶叶同柴、米、油、盐一样，变成了生活必需品。对中国少数民族而言，人们宁可三日无食，不可一日无茶。

Reading Material 阅读材料

Disputation about the Origin of Tea

Millions of people all over the world drink tea. Tea has become an essential part of people's daily life. As you enjoy a refreshing cup of tea, have you ever thought about its origins; who does first discover the delicious beverage and which country is the homeland of tea?

China is the earliest nation of planting, making and drinking tea in the world. It was recorded in *Herbal Canon of Shen Nong*, over two thousand years ago, Shen Nong tasted **various** herbals and was once poisoned 72 kinds of toxins in one day. Eventually he discovered that tea detoxified all the toxins in his body, and he also noted that regular consumption of tea can maintain one's youthful appearance and reinforce vital energy.

Ancient books used the Chinese character "tu" when they referred to tea plant. Today, the popular beverage is known around the world as "tea" and "cha", derived its name from the pronunciation of dialects in Guangzhou and Fujian. So, as tea spread from China to other countries, it retained its Chinese name.

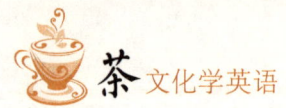

For a long time it was an undisputed fact that China was the homeland of tea, but in more recent times this has been challenged in a series of arguments and disputes. India has been credited by some authorities as the homeland of tea, but the facts substantiate that tea did originate in China.

It is known that a Japanese Buddhist monk, called Deng, studied in China and brought tea to Japan in 805 AD. He was the pioneer for growing tea outside of China. India, in spite of a country with great history, did not engage in tea planting and drinking in ancient times.

In 1610, tea was first taken to Europe by a Dutch merchant, and it rapidly gained popularity. There were high profits to be made in dealing with tea, and to take advantage of this, Britain started planting tea in India in 1780. To aid this, successive prime ministers sent representatives to China to buy tea and learn about tea plantations. Surviving records indicate that in the eighteenth century, tea was cultivated in at least twelve provinces of China, and two of those(Anhui and Fujian) supplied the largest portion of exports to Europe.

In 1824, the British Major General R. Bruce, once invaded India, claimed that he discovered wild tea trees at Assam in India, somewhere near the border between Burma and Chinese Yunnan. Under his direction, five boxes of black tea were shipped to London and subsequently received the prestigious 'Innovation Award' from the British Technology Institute in 1836. Spurred by General Bruce's discovery, the Indian Tea Committee organized a scientific research group to study the wild tea trees at Assam. Led by botanists Dr. Wallice and Dr. Griffich and geologist Mr. Mcclelland, the group found that the species of wild tea growing in Assam was actually from China; although its quality was poor because of a long period of wild, uncultivated growth.

General R. Bruce vehemently disagreed with the conclusions of the research team, and he wrote a pamphlet in India listing the 108 wild tea trees he had found in Assam including a 43-foot high by 3-foot diameter specimen. Thus India was promulgated as the original homeland of tea, starting a dispute which has persisted right through to this century.

There are five schools of thought on the subject:

(1)Indian School: Represented by an Englishman, Samuel Baildon, who opposed the historical theory of Chinese origin in his book *Tea in Assam* written in

1877. Mr. Baildon advocated that tea originated in India. Also from this school, another Englishman John H. Blake wrote a book *Guide to Tea Merchants* to promote Indian tea sales in 1903. Edith A. Browne was the other prominent figure who supported the Indian School.

(2) Persistent School: Numerous scholars of the Persistent School insist that tea was sourced from China. Notable works supporting this include Russian scholar E. Brets-cheider's *Botanic Science*, French Decandle Oenine's *Natural Systematic Botany* and A. Wilson's *The Traveller's Tale of Estern China*.

(3) Bioriginism: A Java tea classifier named Cohen Stuatt indicated in his book that there are two types of tea leaves, differentiated by their separate origins. He believed the large-leaf species originated in India whereas the small-leaf varieties came from China.

(4) Multi-originism: William H. Ukers, an American tea expert, in his publication *A Full Text on Tea*. insisted that tea originated wherever the natural environment favored its survival, thus he proposed a multi-origin theory.

(5) Anony mous Theory: A new theory, which can only be described as "Anonymous" was put forward by T. Eden in his book *Tea* written in 1974. In this publication, Mr. Eden indicated that neither China nor India is the origin of tea.

关于茶叶起源的争论

世界上有很多人饮茶，茶已经成为人们日常生活的一部分。当你享用一杯清茶的时候，是否想过茶叶的起源？谁最先发现了这一美味饮品？哪个国家才是茶叶的故乡？

中国是世界上最早种茶、制茶和饮茶的国家。两千多年前的《神农本草经》中记载：神农尝百草，日遇七十二毒。最终，神农氏发现茶叶可以解毒。神农还认为，经常饮茶有助于人们保持青春容颜，增强自身活力。

古书中使用汉字"荼"来指茶树。现在，人们称这一流行饮品为茶。世界各地茶的发音"tea"和"cha"都是从广东和福建方言中"茶"的发音演变而来。所以，当茶从中国传播到世界各地时仍保留了它的中国名字。

很长时间以来，中国毫无争议地被认为是茶叶的故乡，但是最近这一事实却遭到了一系列争论和质疑。印度曾被许多权威专家认为是茶叶的故乡，但事实证明茶叶确实起源于中国。

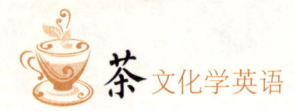

公元805年，一位叫澄的日本僧人来中国学习，并将茶叶带回日本，他是在中国境外种茶的先驱。印度虽然也是一个有着丰富历史的文明古国，但它在古代并没有种茶及饮茶的记载。

1610年，荷兰一位商人第一次把茶叶传入欧洲，此后茶叶得到了迅速普及。茶叶贸易收益巨大，所以英国于1780年开始在印度种茶。为了更好地种茶，历任英国首相都会派代表到中国购买茶叶和学习种茶技术。现存的记载表明：18世纪时，中国至少有12个省种茶，其中安徽、福建两省供应了出口到欧洲的大部分茶叶。

1824年，曾入侵印度的英国少将R·布鲁斯（R. Bruce）宣称：在邻近缅甸与中国云南交界处的印度阿萨姆地区发现了野生茶树。在他的指导下，五箱加工好的红茶被运回伦敦，在随后的1836年他获得了英国技术研究所颁发的颇负盛名的"创新奖章"。受R·布鲁斯发现的启发，印度茶叶委员会组织了一个科研团队，专门研究阿萨姆的野生茶树。在植物学家华莱士博士（Dr. Wallice）和格里芬奇博士（Dr. Griffich）以及地理学家麦克兰先生（Mr. Mcclelland）的领导下，他们发现：这些生长在阿萨姆地区的野生茶树确实来源于中国，由于长时间处于野生状态，没有管理，其茶叶品质低。

R·布鲁斯少将极力反对科研团队的这一结论，他撰写了一本小册子，列举了他在阿萨姆发现的108棵野生茶树，包括一棵高43英尺（约13米）、直径3英尺（约1米）的茶树，因此宣称"印度是茶叶起源地"，开启了一场延续至今的争论。

关于这个话题有五种观点：

（1）印度说：代表人物是一个名叫塞缪尔·拜顿（Samuel Baildon）的英国人，他在写于1877年的《阿萨姆茶》一书中反对茶起源于中国的历史观点。拜顿提出：茶叶起源印度。持同样观点的英国人约翰·H·勃拉克（John H. Blake）于1903年写了《茶商指南》一书，来提高印度的茶叶销售量。艾迪斯·A·布朗（Edith A. Brown）是支持印度派的另一位主要人物。

（2）传统说：大量传统说学者坚持认为：茶起源于中国。支持这一观点的著作有俄国学者E. Brets－cheider的《植物科学》，法国Decandle Oenine的《自然系统植物学》以及A·威尔森（A. Wilson）的《中国东部旅行游记》。

（3）双元说：一位爪哇的茶叶分类员科恩·斯图尔特（Cohen Stuatt）在他的书中称：两种叶片类型的茶树有着各自的起源。他认为大叶种茶树起源于印度，小叶种茶树起源于中国。

（4）多元说：一位美国的茶叶专家威廉·H·尤科斯在他出版的《茶叶大全》中坚持认为：茶叶可以起源于任何自然环境允许其生长的地方，由此产生了多元说。

（5）无名说：1974年，T·艾登在其书《茶》中提出了一种我们可以称之为无名说的新理论。在书中，艾登先生认为中国和印度都不是茶叶的起源地。

Lesson 2
Chinese Tea Books

It has been more than 1200 years since the publication of Lu Yu's *The Classic of Tea Ch'a Ching* in the eighth century. Since then, a lot of books were published in many dynasties. These writings are of rich content and wide range, varying from science to economics, as well as from philosophy to literature etc. Even the group of the writer is **embracive**, including the emperors, nobles, officials and ordinary civilians. Thus it can be concluded that the tea industry is really **multifacet** and far-reaching in China.

Profiles of Classical Tea Books

1. Tea books in Sui, Tang and Five Dynasties

In this period, thirteen kinds of books came out but only four types are exisfeat now. The most famous one is Lu Yu's *The Classic of Tea (Ch'a Ching)*, which was not only pioneering, but also in high level. It was called "the encyclopedia of ancient tea matter".

2. Tea books in Song and Yuan Dynasties

During this period, thirty-one types of tea books were published with fifteen left and ten recovered. Among those twenty-five books, twenty-three are regional and professional except *Treatise on Tea* and *Supplement of Tea*. For example, *The Record of Beiyuan Tea* concentrates on Jian'an Tea, and *Tea Ware Pictorial* was specifically for tea ware. During this phase, *Treatise on Tea*, written by Emperor Huizong of Song Dynasty, is the most distinguished one that recorded vividly as well as strictly the procedure of gambling for tea. Huizong Zhao Ji was the only emperor of the entire feudal dynasties who wrote tea books.

3. Tea books in Ming Dynasty

The publication of tea books is the most numerous in Ming Dynasty. There are sixty-eight in the short 250 years, with forty-six left. With the arrival of the reform on tea plucking, books of that age were thriving. Zhang Yuan's *The Record of Tea* and Zhu Quan's *Tea Manual* were all famous works through their long-term practice. The characteristics of tea books in Ming Dynasty were that a great amount of them were compiled based on previous works, Such as *Discrimination on Tea Water* based on Ouyang Xiu's *On Da Ming Water and Record on Fuchashan Mountain Water*.

4. Tea books in Qing Dynasty

Since Qing Dynasty tea-plucking and tea-tasting mainly followed the former generations, writings of tea were in a small number. There are total twenty-six books with twenty-three left. Among these books, three features are noteworthy. First, the only book about the procedure of Longjing tea *On Visiting Longjing Tea* appeared in the period. Second, there was the first book about tea imports and exports named *Rectification on Wan Tea Documents*. The third one, *Supplement to the Classic of Tea*, was the longest tea book in ancient times with one hundred thousand words.

5. Tea books in modern times

It can be divided into two phases. The first stage was from 1912 to 1949. In this period, tea culture hit rock bottom because of chaos and wars. Thus only ten types of tea books appeared, with three of them written by Contemporary Tea-Sage Wu Juenong. The second stage was from 1949 up to now. In this phase, tea culture was renewed and developed especially after China's implementation of reform and opening up. Thousands of tea books were published with rich content and themes. The representatives were Wu Juenong's *Review on Tea Classics*, Chen Zongmao's *Tea Classics of China*, etc.

The World's First Tea Book: *The Classic of Tea*

Even thought the tea was welcomed by the western people, it never achieve the value that it means to the Eastern people, no matter in the past or the pres-

ent.

Despite of its popularity, tea never became what it had meant in the West and still means to East. If it was an extrinsic detail in the culture of the West, it was intrinsic to that of the East. The culture and the drink lived **symbiotically**, we acquire **mystique** from the tea culture as it added new meanings and dimensions to life within the culture.

There's no doubt that Lu Yu's works was crucial in the development of tea's culture. Tea was rather an ordinary thing before the Lu Yu's tea works came out. His book has only three parts, teaching people how to manufacture tea, how to lay out the **equipage** and how to make a good cup of tea. Actually when it comes to tea, it is Lu Yu who has every detail. No wonder thathe was named "the sage of tea".

He was a leader in his time who helped create a culture. Lu was born probably in 40s to 50s of the eighth century and died in 804. His name is an interesting one, for it is closely bound to one of the most respected book of China's early classics, the *Book of Changes*.

At some time between 760 and 762, he went to lived in **seclusion** in a place called T'iao Ch'I in Chekiang Province. Once, it is said, while living there alone, he walked in the wilderness **chanting** a poem about a fallen tree. Moved to tears, he came home for tea and wrote *The Classic of tea*. Although The Classic of Tea establish him his present fame, he seemed to have produced a wealth of other materials, now were lost. We know, for instance, that Chang Youxin, in a book called *A Record of Waters of Boiling Teas*, cited another work by Lu describing some twenty different sources of superior water. Some are still famous, one of the sources in Kiangsu Province was named Lu Yu Spring. It is the world's misfortune that they are missing. Even *The Classic of Tea* is available to us now only in editions published as late as the Ming dynasty (1368—1644). At that time, it was included in two different compendia; and its original edition was developed, extended and illustrated not until 1735 when Lu T'ing-ts'an wrote a ten volume *Supplement to the Classic of Tea*.

Now it is time to turn to *The Classic of tea*. Let us approach it as Lu Yu would have wished with tea kettle chattering amiably, let us find our own delight in his eternal fragile moment which stands at the crossing of time and space.

Unit 1 General Description of Tea

The book is divided into three volumes with a total of 10 chapters of about 7000 words. Part one consists of *The Beginnings of Tea*, *The Tools of Tea*, and *The Manufacture of Tea*. Part two includes only one chapter, *The Equipage*. Part three contains six chapters, i. e. *The Brewing of Tea*, *Drinking the Tea*, *Notations on Tea*, *Tea-Producing Areas*, *Generalities of tea*, and *Plan of the Book*.

In chapter one, *The Beginnings of Tea*, it explains the producing areas, the growth characteristics of tea plant, functions of tea leaves, the cultivation of tree plant, the identification methods of fresh leaves and the **etymological** analysis of the character for tea in Chinese.

In chapter two, *The Tools of Tea*, it introduces eighteen tools including ying, furnace, cauldron, tseng, ch'uan, and chan etc.

In chapter three, *The Manufacture of Tea*, it includes the picking of tea, the manufacture of tea cakes in Tang Dynasty (picking, steaming, pounding, shaping, drying, tying and sealing), the process of tea production, the development of various teas, and the examination of tea quality.

In chapter four, *The **Equipage***, it specifying 28 tea-brewing and tea-drinking utensils including brazier, basket, stoker, fire tongs, cauldron, stand, pincers, paper sack, measure, water dispenser, water filter, water ladle, bamboo pincers, salt dish, heating basin, tea bowl, basket for cups, brush, scouring box, container for dregs etc.

In chapter five, *The Brewing of Tea*, it illustrates **concocting** of tea soup from the perspective of drying, grinding, heat controlling etc. The water in cauldron should be brought to the boil in three stages: "fish eyes," "pearls from a **gushing** spring along the rim," and "**galloping** waves." It also explains the water for tea. Tea made from mountain streams is best, river water is all right, but well-water is quite inferior. And "if you must use river water, take only that which man has not been near; and if it is well water, then take only that which has been used alot before".

In chapter six, *Drinking the Tea*, it mainly deals with the spread of tea drinking customs especially that of Buddhist monks and drinking habits in Tang Dynasty. It is said that "tea, used as a drink, was first discovered by the Emperor Shen Nong and then spread out by Duke of Chou in the state of Lu. While the

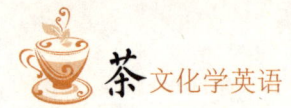

State of Ch'i had Yen Ying. During the Han Dynasty there were Yang Hsiung and Ssu Ma Hsiang ju. During the Wu, there was Wei Yao. During the Chin there were Liu Kun, as well as Chang Ts'ai, Lu Yu's distant ancestor Lu Na, Hsieh An. and others pulled out of memory at random, all of whom drank tea." "Tea has been traditionally taken so extensively that it is immersed in our customs and flourishes in the present Dynasty both North and South. From Ching to Yu, it is the common drink of every household." Lu also put forward that there are nine ways when he has to do with tea. e. g.

He must manufacture it.

He must develop a sense of selectivity and discrimination about it.

He must provide the proper implements.

He must prepare the right kind of fire.

He must select suitable water.

He must roast the tea.

He must grind it well.

He must brew it to its ultimate perfection.

He must, finally, drink it.

In chapter seven, Notations on Tea, it chiefly records some important people (Shen Nung, the Duke of Chou etc.) and books (Er Ya, Kuang Ya, etc.). It also records the reforms on tea affairs of past dynasties.

In chapter eight, Tea-Producing Areas, it demonstrates the producing areas of tea in Tang Dynasty, broken into eight sections, e. g. Shan Nan, Huai Nan, Che His, Chien Nan, Che Tung, etc. At the same time, it indicates different quality in different areas. For instance, in Shan Qian, Sha Chou has the best quality and in Huai Nan, Kuang Chou has the best quality.

In chapter nine, Generalities, it is about under what circumstance tea instruments can be eliminated. For example, if he uses dry firewood and a tripod frame, then the brazier, cinder receptacle, stoker, fire tongs and stand can be eliminated. Or should one be lucky enough to discover a clear spring or happen upon a fast-running stream, he need not to use water dispenser, scouring box or water filter.

In chapter ten, plan of the Book, narrates that on white silk of four or six rolls, copy it so that it can be hung on walls. In this way, people can take a glance and remind in memory.

Summary

This article includes two parts, the first part makes a review of classical tea books of past times and the second part concentrates on a typical tea monograph, Lu Yu's *The Classic of Tea*.

Through thousands of years' development, Chinese tea culture has formed unique cultural patterns and norms and turned into cultural **integration** of a multi-ethnic and multi-level system. The growth and development of tea classics is a changing process with three turning points: the emergence and popularity of tea-drinking; the establishment and enhancement of the status of tea-drinking; the awareness and intensification of tea culture awareness. On the whole, the ancient history of tea books mainly undergoes three stages synchronizing with the history of tea culture. That is the beginning period (from the pre-Qin to the Northern and Southern Dynasties), the shaping period (Tang Dynasty) and the developing period (from Song Dynasty to Qing Dynasty).

Chinese tea books are one of the most precious treasures in the whole world. Only after full understanding of the value of tea classics can we carry the profound tea culture forward.

New words and expressions 生词和短语

embracive [ɪmˈbreɪsɪv] *adj.* 包括一切的
multifacet [mʌltrˈfæsɪt] *adj.* 多层面的
exisfeat [ɪgˈzɪstənt] *adj.* 目前的;现行的
symbiotically [ˌsɪmbaɪˈɒtɪkəlɪ] *adv.* 共生地
mystique [mɪˈstɪk] *n.* 奥秘,秘诀;神秘性
equipage [ˈekwɪpɪdʒ] *n.* 装备,用具
integration [ɪntɪˈsreɪʃn] *n.* 综合;同化
seclusion [sɪˈkluːʒ(ə)n] *n.* 隔离;隐退
chanting [tʃæntɪŋ] *n.* 诵唱
etymological [ˌetɪməˈlɒdʒɪkəl] *adj.* 词源的
concocting [kənˈkɒkt] *adj.* 捏造的;混合而制的

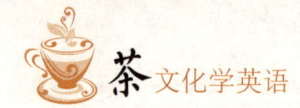

gushing [ˈgʌʃɪŋ] *a.* 涌出的

galloping [ˈgæləpɪŋ] *a.* 飞驰的；急性的

Give answers to the following questions in your own words and complete sentences as far as possible.

1. When was Lu Yu's *The Classic of Tea* been written?
2. What is Zhu Quan's master work?
3. Who is the Contemporary Tea-Sage?
4. How many chapters are there in Lu Yu's *The Classic of Tea*?
5. Please sketch the stages of tea books.

中国茶书典籍

从公元 8 世纪陆羽第一本《茶经》问世，距今已有 1200 多年了。自此之后，各朝各代出版了不少茶叶经典著作。这些著作内容丰富、涉及面广，涵盖从科学到经济，从哲学到文学等多方面的内容。而作者队伍从皇帝、贵族、官员到平民，无所不包。这说明了茶叶在中国涉及面之广，影响之大。

茶书经典概况

1. 隋唐五代茶书

这一时期共出版茶书 13 种，现存的只有 4 种，以陆羽的《茶经》最著名。它开创了茶书先河，并且水平极高，被称为古代茶事的百科全书。

2. 宋元两代茶书

这一时期共出版了 31 种茶书，现存只有 15 种，辑佚 10 种。在这 25 种书中，除《大观茶论》和《补茶经》外，其他 23 种都是地域性和专业类书籍。如《北苑茶录》是专讲建安茶的，《茶具图赞》是专讲茶具的。这一时期宋徽宗赵佶的《大观茶论》最著名，它详细记载了生动而又严格的斗茶程序。宋徽宗是

整个封建王朝中唯一一个写茶书的皇帝。

3. 明代茶书

明代是我国历史上出书最多的朝代，在250年里出书68种，现存46种。随着"创新茶叶采制"的改革，适合时代潮流的茶书不断涌现。如张源的《茶录》、朱权的《茶谱》等，都是作者长期研究实践的结果。明代茶书的特点是：编辑都是在搜集前人资料的基础上成书的，如在欧阳修的《大明水记》及《浮槎山水记》基础上编辑而成的《茶经水辨》。

4. 清代茶书

清代茶叶的采制、品饮多沿袭前代的方法，因此茶书较少。共有茶书26种，现存23种，其中有三大特点值得关注：一是有古代唯一写龙井茶采制的《龙井访茶记》；二是有专门写茶叶进出口的《整饬皖茶文牍》；三是有古代最长的茶书《续茶经》，全书共十万字。

5. 现代茶书

我国现代可分为两个阶段，第一阶段为1912年到1949年。由于战乱，茶文化陷入低潮。出版茶书仅10种，其中3本均为当代茶圣吴觉农所写。第二阶段是1949年新中国成立以后到现在，这一阶段是茶文化恢复和发展阶段，特别是改革开放以后，出版了上千种题材多样、内容丰富的茶书。代表作有吴觉农主编的《茶经述评》和陈宗懋主编的《中国茶经》等。

世界第一部茶叶专著——《茶经》

尽管茶在西方很受欢迎，但不论是过去还是现在，它永远达不到茶在东方的价值。如果说在西方文化中，茶是外在的，那么对于东方文化来说，茶则是内在的。茶文化与饮茶是共生的，"因为文化赋予了茶以新的含义和难度，所以品茶能给人带来一种历史感。"

陆羽的著作对于茶文化的重大意义不容置疑。在陆羽之前，茶不过是普通的东西，但陆羽在这本仅仅包含三部分的著作中，传授了如何制茶，如何选用茶具，如何恰到好处的泡茶技巧。实际上，一谈到茶，不论是周朝衰败之后还是在现代，陆羽的描述最为详细。人们给予他茶圣的称号也就毫不奇怪了。

在他那个年代，陆羽作为一个领军人物，帮助人们创造了一种文化。他大

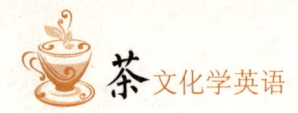

约生于公元八世纪四五十年代，卒于公元804年。他的名字非常有趣，与中国人非常崇敬的经典著作《易经》有关。

公元760到762年，他在非常闭塞的浙江苕溪居住。据说在他独居的时候，有一次他在野外吟一首关于枯树的诗时感动落泪，回家饮茶时写下了《茶经》。虽然《茶经》奠定了他现在的地位，但他还有其他大量著作，均已失传。例如，张又新的《煎茶水记》曾引用陆羽的另一部著作，其中陆羽详述了20余种不同水源的优质水，有一些至今仍非常有名，如江苏有一眼泉水被更名为陆羽泉。它们的失传是世界的遗憾，而且即使是《茶经》，我们所获得的版本也是在明代才刊印发行的。那时，《茶经》被收录到两部不同的集子里，直到1735年陆廷灿十卷《续茶经》的出现才发展、扩充并详述了原版本。

现在，让我们转向《茶经》。让我们像陆羽所希望的那样去接近它，伴随着茶壶那醉人的颤动，让我们在他那经受过时间与空间考验的永恒的碎梦中寻求愉悦。

全书共分上、中、下三卷共10章约7000字。上卷分一之源、二之具、三之造。中卷只有一章，四之器。下卷分茶之煮、茶之饮、茶之事、茶之出、茶之略、茶之图。

第一章，茶之源，阐述了茶叶的产地，茶树的生长特性，茶叶的功能，茶树的栽培方法，鲜叶品质的鉴别方法和"茶"字的字源。

第二章，茶之具，共讲了18种采制工具，包括籝、灶、釜、甑、杵、檐等。

第三章，茶之造，讲了茶的采摘，唐代茶饼的制造方法（采、蒸、捣、拍、焙、穿、封），制茶工艺和茶类的发展，茶叶的品质审评。

第四章，茶之器，详列了28种煮茶和饮茶的用具，包括风炉、筥、火䇲（炭檛）、鍑、交床、竹夹、纸囊、则、水方、漉水囊、瓢、竹钳、鹾簋、熟盂、茶碗、都篮、刷、涤方、滓方等。

第五章，茶之煮，论述了茶汤的调制，从烤茶、碾茶、火候、燃料选择以及煮茶用水都做了详细论述。煮汤有三阶段："鱼眼""连珠""鼓浪"。其中还详细讲了煮茶用水："山水上，江水中，井水下""江水取上游去人远者，井水取汲多者。"

第六章，茶之饮，讲了饮茶风尚的传播，特别是佛教僧侣对饮茶风尚的传播等，以及唐代的饮茶习惯。六之饮中说："茶之为饮，发乎神农氏，闻于鲁周公。齐有晏婴，汉有杨雄、司马相如，吴有韦曜，晋有刘琨、张载、远祖纳、谢安、左思之徒，皆饮焉。""两都并荆俞间，以为比屋之饮。"陆羽还提出茶有九难："一曰造，二曰别，三曰器，四曰火，五曰水，六曰炙，七曰末，八曰煮，九曰饮。"

第七章，茶之事，主要是记录了与茶有关的人和著作。如人物提到了神农、周公等。著作提到了《尔雅》《广雅》等。它还记载了历代茶政的改革。

第八章，茶之出，主要是论证了唐代的茶叶产地，主要有八大茶区，如山南茶区、淮南茶区、浙西茶区、江南茶区、浙东茶区等。同时，还指出了各地区茶叶品质的好坏，如山南茶，以峡州为上；淮南茶，以光州为上。

第九章，茶之略，是写茶具和茶器在什么样的情况下可以省略。例如，如果用干柴和三脚架，就不需要用风炉、滓方、司炉、火䇲、茶架，或者煮茶人碰巧发现了一眼清泉或是一道急流的溪水，就不需要水方、涤方和漉水囊了。

第十章，茶之图，讲述了可以将前九章记载在四到六卷的绢上，并挂在墙上。用这种方式，人们可以熟记《茶经》。

总　结

本文包括两部分，第一部分概览古今茶书经典，第二部分集中阐述了经典茶书著作陆羽的《茶经》。

经过数千年发展演变，中国茶文化形成了独特的文化模式和规范，是多民族、多层次的文化整合系统。中国茶文化典籍文献的兴起与发展，有一个历史的流变过程。其契机则有三个方面：一是饮茶事项的出现与饮茶风尚的演进，二是饮茶在社会中地位的确立和提高，三是茶文化意识的自觉和深化。从整个中国茶文化典籍文献来看，大致与中国茶文化的历史进程同步，经历了滥觞（先秦到南北朝）、定型（唐代）和发展（宋代至清代）三个时期。

中国茶书是世界文化宝藏中的珍品，只有全面认识和把握中国茶文化典籍文献的价值所在，才能真正把博大精深的茶文化发扬光大。

Lesson 3
Spread of Tea to Other Countries

The spread of tea from China to other parts of the world is said to have commenced as early as 221 BC With the migration of minority nationalities from China to Vietnam, Burma, Laos, and Thailand, which was the result of incessant internal wars which prevailed at that time, tea also was spread to these contries. Centutries past, the methods of tea processing used in some of the mountainous areas of these countries today are still similar to those employed in ancient China, such as the addition of condiments during the steaming of tea leaves and the use of tea as food dishes and medicines.

During the fifteenth century AD, China had already a well-established tea trade with Turkey. Many foreign buyers, especially from India, had established trading posts in Luoyang. In the middle of the cixteenth century AD, thousands of Turkic people—whose country once extended across **Eurasia** from Baikal Lake in the north to the Caspian Sea in the west and was later under the **jurisdiction** of the Tang Dynasty—entered China each year to trade in tea. In that era, China had begun communication with Rome, Arabia, Iran, India, Afghanistan, Pakistan, Korea and Japan; and she enjoyed a flourishing barter trade, with tea as one of the principle barter items. It was at this time that trade on the famed Silk Road prospered. The opening of sea lanes led to further expansion of trade with China. In about the seventh century AD, many travelers, especially students and Monks from Korea and Japan, visited China to study the Buddhist and took back with them the Chinese custom of drinking tea. In 646 AD, special tea ceremonies were held in Korea, and soon these practices found their way to Japan. In 805 AD. tea seeds and techniques of tea cultivation were imported to Japan from China, and in 828 AD tea seeds from China were planted on Mt. Jiri in Korea.

Earliest records of tea in the West are contained in the travel notes *Chai Cattai* and *Nayigatione et Viaggi* made by an Arab traveler, Soliman(85 AD) and a Venetian writer Giambatista Ramasio (1559). Tea was exported to Europe in 1610, to Russia in 1628, to Indonesia in 1648, to England in 1637, and to America in 1657. The first tea packet was sold by Galway Coffee House in London. These were exciting days when the three-mastered **clipper** sailing ships raced across the oceans carrying precious cargoes of tea. Speedy transport was essential because the first Chinese tea that landed in London fetched a **premium** price.

Tea became very popular in the West, and the afternoon tea is taken as a British habit. With the rapidly growing popularity of tea, cultivation of tea was introduced to several countries. Indonesia in 1684, India in 1780, Russia in 1833, Sri Lanka in 1839, Malaysia in 1875, Iran in 1900, Kenya in 1903, Turkey and Argentina in 1924. Tea was an imported trading commodity of huge **cartels** such as the Dutch East India Company and the British East India Company. The latter was granted a charter in 1669 by Elizabeth I to carry tea in their cargo, and the Tea Act of 1778 enabled the British East India Company to trade directly from China to America, thus bypassing other European exporters and American importers. This gave the British East India Company a virtual **monopoly** in tea trading to America and was the cause of the Boston Tea Party. The incident in which citizens of Boston boarded the British East India Company ships, dumped their tea cargoes into the sea, and sparked the American War of Independence. All these events illustrate the central role tea has played in shaping trade and history in various parts of the world.

Speaking of the name, the Chinese word "cha" is the origin of the word "tea". Cha is still used in most areas of western and northern China. In the past, tea was transported overland from northern China to Mongolia, Russia, and the Middle and Near East, as well as to countries in Europe, and in these regions tea is referred to as *cha* or *chai*, as in Russia. The pronunciation tay or tea has been adopted in Xiameng, Fujian province of China, as well as in most Western and Northern European countries, to which tea had been transported by sea in later

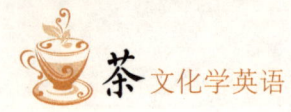

years. "Tea" is widely used in the United Kingdom.

At present, more than fifty countries cultivate tea. The experiences of tea planting and drinking spread out from China, whether directly or not, to the world. So we can conclude that "Tea came out of China and spread over the world".

New words and expressions 生词和短语

Eurasia [juəˈreɪʃə] *n.* 亚欧大陆
jurisdiction [ˌdʒʊərɪsˈdɪkʃ(ə)n] *n.* 司法权
clipper [ˈklɪpə] *n.* 旧时的快速帆船
premium [ˈpriːmɪəm] *v.* 涨价
cartel [kɑːˈtel] *n.* 卡特尔，同业联盟
monopoly [məˈnɒp(ə)lɪ] *n.* 垄断

Comprehension 理解

Give answers to the following questions in your own words and complete sentence as far as possible.

1. What is the reason that tea began to be spread to other areas from China?

2. When did Turkjc people begin to enter China each year to trade in tea?

3. List the time when tea was exported to those countries: Russia, Indonesia, England and American.

4. Why is it said that tea has played a central role in shaping trade and history in various parts of the world, according to the passage?

5. Can you make a brief summary about the process of the spread of tea from China to other areas in the world?

Notes on the text 课文注释

1. Baikal Lake：贝加尔湖，世界上最深，容量最大的淡水湖，被称为"西伯利亚的蓝眼睛"。其位于俄罗斯西伯利亚南部伊尔库茨克州及布里亚特共和国

境内，距蒙古国边界111公里，是东亚地区许多民族的发源地。1996年被联合国教科文组织列入《世界文化遗产名录》。

2. Caspian Sea：里海位于欧洲和亚洲的交界处，是世界上最大的湖泊。

3. Silk Road：丝绸之路简称丝路，是指西汉（公元前202年—公元8年）时，由张骞出使西域开辟的以长安（今西安）为起点，经甘肃、新疆到中亚、西亚，并联结地中海各国的陆上通道（这条道路也被称为"西北丝绸之路"以区别日后另外两条冠以"丝绸之路"名称的交通路线）。因为由这条路西运的货物中以丝绸制品的影响最大，其基本走向定于两汉时期，包括南道、中道、北道三条路线。

4. Mt. Zhivi：智异山，位于今朝鲜境内。

5. Boston Tea Party：波士顿倾茶事件，又称波士顿茶党事件，发生在1773年12月16日的政治示威中。因北美被殖民者不满英国对茶叶贸易的垄断，因而当地居民在马萨诸塞州波士顿倾倒茶叶，来对抗英国国会，最终引起著名的美国独立战争。它是美国革命的关键点之一，也是美国建国的重要历史事件之一。

茶向其他国家的传播

茶从中国向世界其他各国传播，最早可以追溯到公元前221年。那时中国境内内战频繁，导致少数民族向越南、缅甸、老挝和泰国迁徙，同时将茶传播到这些国家。几个世纪过去了，这些国家的山区至今还保留着与古代中国十分相似的制茶工艺，比如在蒸煮茶叶的过程中添加佐料以备食用和药用。

公元15世纪，中国与土耳其之间茶的交易已经初具规模。许多外国商人，尤其是印度商人在洛阳建立了交易点。公元16世纪中叶，每年都有成千上万的突厥人来到中国做茶叶买卖，突厥曾经横跨亚欧大陆，北到贝加尔湖，西抵里海地区，后来为唐朝管辖。那时，中国以茶为中心的易货贸易非常繁盛，并已经和罗马、阿拉伯、伊朗、印度、阿富汗、巴基斯坦、朝鲜及日本开始交流。丝绸之路也正是从此时开始兴盛。海上交通使中国的贸易进一步扩大。在17世

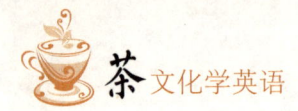

纪左右，大量的游者来到中国参观访问，特别是来自朝鲜和日本的学生和僧人学习佛教，同时把喝茶这一中国习俗带回了本国。646 年，朝鲜为茶制定专门的仪式，并很快传播到了日本。805 年，茶种和种茶的技艺由中国传到日本。828 年，从中国带去的茶种种在了朝鲜的智异山下。

西方关于茶最早的记载见于一名阿拉伯游客索里曼（Soliman）的旅行日记中（公元 85 年）以及一位威尼斯作家 Giambatista Ramasio（1559）的"Chai Cattai"和"Nayigatione et Viaggi"两本书中。茶出口到欧洲是在 1610 年，出口到俄国是 1628 年，印度尼西亚是 1648 年，英国是 1637 年，美国是 1657 年。第一包茶是由伦敦的高威咖啡屋（Galway Coffee House）售出的。那时驾驶着三桅帆船，装载着珍贵的茶在海上乘风破浪的日子令人激动。因为最早运到伦敦的中国茶可以高价销售，而快捷的海运至关重要。

茶在西方很受欢迎，特别是在英国喝下午茶成为了时尚。在饮茶迅速流行的同时，茶的种植被引进到几个国家：印度尼西亚（1684 年）、印度（1780 年）、俄国（1833 年）、斯里兰卡（1839 年）、马来西亚（1875 年）、伊朗（1900 年）、肯尼亚（1903 年）、土耳其和阿根廷（都是 1924 年）。茶叶成为了荷兰东印度公司和英国东印度公司等同业联盟的重要进口商品。1669 年，英国的东印度公司获得伊丽莎白一世制定的宪章批准可以运输茶叶，之后 1778 年的茶叶法案使其能够绕开其他欧洲出口商和美国进口商直接把茶叶从中国运到美国进行交易。东印度公司实际上垄断了美国的茶叶交易，因此引发了"波士顿茶党"事件：波士顿人登上英东印度公司的船只，并把茶叶货物倾进大海，由此引发了美国独立战争。上述事实表明，茶在世界各国贸易和历史发展过程中起到了非常重要的作用。

关于命名，英语单词"tea"源于汉字"茶"，欧洲许多国家和中国北方地区仍使用"茶"。早期，茶由中国北方传入蒙古、俄国和中东、近中东地区，以及欧洲，在这些地区茶被叫作"cha"或"chai"，比如俄国就称茶为"chai"。在中国福建厦门和后来经海路引进茶的西北欧多国，茶被叫作"tay"或"tea"，像英国就说"tea"。

目前，全球有五十多个国家在种植茶叶。不论直接还是间接，种茶和喝茶的经验都从中国传播到世界各地的，所以，我们可以这样总结：茶源于中国，传向世界。

Unit 2
Custom of Tea Drinking

Lesson 4
Tea in Chinese Daily Life

Tea drinking is a part of Chinese daily life and plays an important role in Chinese emotional and social life. For instance, tea is one of necessities in Chinese daily life, which is expressed in a proverb: "On opening the gate, there are seven matters you encounter: **fagots**, rice, oil, salt, sauce, vinegar and tea." Traditional social **decorum** has it that to every visiting guest a cup of tea should be served, and *etc*.

1. Serving a Cup of Tea to Guests

China is a country with a time-honored civilization and a land of ceremony and decorum. Whenever guests visit, it is necessary to make and serve tea with proper decorum to them. Before serving tea, you may ask them for their preferences as to what kind of tea and tea set. In the course of serving tea, the host should take careful note of how much water is remaining in the cups and in the kettle. Usually, if the tea is made in a teacup, boiled water should be added after half of the cup has been taken; and thus the cup is kept filled so that the tea retains the same taste and remains pleasantly warm throughout the entire course of tea-drinking. Snacks, sweets and other dishes may be served at tea time to complement the fragrance of the tea and to allay one's hunger.

Serving a cup of tea is more than a matter of mere politeness. It is also a symbol of togetherness, a sharing of something enjoyable, and a way of showing respects visitors. There are several special circumstances in which tea is prepared and consumed.

Unit 2 Custom of Tea Drinking

As a sign of respect: In Chinese society, the younger generation always shows their respect to the older generation by offering a cup of tea. Inviting and paying for their elders to go to teahouse for tea is a traditional activity on holidays. In the past, people of lower rank served tea to higher ranking people. Today, as Chinese society becomes more liberal, sometimes at home parents may pour a cup of tea for their children, or a boss may even pour tea for his subordinates at restaurants. However, the lower ranking person should not expect the higher rank person to serve him or her a cup of tea on formal occasions.

For a family gathering: When sons and daughters leave home to work and get married, they may seldom visit their parents. As a result, parents may seldom meet their grandchildren. Going to restaurants or teahouse and drinking tea, therefore, becomes an important activity for family gatherings. Every weekend, Chinese restaurants or teahouses are crowded, especially when people celebrate festivals. This phenomenon reflects Chinese family values.

To apologize: In Chinese culture, people make serious apologies to others by pouring them a cup of tea. That is a sign of regret and submission.

To express thanks to elders on one's wedding day: In the traditional Chinese marriage ceremony, both the bride and groom kneel in front of their parents and serve them tea. That is a way to express their gratitude. Moreover, the married couple should say, "Thanks for bringing us up. Now we are getting married. We owe it all to you." The parents will usually drink a small portion of the tea and then give them a red envelope, which symbolizes good luck.

To connect families on wedding days: The tea ceremony during weddings also serves as a means for both parties in the wedding to meet with members of the other family. As Chinese families can be rather extended, it is entirely possible during a **courtship** to not have been introduced to someone. As such, during the tea ceremony, the couple would serve tea to all family members and call them by their official title. Drinking the tea symbolizes acceptance into the family. Refusal to drink would symbolize opposition to the wedding and is quite unheard of since it would result in a loss of "face". Older relations so introduced would give a red envelope to the **matrimonial** couple while the couple would be expected to give a red envelope to younger, unmarried relations.

To pass on the tradition: Gongfu Tea is drunk in Chaoshan because it is part

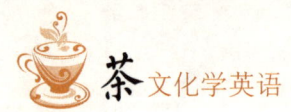

of the Chaoshan culture. While friends and family get together to drink Gongfu Tea and chat, the tradition and culture are passed on to the younger generations.

2. Savoring Tea as a Style of Life

Chinese people, in their drinking of tea, place much significance on the act of "savoring." "Savoring tea" is not only to **discern** good tea from **mediocre** one, but also to take delight in their **reverie** and in tea-drinking itself. **Snatching** a bit of leisure from a busy schedule, making a kettle of strong tea, securing a serene space, and serving and drinking tea by yourself can help banish **fatigue** and frustration, improve your thinking ability and inspire you with enthusiasm. You may also **imbibe** it slowly in small sips to appreciate the **subtle allure** of tea-drinking, until your spirits **soar up** and up into a **sublime** aesthetic realm. Buildings, gardens, ornaments and tea sets are the elements that form the ambience for savoring tea. A **tranquil**, refreshing, comfortable and neat **locale** is certainly desirable for drinking tea. Chinese gardens are well known in the world and the beautiful Chinese landscapes are too numerous to count. Teahouses **tucked away** in gardens and nestled beside the natural beauty of mountains and rivers are enchanting places of **repose** for people to rest and recreate themselves.

New words and expressions
生词和短语

fagot [ˈfægɒt] n. 柴把；柴捆
discern [dɪˈsɜːn] v. 辨明，分清
reverie [ˈrev(ə)rɪ] n. 幻想，遐想
fatigue [fəˈtiːg] n. 疲劳，劳累
subtle [ˈsʌt(ə)l] adj. 微妙的；精巧的
courtship [ˈkɔːrʃɪp] n. 求爱；求婚；求爱期
matrimonia [ˌmætrɪˈməʊnɪəl] adj. 婚姻的
savor [ˈseɪvə] vt. 品尝；欣赏（喻）品味；给……加调味品；使有风味
tucked away 藏起来
mediocre [ˌmiːdɪˈəʊkə] adj. 中等的；平凡的
sublime [səˈblaɪm] adj. 崇高的；令人崇敬的
tranquil [ˈtræŋkwɪl] adj. 平静的，安静的
locale [ləʊˈkɑːl] n. （事情发生的）现场

soar up v. 升华
repose [rɪˈpəʊz] n. 安静
snatch [snætʃ] vt. 抓住；攫取
imbibe [ɪmˈbaɪb] vt. 饮，喝
allure [əˈlʊə(r)] n. 迷人之处

Comprehension 理解

Give answers to the following questions in your own words and complete sentences as far as possible.

1. What does the Chinese proverb mean by saying "On opening the gate, there are seven matters you encounter: fagots, rice, oil, salt, sauce, vinegar and tea"?

2. How do Chinese serve their guests tea drinking?

3. What role does tea usually play in a traditional Chinese wedding ceremony?

4. What is "Savoring tea"?

5. What difference is there between drinkingtea and savoring tea?

Notes on the text 课文注释

Gongfu Tea: It is a commercialized show basing on the tea preparation approach originated probably in Fujian or Guangdong. The original term "Gongfu Tea (功夫茶)" literally means "making tea with efforts". Sometimes "功" instead of "工" is used, thus "功夫茶" appears. Today, the approach is used popularly by teashops carrying tea of Chinese origins, and by tea connoisseurs as a way to maximize the taste of a tea selection, especially a finer one. The "ceremony" show aspect has become an entertainment in various fairs, ceremonies and tourist programs. 功夫茶是起源于中国福建或广东的一种备茶表演。最初名为"工夫茶",意为茶的准备很费时间和工夫,后来"工"字被"功"字取代,遂成为"功夫茶"。今天,这种泡茶方法多在中国茶叶专卖店由专业人士来表演,以便于把优质茶叶的美味最大限度地发挥出来。由于"功夫茶"的表演性很强,所以它逐渐成为各种集会、仪式和旅游中很受欢迎的一个娱乐项目。

中国人的日常生活与茶

饮茶是中国人日常生活的一部分,对情感表达和社会交往有非常重要的作用。例如:茶是中国人日常生活中的必需品之一,俗话说:"开门七件事,柴、米、油、盐、酱、醋、茶。"在传统社交礼仪中有"客来敬茶"的习俗等。

1. 客来敬茶

中国是文明古国,礼仪之邦。凡来了客人,沏茶、敬茶的礼仪是必不可少的。在泡茶之前,可了解客人的爱好,选用客人最喜欢的茶叶和茶具招待客人。在饮茶过程中,主人要注意客人茶杯、茶壶中的茶水量,若用茶杯泡茶,如果已喝去一半,就要添加开水,并做到随喝随添,使茶汤滋味保持不变,水温适宜。在饮茶时也可适当佐以茶食、糖果、菜肴等,达到调节口味和餐前开胃的目的。

客来敬茶不仅是一种礼仪的表达,同时它还是聚会、欢庆的一种形式以及对来访者表达敬意的方式。有一些特殊的场合需要备茶和饮茶。

表示尊重:在中国,年轻人通常通过向长辈们奉茶的方式表示尊敬。每逢节假日,也有请长辈到茶楼品茶的传统。过去,下属要为上级沏茶。现在随着社会变得更开放自由,在家中有时父母会为孩子们泡茶,在餐馆也可见老板为下属冲茶的情况。不过,在正式场合下属不应该期望上司为自己斟茶。

家庭聚会:儿女因工作或结婚离家后,很少会去拜望父母,所以父母也很少能见到他们的孙子孙女,因此去餐馆或茶楼品茶成了家庭聚会的一种重要活动。每到周末,中国的餐馆或茶楼都会有很多人,特别是节假日。这种现象反映出了中国人的家庭观念。

表示道歉:在中国,通过给对方敬茶可以表达诚挚的歉意,并有后悔和顺从之意。

结婚时向父母表示感谢:在中国传统婚礼上,新娘和新郎要跪在父母面前并奉茶,以表达感激之情。而且新婚夫妇会说"感谢父母养育了我们,我们现在结婚了,这都是你们的功劳。"父母通常会饮一小口茶,然后给他们一个红包以示吉祥。

结婚期间联系家族成员：在结婚期间举办的茶会通常是双方家庭成员会面的一种方式。因为中国家庭的亲戚很广，在恋爱期间完全有可能没有介绍认识。在茶会上，新婚夫妇要为所有家庭成员奉茶，并用正式称谓称呼他们。喝茶表示接受新人进入家庭，拒绝喝茶将意味着反对婚事。拒绝喝茶的事很少发生，因为这会丢"面子"。长者亲戚们会给新婚夫妇红包，同时新婚夫妇也要给未结婚的年轻人红包。

民俗传承：潮汕地区的功夫茶品饮是潮汕文化的一部分，当朋友和家人聚在一起共同品饮功夫茶和聊天时，民俗和文化就传至了年青一代。

2. 品茶是一种生活方式

中国人饮茶，注重一个"品"字。"品茶"并非仅鉴别茶的优劣，而且还包括在神思遐想和品茶中获得的愉悦。百忙之中偷闲一下：沏一壶浓茶，择一雅静之处，自斟自饮，可以消除疲劳、涤烦益思、振奋精神，也可以细啜慢饮，领略其中的美妙，直到使精神世界升华到高尚的境界。品茶的环境一般包括建筑物、园林、摆设、茶具等。饮茶之处要求安静、清新、舒适、干净。中国园林世界闻名，山水美景更是不可胜数。隐于园林或自然山水美景的茶室，是人们小憩和意趣盎然的静谧之所。

Tea in My Life

Everyone knows that tea is a popular drink in the UK, but when I was a child I never drank a cup of tea, and I would spit it out soon after a quick sip. It was only when I went to study in China in 1987 that I began to drink tea on a daily basis. One reason was that the place I lived was dry and needed to drink a lot of liquids and another was that in winter it was nice to have a warm cup to hold onto. I didn't know much about tea then, and to begin with I bought the cheap jasmine tea.

 茶 文化学英语

Tea in Taiwan of China

Only when I came to Taiwan in 1990 did I begin to learn more about the various different kinds of tea and tea drinking as an art. My first experience of tea in Taiwan was when I stayed with a family in the countryside near Pingdong for a few weeks. They would regularly gather around the stone table in the garden of their old house and drink cup after cup. This was the first time I experienced this kind of **Taiwan-style** "tea ceremony" with the tea made and drunk following the tea drinking "rules".

In the last few years I have spent quite a bit of time in coffee shops. I don't go there for the coffee but for a sit down to read the newspapers or to daydream or to work. Usually I have a cup of coffee, and the reason not I love the drink but it's cheap and also I have to buy something to sit there. I have noticed that whatever the coffee shop chain is, they only have very limited choices of tea and usually have no Chinese teas at all.

The same also applies to the numerous pearl milky tea places——they have various beverages but usually they don't offer a simple tea drink, just tea and hot water. There are lots of places to sit down and have a drink in Taiwan (or other places of China), but not many places where you can sit down and have a cup of Chinese tea for a reasonable price. Teashops are few and far between these days and not really convenient when you just want to sit down for a short time to relax, read the papers or work with out pay too much.

Tea in the Mainland of China

At the moment I usually drink Longjing tea. I notice in the local shop that most of the teas are green teas from Anhui or Zhejiang. Among all the kinds of tea sold, it seems that Longjing tea is a big favorite, in Shanghai anyway. Doing a quick survey of the local supermarket, I found the Tieguanyin was the only Oolong type tea on sale.

Of course you can find a wider choice of tea, including the familiar names from Taiwan, if you go to a specialized tea shop or a large supermarket, dozens of varieties in fact. In fact, just in the local supermarket here in Shanghai if you spend about 30 yuan you can buy Longjing tea that seems to me to be good quality. That's the cheaper end of the scale. Many good teas aren't cheap in Taiwan (especially the kind of **prize-winning** teas to be given as gift) or the mainland of China, but I also have found that you can buy well quality and **highly-drinkable** teas for a reasonable price in China.

Tea Drinking in the UK

Going back to the UK after almost 2 years in China, I kept up the Chinese tea drinking habit while my Chinese tea stocks lasted. I remember when I first went back home and I took a pot of tea to the living room and poured myself a few cups while I was watching TV. My family thought that this was a strange behavior. In fact they thought, some inexpensive Chinese green tea, if I remember correctly, was strange, looked strange and smelled strange. They thought this way because people have a fixed idea about what "tea" is and how it is drunk.

In the UK, tea has been a popular drink for centuries. Fifty years ago it was drunk by most people in the UK (interestingly the slang name for tea in the UK is "cha", which came from the Chinese, and was brought to the UK in the 19th century which has become part of the English language). Today coffee has become more popular, but still about 50% of people in the UK drink tea everyday. However, 99% of the tea is most black tea from India or Sri Lanka. It is now usually in teabag form and either brewed in a pot or in the cup and then sugar and a small amount of milk added to the cup. This is what tea means to most UK people, So any other kinds of tea, even Chinese tea with thousands of years of history, seems strange to many.

Very few people regularly drink "luxury" teas like Earl Grey and even fewer people drink Chinese tea. This is changing though as more people become aware of the benefits of drinking Chinese tea and there is a small but growing market for Chinese and Japanese tea in the UK.

The Future for Chinese Tea

At present the UK market for Chinese teas, including Longjing tea, Puer tea, Oolong tea and Tieguanyin tea, is small. But as more and more people become interested in Chinese culture and they also become aware of the healthy benefits of tea, it can be expected that consumption of Chinese teas will grow strong-

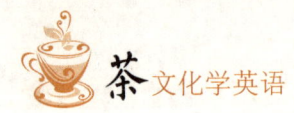

ly in the future. Many Western people lack knowledge about Chinese tea, even those who know something maybe know only the basics. So, there is a lot of educating work to be done to people in the UK. However, I think, with more and more people interested in Oriental culture in the West, they will also be attracted to the "ceremonial" aspects of Chinese tea drinking and discover that sitting around a table with friends unhurriedly following the tea making process step by step, while also showing off their knowledge of another culture, is a fun and relaxing activity, and also a welcome break away from the busy and high-stressed life. Or they can enjoy tea alone in a quiet moment of contemplation. As people become more aware of the benefits of tea, there will be an increased demand for other kinds of good quality of Chinese tea. ①

我生活中的茶

大家都知道茶在英国很受欢迎,不过当我还是个孩子的时候,我一杯茶都没喝过,顶多只喝一小口就很快吐掉。我和茶结缘,是1987年到中国念书时开始的。一方面因为我住的地方相当干燥,必须喝很多水来补充水分,另一方面则是因为冬天手中有杯热茶祛寒感觉挺好的,但由于当时我对茶的了解很贫乏,所以只会买便宜的茉莉花茶。

中国台湾茶

1990年来到台湾之后,我才开始学习更多不同茶业种类的知识以及喝茶艺术。我初次品饮台湾茶是在屏东乡下的一户人家里,他们经常聚在老房子院中的石桌旁,一杯接一杯地喝,那是我初次体验什么是台湾的"茶艺",要按照一定的规矩泡茶和饮茶。

那几年我花很多时间待在咖啡店,不是因为想喝咖啡,只是想有个地方坐下来看报纸,做做白日梦,或是工作一会。之所以点咖啡也只是因为价格比较便宜,而我需要花点钱坐在那里。我发现各级咖啡连锁店供应的茶种类往往十分有限,而且通常不卖中国茶。

同样的情形也发生在数不清的珍珠奶茶店,他们有各式各样的饮料,但却

---

① Written by Kevin Lax from Decorous Collection of Tea Events 2007, December issue

很少供应简单的茶，即热水冲泡的清茶。台湾（或中国其他地方）都有很多地方可以坐下来喝点东西，但是能够以合理的价格坐下来喝杯中国茶的地方反而不多。那时茶店不多且距离太远，当你不想在喝茶上花费太多，只想找个地方坐一会儿轻松一下，看个报纸或工作时，感觉实在不方便。

中国大陆茶

目前我常饮龙井。我注意到上海当地的茶店多半出售安徽或浙江产的绿茶，以所有出售的茶叶产品而言，龙井茶是当地人最喜爱的茶叶。此外，通过对当地超市的调查，我发现铁观音是唯一销售的乌龙茶产品。

当然，如果你去茶叶专卖店或大超市，这里的茶有几十种之多，包括来自台湾的名茶，你将有更多的茶叶可以选择。事实上，在上海的超市你可以花30元买到龙井茶，而且对我来说质量似乎不错，这是价格较便宜的。台湾好茶的价格通常不便宜（尤其是朋友送的那种获奖茶）；在其他地方茶价也挺高，不过我发现也可以用合理价钱买到质量尚可、喝起来不错的茶。

英国的饮茶习俗

在中国待了两年之后回到英国，我保留了喝中国茶的习惯，只要我的茶还有库存。记得第一次返乡，我带着一壶茶到客厅，一边喝一边看电视，我的家人对我的举止感到很奇怪，事实上他们对一些便宜的中国绿茶（如果我没记错的话）感觉陌生，外形和香气都感觉奇怪。他们之所以这样想是因为人们对茶的认识以及如何饮茶已有一种固定的观念和模式。

几个世纪以来，茶在英国一直是很普遍的饮料。50年前几乎所有英国人都喝茶（有趣的是在英国俗称茶为"cha"，这个字就是19世纪来自中国的"茶"字，且成为英国语言的一部分）。今天咖啡虽然更加普遍，但还是有50%的英国人天天喝茶，而99%的茶是印度或斯里兰卡的红茶，其中大多是袋装茶。泡在壶里或杯中，加糖再加些牛奶的泡茶方式是英国人对茶的看法，所以他们对任何其他的茶，甚至具有千年历史的中国茶都是陌生的。

少数英国人会经常喝昂贵的伯爵茶（Earl Grey），饮用中国茶的人就更少。但是这种状况正在改变，因为人们逐渐知道饮用中国茶的益处，虽然目前中国茶和日本茶的市场尚小，但正在扩大开来。

中国茶的未来

在英国,目前中国茶如龙井、普洱、乌龙茶和铁观音等的市场还很小,但随着越来越多的人对中国文化兴趣的增加,以及对茶叶保健作用的逐步认识,可以预期中国茶叶的消费会大幅增长。许多西方人对中国茶缺乏了解,即使懂茶的人也仅略知一二,所以英国需要茶文化的普及。既然西方越来越多的人对东方文化感兴趣,我想人们同样会被中国茶艺所吸引,并发现与朋友围坐一桌,从容地按照茶道程序一步一步泡茶,同时展示自己对其他文化的感知是一种有趣而悠闲的活动,同时也可远离尘世的喧嚣和生活的压力,在静谧中独享茶的芳香。随着人们对茶的益处越来越了解,更多不同种类的优质中国茶将会被人们所品尝。

Lesson 5
Chinese Minorities and Tea

There are 55 ethnic minorities in China. Although serving tea to guests is a common practice, there are some differences among their customs of tea drinking.

1. Tibetan Ethnic Minority: Buttered Tea

Tea is regarded as something belonging to the gods for the Tibetan. In Tibet, from Zanpu (King) to Lama, from the rulers to ordinary citizens, they eat more cheese and meat than vegetable and fruit, so tea becomes an **indispensable** beverage to them in every meal.

Major kinds of tea drunk by the Tibetans include Buttered Tea, Milky Tea, Salty Tea, and Green Tea. According to a survey, the Buttered Tea was voted as the most favorite followed by the Milky Tea. The Buttered Tea takes tea as its main material mixed with some other food, so one will find **various** tastes when drinking it. The tea not only can get one's body warmed up, but also can nourish the drinker.

There is a set of rules to follow when one visits a Tibetan family and drink the buttered tea. One cannot drink up the whole bowl of tea in one breath, but lick the mushy tea while drinking it. The hospitable host often keeps the guests' bowl filled up; so don't touch the bowl if you don't want to drink the tea. If you have had enough and cannot drink anymore, you may leave the bowl full for the moment and drink up the tea when you're leaving. Only one follows these rules in line with the customs and manners of the Tibetans can she/he receive a warm welcome from them.

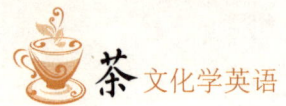

2. Mongolian Ethnic Minority: Salty Tea with Milk

Living in Inner Mongolia and some areas adjoining to the province, the Mongolians mainly live on beef, mutton and dairy, complemented with rice and vegetables. The brick tea is an indispensable beverage to herdsmen and drinking Salty Tea with Milk is a Mongolian tradition. The Mongolians usually have tea three times but only one meal a day. To drink Salty Tea with Milk is not only a way of quenching thirst but also the main source of gaining nourishment. Every morning, the first thing a housewife does is to prepare a pot of Salty Tea with Milk for the whole family. The Mongolians drink tea and eat fried rice in the morning. In order to get hot tea at anytime, they usually leave the pot on the fire. Everyday, Mongolians go out in the early morning and graze the herd for a whole day, so they only have one meal in a day after they return home in the evening, but they drinks Salty Tea with Milk three times a day.

The Salty Tea with milk uses green or black brick tea as its main material and an iron pot as the cooker. The brick tea should be broken into pieces and a irovl pot put on the fire before making The salty Tea. Fill the iron pot with 2~3 kilograms of water, and then put 50−80 grams of brick tea pieces into the pot once the water boils. After another 5 minutes, pour milk into the pot with a ratio of 1/5 to water and stir it, and then add certain amount of salt. When the whole pot of the mixture boils, the Salty Tea with Milk is ready to be served.

3. Bai Ethnic Minority: Three-Course Tea

The Three-Course Tea of the Bai ethnic minority is a special tea ceremony. This ceremony was originally held by the senior members of a family to express their best wishes to juniors when they were going to pursue studies, learn a skill, start a business or get married. Now, to drink Three-Course Tea has become a conventional ceremony when people of the Bai ethnic minority greet guests.

In the past, the ceremony was normally conducted by the senior family members, but now juniors also can take charge of the whole procedure and offer tea to the elder. In Three-Course Tea, the brewing techniques and materials used in each course are different from one and another.

The first course of tea is called Bitter Tea, suggesting that one should suffer a lot before she/he starts his or her career.

The second one is called Sweet Tea. When guests drinking the first course tea up, the host over again put some tea in the tea pot, baking it and cooking it. At the same time, put some brown sugar, milk fan and Chinese cinnamon in the tea cup, and then pour the hot tea in it to 8/10 de.

The third course is called Aftertaste Tea. The brewing method is the same but the raw materials in the cup is replaced by the honey, little fried rice, some dry pepper, few walnuts and pour 60% or 70% full of the cup. When you are drinking the tea, you should shake the tea cup and then drink it up while it is hot. The third course of tea makes the guest fully taste of sweet, acid, bitterness and hot, which let people know that everything has "aftertaste" and let them remember "first bitter and then sweet".

4. Dai Ethnic Minority: Bamboo-tube Tea

The Dai ethnic minority is a group of hospitable people good at singing and dancing. They like to sit at the small round bamboo table to prepare and drink Bamboo-tube tea. Bamboo-tube tea is known as Laduo in Dai language.

The making procedure of Bamboo-tube tea is quite special, which can be divided into three steps.

Step one, Put the tea into bamboo tube. Put the dried spring tea (the tea growing in the spring time) or preliminary-processed tea into the bamboo tube. The bamboo should be freshly chopped down and has a growing period of about one year.

Step two, bake the tea. Put the bamboo tube with tea in it on the fire for 6 to 7 minutes until the tea leaves are softened. Press the tea leaves with a wooden stick, and then fill up the tube again with more tea leaves. Repeat this procedure until tea leaves in the tube are compacted.

Step three, take out the tea. When tea leaves are completely baked, cut open the tube with a knife and take out the column-shaped Bamboo-tube Tea.

After everybody sits at the round bamboo table, the Bamboo-tube Tea can be served. ① Make the tea. Break off some **Bamboo-tube** Tea with fingers and put it into tea cups, then pour boiling water with an amount of 7/10 or 8/10 cup. After 3 to 5 minutes of brewing, the tea is ready. ② Drink the tea. The Bamboo-tube Tea has the pure taste of tea as well as the strong flavor of bamboo. One will feel refreshed when drinking the delicious tea.

5. Dong Ethnic Minority: Oil Tea

As one favorable tea of Dong ethnic minority, Oil Tea is like a kind of dish

which can allay one's hunger, expel the wind and humid air, stimulate the appetite and prevent one from catching cold. For a people living in mountain areas all years round, the Oil Tea really helps to improve one's health.

The procedure of making the Oil Tea consists of four steps.

First, choose tea. There are two kinds of tea which can be used to make Tea: one is specially-baked tea dust, and the other is tender leaves and buds just picked from tea trees. Which one to choose depends on different drinkers' tastes.

Second, prepare other ingredient, including peanuts, popcorns, soybeans, sesames, polished glutinous rice, and dried bamboo shoots.

Third, make tea. If the tea is made for a celebration or a banquet, then the fourth step is required, that is to prepare the tea. One needs to fry the prepared ingredients and put them into bowls, and then filtrate out tea leaves before pouring the brewed hot tea into those bowls.

The final step is to present the tea. Before the housewife finishes preparing the tea, the host serves the guests to sit around the table. One needs chopsticks while drinking the Oil Tea, because there are much food in his tea. So we can call "eating" the Oil Tea rather than "drinking" the Oil tea. For the sake of thanking the hospitable host, the drinker should praise the fresh and delicious tea with a dick of the tongue when enjoy the tea.

Since there are many materials to prepare when making the Oil Tea and the brewing procedure is complicated, many people invite Oil-Tea experts to help them on important occasions.

The most interesting thing is that the saying of "eating the oil tea" also means for the boys to propose to the girls. If a matchmaker comes into a girl's home, say something as "someone lets me ask for a cup of oil tea", and once the girl's parents accept it, the boy and the girl have gotten engaged. So, the saying "eating the oil tea" has more than one meaning.

6. Naxi Ethnic Minority: Dragon and Tiger's Fighting Tea and Salty Tea

Naxi people live on the cold plateau in northwest Yunnan Province where the Jade Dragon Snow Mountain lies and three rivers are running, named the Jinsha River, the Lancang River and the Yalong River. **The Dragon and Tiger's Fighting Tea**, a kind of tea mixed with white spirit, is regarded as a good medicine to dispel cold, so it is favored by the Naxi people.

The brewing method of The Dragon and Tiger's Fighting Tea is also very special. First, and then bake the tea together with the pot. To avoid burning the tea leaves, one needs to keep on turning the pot to let the tea leaves be heated evenly. When the scent of the tea is baked out, pour the boiling water in the pot and cook it for 3～5 minutes. At the same time, pour the white spirit into a tea cup with an amount of half cup, and then add the tea into the same cup. When the two kinds of liquid mix together, they will give out crack sound, which is regarded as a good omen by the Naxi people. Louder the sound is, happier are the people on the spot.

The tea is also believed to be a good medicine to cure cold, so you'd better drink the tea when it is still hot. One can refresh oneself through drinking the delicious and strong tea. When making The Dragon and Tiger's Fighting Tea, one must not pour the white spirit into the tea, but revise verse.

The brewing procedure of the salty tea is similar to that of The Dragon and Tiger's Fighting Tea, just to replace the white spirit with salt. The Naxi people also make other kinds of tea, such as the oil tea which is made by adding cooking oil, and the sugar tea by adding sugar.

New words and expressions
生词和短语

Salty Tea with Milk 咸奶茶
Three-Course Tea 三道茶
Bamboo-tube tea 竹筒茶
Oil Tea 油茶
indispensable [ˌɪndɪˈspens(ə)l] *adj.* 必需的,必不可少的
various [ˈveərɪəs] *adj.* 各种不同的,各式各样
The Dragon and Tiger's Fighting Tea 龙虎斗茶

Comprehension
理解

Give answers to the following questions in your own words and complete sentences as far as possible.

1. Why take Buttered Tea as their favourite drink?

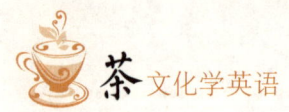

2. How to make the Salty Tea with Milk?
3. On which occasions will Bai people drink Three-Course Tea?
4. What does the Bamboo-tube Tea look like?
5. What special meaning does the Oil Tea have to Dong people?
6. What Dragon and the Tiger refer to in Naxi people's drinking tradition?
7. How much tea should be poured into the tea cup usually?

Notes on the text 课文注释

Chinese Minorities: Ethnic minorities in China are the non-Han Chinese population in the mainland and Taiwan. The People's Republic of China (PRC) officially recognizes 55 ethnic minority groups within China in addition to the Han majority. As of 2010, the combined population of officially recognized minority groups comprised 8.49% of the population of mainland China. By definition, these ethnic minority groups, together with the Han majority, make up the greater Chinese nationality known as *Zhonghua Minzu*. 中国少数民族，是指中国大陆和台湾境内除汉族以外的民族，经官方认定，共有55个。至2010年，少数民族人口总数占中国大陆人口的8.49%。这些少数民族连同汉民族共同构成了中华民族。

Translation 参考译文

中国少数民族与茶

中国有55个少数民族，虽然都有客来敬茶的习俗，但各民族之间还是有许多不同的饮茶习俗。

1. 藏族酥油茶

藏族人民视茶为神之物。从历代的"赞普"至喇嘛，从土司到普通百姓，因其食物结构中乳肉类占很大比重，而蔬菜、水果较少，故藏民以茶佐食，餐餐必不可少。

藏族饮茶主要有酥油茶、奶茶、盐茶、清茶几种类型，调查结果表明：酥油茶最受欢迎，其次是奶茶。酥油茶以茶为主料，并加有多种食物混合而成，所以滋味丰富，既可暖身御寒，又能补充营养。

藏族喝酥油茶是有一套规矩的，到藏民家去做客就应遵守这套规矩。这就是：在藏民家喝酥油茶一般是边喝边舔，而不能一口气喝完。主人总是随时会把客人碗里的酥油茶添满的。假如你不想喝，就别动它；假如喝了一半，再也喝不下了，当主人把碗里的茶添满，你就摆着，告辞时再一饮而尽，这样做才符合藏族人民的习惯和礼貌，才会受到藏族人民的欢迎。

2. 蒙古族咸奶茶

蒙古族主要居住在内蒙古自治区及其毗邻的一些省、区，蒙古族牧民以食牛、羊肉及奶制品为主，粮、菜为辅。砖茶是牧民不可缺少的饮品，喝由砖茶煮成的咸奶茶，是蒙古族人们的传统饮茶习俗。在牧区，他们习惯于"一日三餐茶、一顿饭"。所以喝咸奶茶，除解渴外也是补充人体营养的主要方法。每日清晨，主妇的第一件事就是先煮一锅咸奶茶，供全家整天享用。蒙古族喜欢喝热茶，早上，他们一边喝茶一边吃炒米，将剩余的茶放在微火上暖着，以便随时取饮。通常一家人只在晚上放牧回家才正式用餐一次，但早、中、晚三次喝咸奶茶，一般不可缺少。

蒙古族喝的咸奶茶，多以青砖茶或黑砖茶为原料用铁锅煮咸。煮咸奶茶时，应先把砖茶打碎，再将洗净的铁锅置于火上，盛水2～3千克，烧水至刚沸腾时，加入打碎的砖茶50～80克。当水再次沸腾5分钟后，掺入牛奶，用奶量为水量的1/5左右，稍加搅动，再加入适量盐巴。等到整锅咸奶茶开始沸腾时，才算把咸奶茶煮好了，即可盛在碗中待饮。

3. 白族三道茶

白族三道茶是一种独特的饮茶方式。喝三道茶，当初只是白族用来作为求学、学艺、经商、婚嫁时长辈对晚辈的一种祝愿。如今，应用范围已日益扩大，三道茶成了白族人民喜庆迎宾时的饮茶习俗。

以前，一般由家中或族中长辈亲自司茶，现今也有小辈向长辈敬茶的。制作三道茶时，每道茶的制作方法和所用原料都不一样。

第一道茶称为"清苦之茶"，寓意做人的哲理："要立业，先要吃苦。"

第二道茶称为"甜茶"，当客人喝完第一道茶后，主人重新用小砂罐置茶、烤茶、煮茶，与此同时，还得在茶盅内放入少许红糖、乳扇、桂皮等，将煮好的茶汤倾入八分满为止。

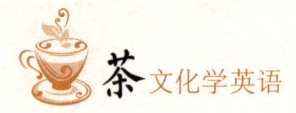

第三道茶称为"回味茶"。其煮茶方法虽然相同，只是茶盅中放的原料已换成适量蜂蜜，少许炒米花，若干粒花椒和一撮核桃仁，茶容量通常为六、七分满。饮第三道茶时，一般是一边晃动茶盅，使茶汤和佐料均匀混合；一边口中"呼呼"作响，趁热饮下。这杯茶喝起来甜、酸、苦、辣各味俱全，回味无穷。它告诫人们，凡事要多"回味"，切记"先苦后甜"的哲理。

4．傣族竹筒茶

傣族是一个能歌善舞而又热情好客的民族。他们喜欢围坐在小圆竹桌四周泡饮竹筒茶。竹筒茶，傣语称为"腊跺"。

竹筒茶的制作分三步进行。第一步：装茶。用晒干的春茶（春季采制的茶叶），或经初加工而成的毛茶，装入刚刚砍回的生长期为一年左右的嫩香竹筒中。第二步：烤茶。将装有茶叶的竹筒，放在火塘三脚架上烘烤，约6～7分钟后，竹筒内的茶便软化。这时，用木棒将竹筒内的茶压紧，尔后再填满茶烘烤。如此边填、边烤、边压，直至竹筒内的茶叶填满压紧为止。第三步：取茶。待茶叶烘烤完毕，用刀剖开竹筒，取出圆柱形的竹筒茶，以待冲泡。

当每个人都坐在竹圆桌旁时，开始泡饮竹筒茶。① 泡茶。先取少许竹筒茶，放在茶碗中，冲入沸水至七八分满，3～5分钟后，就可开始饮茶。②饮茶。竹筒茶饮起来，既有茶的醇厚滋味，又有竹的浓郁清香，非常可口，让人神清气爽。

5．侗族油茶

类似菜肴的油茶可以充饥健身、祛邪去湿、开胃生津，还能预防感冒。对长期居住在山区的民族而言实在是一种健身饮料。

打油茶一般经过四道程序。

首先是选茶。通常有两种茶可选用，一是经专门烘炒的末茶；二是刚从茶树上采下的嫩梢，根据个人口味而定。

其次是配料。打油茶用料通常有花生米、爆玉米花、黄豆、芝麻、糯粑、笋干等。

第三是煮茶。如果打的油茶供作庆典或宴请用的，那么，还得进行第四道程序，即备茶。备茶就是将事先准备好的食料，先行炒熟，取出放入茶碗中备用。然后将油炒煮好而成的茶，捞出茶渣，趁热倒入备有食料的碗中供客人吃茶。

接着是奉茶。一般当主妇快要把油茶打好时，主人就会招待客人围桌入座。由于喝油茶时，碗内加有许多食物，因此，还得用筷子相助，所以，说是喝油茶，其实是吃油茶。吃油茶时，客人为了表示对主人热情好客的回敬，赞美油茶的鲜美可口，称道主人手艺不凡，总是边喝、边啜、边嚼，在口中发出"啧啧"声响，表示称赞。

由于油茶加有许多配料，操作较为复杂，所以有的家庭，每当贵宾进门时，还得另请村里做油茶高手制作。

最有趣的是"吃油茶"一词，还是侗族未婚青年向姑娘求婚的代名词。倘有媒人进得姑娘家门，说是"某某家让我来你家向姑娘讨碗油茶吃"。一旦女方父母同意，男女青年婚事就算定了。所以，"吃油茶"一词，其意并非是单纯的喝茶之意。

6. 纳西族的"龙虎斗"和盐茶

纳西族聚居于滇西北高原的玉龙雪山和金沙江、澜沧江、雅砻江三江纵横的高寒山区，用茶和酒冲泡调和而成的"龙虎斗"茶，被认为是解表散寒的一味良药，因此，"龙虎斗"茶总是受到纳西族的喜爱。

纳西族喝的"龙虎斗"，制作方法也很奇特。首先用水壶将水烧开，再另选一只小陶罐，放上适量茶，连罐带茶烘烤。为免使茶叶烤焦，还要不断转动陶罐，使茶叶受热均匀。待茶叶发出焦香时，罐内冲入开水，烧煮3～5分钟。同时，另准备茶盅，一只放上半盅白酒，然后将煮好的茶水冲进盛有白酒的茶盅内。这时，茶盅内就会发出"啪啪"的响声，纳西族将此看作是吉祥的征兆。声音愈响，在场者就愈高兴。

纳西人认为"龙虎斗"还是治感冒的良药，因此，提倡趁热喝下。如此喝茶，香高味酽，提神解渴。但纳西族认为，冲泡"龙虎斗"茶时，只许将茶水倒入白酒中，切不可将白酒倒入茶水内。

纳西族喝的盐茶，其冲泡方法与"龙虎斗"相似，不同的是在预先准备好的茶盅内，放的不是白酒而是食盐。此外，也有不放食盐而改换食油或糖的，分别称为油茶或糖茶。

Lesson 6
English Time for Tea

Tea drinking has been a well-respected tradition in England and tea time for English is much varied. Different time for tea even reflects the class gap which is always characteristic of English society.

1. Afternoon Tea

When related to afternoon tea, what would you think of? A cup of tea, a piece of cake and a good mood, what a good enjoyment! But do you know how does the afternoon tea come?

We should thank for a lady, who had created the custom of afternoon tea in the year 1840. She is Anna, the seventeenth Duchess of Bedford. At that time, people of upper class usually had supper at around 8 o'clock in the evening. But Anna began to feel hungry at round 4 in the afternoon. This had left her a good long time of 4 hours. Therefore, she told the servant to bring **a tray of** tea, bread, butter and cake to her room during the late afternoon. It became a habit of hers. Soon the Duchess invited guests to join her for afternoon tea at 5 o'clock. But it did not become instantly popular elsewhere though, partly because in fashionable circles dinner was eaten earlier, leaving less of a gap to be filled by afternoon tea. But by the 1860s the fashion for afternoon tea had become widespread.

Afternoon tea was favored by women mostly, because they then had reason to get together and killing the leisure time more meaningfully. After Anna's launch of the afternoon tea, women of the **aristocracy** did the same in their homes and it later became a fashionable social event, providing an opportunity for people to meet new friends and get new information, and it is the enjoyment of elegant with tea drunk from the best china and small amounts of food presented perfectly on little china plates.

The traditional afternoon tea usually contains a teapot of tea, several teacups and **pastries**. There are different types of pastries: **a selection of dainty** sandwiches, scones served with clotted cream and preserves, teacakes etc. English tea is mainly or **Ceylon**, which was originally transported by the East India Company. Today, afternoon tea has been simplified because of the change of lifestyle. People use tea bags instead of infusing tea leaves. Pastries are no longer as various and sophisticated as that of long time ago. They usually are some pieces of biscuits or cakes. But if you want to experience a real English afternoon tea, I would advise you to Devonshire, where produces good clotted cream and famous cream tea. Afternoon tea consists of cups of hot and sweet tea served in china teacups and scones, strawberry jam as well as the fine clotted cream(the vital ingredient of cream tea). You may enjoy yourself for a whole afternoon to enjoy the best tradition.

Contemporary handbooks on etiquette and good housekeeping are full of advice on how to conduct a correct afternoon tea. The idea of needing an instruction book in order to enjoy a cup of tea and a biscuit with some friends seems rather alarming these days, but although nineteenth century afternoon teas were elaborate affairs from our point of view, in those days they were considered relatively informal occasions. Invitations were issued verbally or by note, and guests were free to pop in when it suited them and likewise leave when they wanted to. The hostess would pour the tea, but it was the responsibility of the men to hand the cups round. If there were no men present, this job fell to the daughters of the hostess or other young women present (goodness knew what happened if there were no men and no daughters available). There was a fashion for women to wear tea gowns, and these were softer and less restrictive than evening gowns, and it was not always deemed necessary for women to wear gloves. Nonetheless many did, and the author of *The Etiquette of Modern Society* points out that a thoughtful hostess should always provide biscuits with tea, since these can be eaten more easily than sandwiches without removing one's gloves. Moreover, people should take the teacup's handle with thumb and first finger, and little finger is upswept

to maintain the balance of the teacup (called orchid fingers), which is indeed a good way to prevent the splash from tea. You will never buckle your fingers on the handle of the cup or take the cup to drink directly. The putting for napkin for the traditional afternoon tea has the unique way, featuring one laying position on the table only, i.e. the folded heads for left and the opened towards right. Actually, people should lightly put napkin on the left of the table when drinking or leaving the table. It is an absolutely improper manner that **churning** tea in the teacup forms a circle. The correct way is to put the teaspoon on the 6 o'clock position of the teacup, and then to turn slowly towards the direction which is zoned to 12:00 p.m., to return two or three times. Teaspoon should be put on the right of the saucer when it is not used. Taking the teacup to talk with others is also impolite. Moreover, the teacup should be put on the saucer after nipping tea for showing your "gentleman" or "lady" feelings.

2. High Tea

Some poorer households also adopted the practice of afternoon tea, and in some areas women **pooled** their resources and equipment in order to make such occasions affordable. But more common among the working classes was "high tea". During the seventeenth and early eighteenth centuries, when most people worked in agriculture, the working classes tended to have the main meal of their day at midday, with a much lighter supper late in the evening. But after the industrial revolution, more and more people were employed for long shifts in factories or mines, and hot midday meals were thus less convenient. They were also not appropriate for the increasing number of children who were at school during the day. The custom developed of having a high tea in the late afternoon, at the end of the working day, consisting of strong tea, and hearty, hot food. Unlike afternoon tea, high tea was the main meal of the day, rather than a stop-gap between lunch and dinner.

3. Tea Shop

In 1864, a woman manager of an Aerated Bread Company shop persuaded her directors to allow her to serve food and drinks in the shop. She dispensed tea to her more favored customers and soon attracted more clients.

Not only did she start the fashion for tea shops but also **unwittingly** liberate the women, since an unchaperoned lady could meet friends in a tea shop without **sullying** her reputation. Tea shops spread throughout Britain, becoming as much a tradition as tea itself; and even today, despite the plethora of fast food and drink outlets, this tradition remains, and attracts huge number of UK and foreign tourists.

4. Tea Gardens and Tea Dances

As the popularity of tea spread, it also became an essential part of people's entertainment outdoors. By 1732 an evening spent dancing or watching fireworks in Vauxhall or Ranelagh Gardens would serve tea. Tea gardens then opened all over the country on Saturdays and Sundays, with tea being served in the afternoon. The charge for entrance to such fashionable gardens as Vauxhall or Ranalagh Gardens included tea with bread and butter. But rapid urban growth in the early 1800s led to the closure of the gardens and the only places left serving tea were the inns, **taverns** and hostelries.

Dancing was included as part of the day's festivities, so from the tea gardens came the idea of the tea dance, which remained fashionable in Britain until World War II. Tea dances are still held today.

5. Tea Breaks

Tea breaks is a tradition which has been with us for **approximately** 200 years. Initially when workers commenced their day at around 5 or 6 a.m., employers allowed a break in the morning when food and tea were served. Some employers repeated the break in the afternoon as well.

Between 1741 and 1820 industrialists, landowners and clerics tried to put a stop to the tea break, maintaining that tea drinking and rest made working people slothful. Modern thinking couldn't be further away from this — regular tea breaks can play a vital part in the day to help maintain a positive attitude towards work and fluid intake.

6. Tea at Home

Later in the nineteenth century then, going out to a tea shop became a popular pastime for women. But tea that was mostly drunk at home. Tea was drunk at breakfast by all social classes. Among the rich, it would typically be accompanied by a vast spread of bread or toast, cold meats and pies, eggs and fish. Of course some families favored a lighter breakfast, and lower down the social scale this was a necessity rather than an option. Poor families usually began the day with a cup of tea, as well as bread with butter, or perhaps porridge or gruel. Tea was then

 文化学英语

drunk at regular intervals throughout the day.

Tea features often in the works of the great nineteenth century author and social commentator Charles Dickens. His books make it clear that tea-drinking was ubiquitous among the working classes and through the eyes of Pip, the hero of *Great Expectations*, we can sense Dickens' affection for it: "... we returned into the Castle, where we found Miss Skiffins preparing tea. The responsibility of making toast was delegated to the Aged [an elderly man]... The Aged prepared such a haystack of buttered toast, that I could scarcely see him over it... while Miss Skiffins prepared such a jorum of tea, that the pig in the back premises became strongly excited... We ate the whole of the toast, and drank tea in proportion, and it was delightful to see how warm and greasy we all got after it." On the other hand, in *Oliver Twist*, Dickens uses the precise tea-making ceremony of Mrs. Corney, the matron of workhouse, to display her self—satisfaction, and she is wooed over a cup of tea by the tyrannical and grasping beadle, Mr. Bumble, who, when she has left the room, inspects her tea-making equipment to check whether it is genuine silver or not.

New words and expressions
生词和短语

approximately [əˈprɒksɪmətlɪ] adv. 大约
aristocracy [ˌærɪˈstɒkrəsɪ] n. 贵族
dainty [ˈdeɪntɪ] adj. 美味的,可口的
Ceylon [sɪˈlɑn] n. 锡兰,现称斯里兰卡
churn [tʃɜːn] v. 搅动;粗制滥造
tavern [ˈtæv(ə)n] n. 酒馆
unwittingly [ʌnˈwɪtɪŋlɪ] adv. 不知情地

a tray of 一碟
pastries [ˈpeɪstrɪz] n. 甜点
a selection of 有……可供选择
pool [puːl] v. 合伙使用,共用
sully [ˈsʌlɪ] v. 玷污,弄脏

Comprehension
理 解

Give answers to the following questions in your own words and complete sentences as far as possible.

1. How did Tea breaks come into being?
2. What households could afford an afternoon tea in the 19th century?

3. Why tea shop is so popular in England?

4. What would they have during a High tea?

5. Why did Charles Dickens describe tea drinking so closely in *Great Expectations*?

Notes on the text 课文注释

1. scones: The scone is a small British quick bread of Scottish origin. They are usually made of wheat, barley or oatmeal, with baking powder as a leavening agent. The scone is a basic component of English afternoon tea. 英国茶饼、司康饼，起源于苏格兰。它由小麦、大麦或麦片制成，通常用烘焙粉作发酵剂用。是英式下午茶常见的点心。

2. High Tea: For the working and farming communities, afternoon tea became high tea. As the main meal of the day, high tea was a cross between the delicate afternoon meal enjoyed in the ladies' drawing rooms and the dinner enjoyed in houses of the gentry at seven or eight in the evening. With the meats, bread and cakes served at high tea, hot tea was taken. 主餐茶，就工人阶层和农耕群体而言，下午茶就是主餐茶。作为一天中的主餐，主餐茶介于贵族女士们在客厅里吃的精致的下午茶点和绅士们在晚上7~8点钟吃的晚餐之间，有肉、面包和蛋糕，佐以热茶。

3. Charles Dickens: Charles Dickens (1812—1870) was an English novelist, generally considered the greatest of the Victorian period. Dickens enjoyed unrivaled popularity and fame during his career, and he remains popular, being responsible for some of English literature's most iconic novels and characters. His great works chiefly include *Great Expectations*, *Oliver Twist*, *David Copperfield*, *The Hard Times* and *A Tale of Two Cities*. 查尔斯·狄更斯（1812—1870）是英国维多利亚时期最伟大的小说家。在世期间狄更斯享有无可争议的荣誉，由于他塑造了英国文学史上最有标志性的小说和人物，迄今仍被广泛阅读。他的主要作品包括《远大前程》《奥利弗·退斯特》《大卫·科波菲尔》《艰难时世》和《双城记》。

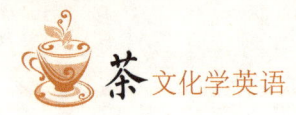

英国人的喝茶时光

在英国喝茶是一项一直得到良好保持的传统,而且英国人喝茶的时间也各有讲究,喝茶的时间都带有英国社会特有的阶级特色。

1. 下午茶

提到下午茶,你想到了什么?一杯茶,一块蛋糕,一份好心情,那是多么好的享受啊!那么你知道下午茶的来历吗?

我们得感谢一位女士,是她在1840年开创了喝下午茶的习俗,那就是安娜,第十七世贝德福德公爵夫人。那时,上流社会的晚饭通常在晚上8点开始。但是安娜下午4点就感觉饿了,要等4个小时才能吃晚饭,这对她来说实在太长了。因此她让侍女把茶、面包、黄油和蛋糕送到客厅里来,逐渐成了她的习惯。不久公爵夫人开始邀请客人在5点钟和她一起喝茶,但是这并没有马上在别的地方也流行起来,部分原因是时髦圈子里的晚饭吃得较早,留给下午茶的空间较小。到了19世纪60年代,下午茶才推广开来。

下午茶备受女士欢迎,她们可以借此聚会消磨时间,让闲暇时间过得有意义。在安娜推出下午茶后,贵族女士们也纷纷效仿,下午茶逐渐成了时尚的社交活动,成为人们结识新朋友、获得新信息的渠道。同时,用最好的瓷器喝茶,吃着用精美的瓷碟拼装的精致点心,也是一种高雅的享受。

下午茶一般包括一壶茶、几个茶杯和一些点心。点心的种类很多:精致小巧的三明治、配有凝乳和果酱的司康饼、蛋糕等。当时英国的茶叶多是由东印度公司自印度和锡兰(今斯里兰卡)进口的。今天的下午茶已经随着生活方式的变化而简化了,袋装茶代替了冲泡茶叶,茶点也远不如从前那样雅致和花样多,通常只是几片饼干或蛋糕。若想享受一份纯正的下午茶,建议你去德文郡,那里的凝乳和乳茶质量上乘。热腾腾、甜滋滋的茶盛在搪瓷杯中,配以司康饼、草莓酱和上乘的凝乳(乳茶的主料),你可以在最好的传统中尽情享受一个下午。

当代的礼仪手册和家务料理手册上满是如何准备下午茶的建议和指导。现在和朋友一起喝杯茶、吃块饼干却需要手册的指导好像有点让人焦虑。虽然从我们的观点来看,19世纪的下午茶是精心准备的,其实那时的喝茶不那么正式。邀请是口头的或是通过便条,客人可以随时来,随时走。喝茶时,由女主人倒茶，男士们送茶，若无男士在场就由女主人的女儿或其他年轻女士送茶（不知道如果没有男士也没有女儿在场的话会怎么办）。当时流行穿茶服，这种衣服要比晚礼服更轻柔，更随意，而且也不要求女士一定戴手套，但是多数女士会戴手套。《现代社会礼仪》的作者指出体贴的女主人会提供饼干作为茶点，因为饼干吃起来不用像吃三明治一样得脱手套。而且，人们需用大拇指和食指拿住杯柄，小指上翘以保持茶杯的平衡（这很像通常人们说的"兰花指"），这是防止茶水外溅的一种好方法。你千万不要把你的手指环扣在杯柄上或整个手掌拿起杯子来喝！传统下午茶的餐巾摆设非常独特，喝茶的时候餐巾只有唯一的摆放位置：在你座位左边的桌上，折起的一头朝左，张开的一头朝右。实际上，不论在喝茶时或是结束后，当你要起身离开时，都需把餐巾轻轻放在你座位的左边桌上。千万别用茶匙在茶杯中有圆圈式的搅动，正确的方法是将茶匙放在茶杯的6点钟位置，然后慢慢在茶水中划向12点方向，来回2到3次。当你不用茶匙的时候，把它放在茶碟的右边。举着茶杯与人交谈是不礼貌的，喝完一口茶后你应把杯子放回茶碟，举手投足中尽显您的"绅士"风度和"淑女"情怀。

2. 主餐茶

一些不那么富有的家庭也开始喝下午茶，在一些地方，女人们合伙使用茶会要用的东西，单独一个家庭无力承担茶会所需。然而工人阶级中更流行喝主餐茶。17世纪和18世纪早期，人们大多从事农业劳动，午饭是一天中的主餐，晚餐较为清淡。工业革命后，越来越多的人受雇于工厂或矿井，当班时间较长，吃一份热乎乎的午餐也越来越不方便了。午餐作为主餐对孩子们也越来越不方便，因为他们白天要待在学校里。因此，在下午晚些时候喝一杯浓茶，吃一顿丰盛的、热乎乎的饭菜就成了一种风俗。主餐茶不同于下午茶，它是一天中的主餐，而不是午餐和晚餐之间的小插曲。

3. 茶馆

1846年，充气面包公司的女经理说服董事会允许她在店里供应食品和饮料。她让常来购物的顾客在店里喝茶，很快就吸引了更多的顾客。

这位女经理不但开创了经营茶馆的先例，而且不经意地解放了女性，女士可以不用监护就可以在茶社里会见朋友，并且不必担心丧失名誉。茶馆迅速流行全国，和茶叶一样成了一种传统。直到今天，虽然快餐店和饮料零售店多如牛毛，但是到茶馆喝茶仍然吸引着大量英国人和外国游客。

4. 花园茶会和舞会

随着茶叶的普及，喝茶也成一项重要的户外娱乐活动。到1732年，在伦敦著名的沃斯豪花园和莱乃拉夫花园里举办舞会和观赏烟花都会伴有喝茶的活动。

周末，英国各地的花园都会举办茶会并且在下午供茶。像沃斯豪花园和莱乃拉夫花园这样的时尚公园，入园门票就包括了面包和黄油的费用。然而19世纪初期随着城市人口的剧增，很多公园关闭了，喝茶的地方只剩各类小饭馆和酒吧。

庆祝活动总会包括舞会，因此从花园茶会派生出了茶舞会，直到第二次世界大战，茶舞会在英国一直非常盛行，直到现在仍有茶舞会举行。

5. 茶歇

茶歇的传统大概有200年的历史了。起初，工人们在早上5点或6点上班，上午雇主会在休息时提供茶和一些食品，有些雇主下午也这样做。

1741年到1820年间，工厂主、地主和牧师试图阻止茶歇这一传统，认为茶歇让工人们变懒了。现代观点正好相反，认为有规律的茶歇能帮助工人们保持积极的态度进行工作和补充水分。

6. 家中喝茶

19世纪后期，虽然出去喝茶成了女士们很喜欢的消遣，但是喝茶主要还在家里。各个阶层的人在早餐时都喝茶。有钱人家会伴以丰富点心：面包或吐司，冷肉和馅饼，鸡蛋和鱼等等。当然，有些家庭喜欢清淡的早餐，而这在低收入阶层是唯一的选择。贫穷之家通常早餐时喝一杯茶，也吃一块黄油面包，或者喝粥或麦片，然后一天中定时喝茶。

喝茶也经常出现在19世纪伟大作家和社会评论家查尔斯·狄更斯的作品中。他的作品证明当时喝茶在工人阶级中非常普遍，通过《远大前程》主人公匹普的眼睛，我们能感受到狄更斯对茶的热爱："我们回到城堡，发现斯格芬斯小姐在备茶。烘烤吐司的活就给了老头……老头在吐司上堆了像干草堆那么高的黄油，我几乎都看不见他了……斯格芬斯小姐准备的茶这么丰盛，养在后院的小猪都兴奋极了，我们吃掉了全部的吐司，茶没喝完，饭后我们全都浑身热乎乎的，嘴巴油腻腻的，高兴极了。"在《奥利弗·退斯特》中，狄更斯通过对喝茶仪式的精确描写体现了女管家考尼夫人的自我满足感。在喝茶期间，专制又贪婪的教堂执事巴木鲍先生向她求婚，当女管家不在厨房时，他检查她的喝茶用具以确定是否为纯正的银器。

Unit 3
Tea Tree and Its Cultivation

Lesson 7
Botanical Characters of Tea Plant

The tea plant is an evergreen, perennial shrub of the genus *Camellia*, which thrives in subtropic and highland tropic regions. ***Camellia sinesis*** is one of genus Camellias over 80 species. In natural conditions, tea grows into a small tree about thirty feet high.

The form of the tea plant is described as follows:

1. Root

Tea plant is tap-root dominant and puts out strong **lateral** roots. The root distribution pattern is distinctly variable, to some degree, the variation was a clonal characteristic. Whilst some bushes develop deep laterals, others persist in putting out almost **horizontal roots** which can penetrate to any great depth. The extensive roots give rise to prolific **feeding roots**, which when fully developed,

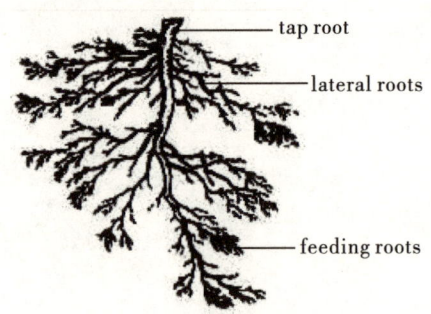

The root of the tea tree

are devoid of **root hairs**. Within a short distance of the **root-cap**, these feeding roots suberized. An **endotrophic mycorrhiza** has been found in the feeding roots. In plantation conditions, the **feeding roots** are confined to a relatively shallow layer irrespective of whether or not cultivation is carried out. Apart from the recognized function of absorbing and conducting water and nutrients, the roots, when they reach a diameter of between one and two millimeters, lay down starch **granules** in their cells, thus becoming important storage organs. This stored carbohydrate has a critical function after pruning operations.

2. Leaf

The development of the aerial portion of the plant proceeds from the **main axis** of the seedling, or vegetative propagation, which puts out leaves whose **phyllo**taxy is alternate. New leaves are evergreen, obovate-lanceolate in shape, and **acuminate**. Normal mature leaves are aerated at

Hairs on the under surface of bud and leaves

the margin. Their size differs according to variety. Those produced in the early stages of growth, after pruning, are large than those subsequently formed. Leaves ranging in size from one to ten inches can be found in fields of mixed race and age. Leaves are generally **glabrous** with some sparsely distributed hairs on the **under surface**. The buds and internodes are more profusely hairy. Old leaves are leathery in texture, highly polished on the upper surface and deep green in color.

A transverse section of the leaf discloses that a heavily cuticularized epidermis, which gives the characteristic glossy shine, and one or two layers of rectangular palisade cells Beneath this regular array is the spongy mesophyll of squat irregular-shaped cells and the lower epidermis. The stomata with prominent guard cells are on the lower surface. Embedded in the mesophyll areoccasional cells, **sclereids**, exhibiting marked **lignifications**. These sclereids are typical and are easily recognized in manufactured leaf. They are of use in diagnosing the presence or absence of **adulteration** of made tea by other leafy material. Fatty bodies and inorganic salt crystals can be distinguished under a low power magnification amongst the cell contents.

3. Flower, Fruit and Seed

The globular flower-buds are borne in the **axils** of scale-leaves, and develop either singly or in clusters. In*camellias* the flowers have **pedicels** that may be either long or short: *Camellia sinensis* has a short pedicel. The fully developed flower has a persistent **calyx** with a variable number of sepals usually 5 to 7. The petals, corresponding in number to the sepals, are white with a smooth waxy appearance. The shape of the petals are obovate, emarginated and internally concave. The **stamens** are long with yellow twin-celled **anthers**. At the base they are fused to one another. but free above two or three millimeters. The **ovary** is hairy and has a single style which split into 3 to 5 arms. The green fruit is three celled and thick-walled, shiny at begining but duller and slightly rough later. According to Sealy this thick wall is characteristic of the Camellia species that have short pedicels naked at anthesis. The fruit dehisces by splitting from the **apex** into three valves. The brown seed is typically thin-shelled, about half an inch in diameter, **semi-globose** in shape or rounded at the back and **wedge-shaped** in front. It contains two large cotyledons which when separated clearly show the embryonic radicle and **plumule**. The cotyledons are notable for their high oil content (up to 20 percent by weight). The fatty acid ester components of this oil are similar to those of olive oil for which it is a recognized **culinary** substitute.

Tea flowers　　　　　　　Tea fruits and seeds　　　Tea seeds

4. Periodic Shoot Growing

One of the most interesting characteristics of tea shoots is the distinct periodicity of growth, which is basically unconnected with climate or other environmental conditions. These rhythms are well known to tea planters for their maxima in "flushing" periods and their minima in dormant "banjhi" periods.

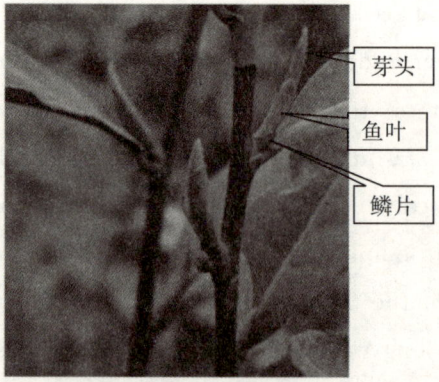

Tea shoots in primary flushing period

Unit 3 Tea Tree and Its Cultivation

Tea new shoots in flushing period

Tea new shoots come into the "banjhi" periods

At the period of dormancy the terminal leaf of the shoot has attained full size and discloses a young "banjhi" bud which is about 5 mm. long and is neither so long nor so fat as a normal active "flush" bud, i. e. a bud that will develop into apluckable shoot. The bud **swells** but shows no sign of breaking for a considerable time. Then the outermost appendage breaks free and produces, not a normal leaf but a mere scale-leaf. This is followed by the unfolding of a second appendage similar to the first; the first scale-leaf commonly drops off. At the breaking of the second scale-leaf the tip of a new leaf becomes visible within; and, as this develops, it is seen to be larger than a scale-leaf but neither in size nor shape similar to a normal flush—leaf. It is smaller, blunter, and has not the usual closely **serrated** margin. This is the so-called fish-leaf. Its position on the shoot is of the very greatest importance when considering standards of plucking. As the bud continues to unfold, normal leaves are produced which grow in size to that of mature flush—leaves with elongating internodes. After the development of a number of normal

leaves the shoot again goes banjhi, thereby ending one complete period, which is followed by further ones of the same type. This periodicity is independent of plucking, and during a single phase, the typical growth consists of two scale-leaves, one fish-leaf and four flush-leaves. At the time when a banjhi bud begins to break, all the initials of the appendages will emerge, before the next banjhi period occurs, are already formed. In other words, the number of appendages between one banjhi pause and the next is predetermined and unalterable, and can be found by dissecting the banjhi bud. Superficially, the banjhi period appears to the agriculturist to be one of inactivity. In fact, it is not so because it is at this time that the **primordial** related to the ensuing flushing cycle are being laid down. The ordered emergence of appendages-scale- or flush-leaves-when plotted against time gives a series of **exponential** curves, illustrating the slow development of the bud and scale-leaves, and the more rapid development of the flush proper. In Bond's view that the determinant of whether a scale-leaf, fish-leaf and a normal flush-leaf will be produced or not depends upon growth rate as affected by the supply of nutrients in general, and of nitrogen in particular. In the event of positive nitrogen deficiency a shoot, instead of growing a normal flush, will throw out an extended series of undeveloped appendages. Contrariwise of flush-leaves may emerge such as are seen in the leading shoots that appear from time to time on vigorous bushes.

The general pattern of rhythmic growth is modified in detail by extraneous factors. That of nutrition has been touched upon: in addition climate is of obvious importance and is also the artificial procedure of plucking. It is impossible to regulate pluckingaccording to the niceties of this elegant demonstration of periodicity. But when its nature is understood and empirical, the solution is possible. The frequency of plucking operation must dovetail into the rhythm of this periodicity so that banjhi periods will not upset the regular plucking rounds: and, equally, so that the rapid growth periods of flush will not be truncated, thus throwing the shoots back into the slow development phase of immature scales and fish-leaves.

Camellia sinesis 茶树学名　　　　　　lateral [ˈlætərə] adj. 侧面的；横向的

Unit 3 Tea Tree and Its Cultivation

feeding roots 吸收根
root-cap 根冠
lateral root 侧根
phyllotaxy [ˌfɪləˈtæksɪ] n. 叶序
under surface [植物]下表皮
axil [ˈæksɪl] n. 叶腋
stamen [ˈsteɪmən] n. 雄蕊
ovary [ˈəʊvərɪ] n. [植]子房
swell [swel] vt. & vi. 增强；膨胀
prolific [prəˈlɪfɪk] adj. (植物、动物等)丰硕的
granule [ˈɡrænjuːl] n. 小颗粒,小硬粒
main axis [meɪn ˈæksɪs] n. [植物]主茎
lanceolate [ˈlɑːnsɪəleɪt] adj. 披针状的
acuminate [əˈkjuːmɪmeɪt] adj. 尖形的
glabrous [ˈɡleɪbrəs] adj. 无毛的,光洁的
lignification [ˌlɪɡnɪfɪˈkeɪʃən] n. 木质化
adulteration [əˌdʌltəˈreɪʃn] n. 掺假；掺杂
calyx [ˈkeɪlɪks] n. 花萼

root hairs 根毛
endotrophic mycorrhiza 内生菌
horizontal roots 水平根
obovate [ɒbˈəʊveɪt] adj. 倒卵形的
sclereid [ˈsklɪːrd] n. 石细胞
pedicel [ˈpedɪsl] n. 花梗；蒂
anther [ˈænθə(r)] n. 花药
apex [ˈeɪpeks] n. 顶端；尖端
serrate [ˈsereɪt] adj. 锯齿状的

persistent calyx n. 宿存萼,萼片的一种,花开过后萼片不脱落,留存至果实成熟。

plumule [ˈpluːmjuːl] n. 胚芽,胚茎；幼芽
culinary [ˈkʌlɪnərɪ] adj. 烹饪的；烹调用的
primordial [praɪˈmɔːdɪəl] adj. 初生的,初发的,原始的
exponential [ˌekspəˈnenʃl] n. 指数 adj. 指数的,幂数的

Comprehension 理 解

Give answers to the following questions in your own words and complete sentence as far as possible.

1. What is the tea tree's root distribution pattern like?
2. Please describe the characteristics of the tea tree's leaves.
3. Please describe the characteristics of the tea tree's flowers.
4. What affects the tea shoots' periodic growth?

5. Could people change the pattern of the tea shoots' growth?

Notes on the text
课文注释

Camellia：山茶科植物，属常绿灌木和小乔木。山茶品种大约有 2000 种，可分为 3 大类，12 个花型，《本草纲目》曰："山茶花其叶类茶，又可作饮，故得名。"

Translation
参考译文

茶树的植物特征

茶树是一种常绿、多年生的山茶属植物，生长在亚热带和热带地区的高山地区。茶树是 80 多种山茶属植物中的一种，在野生状态下，茶树能长到约 30 英尺（约 19 米）高。

茶树的形态描述如下：

1. 根

茶树主根发达，侧根也很发达。根系分布特征在一定程度上与品种特性有关。有些茶树能发育出纵向侧根，而有的不断发出水平根，很难达到一定的深度。如此发达的根系可生出众多的吸收根，但当吸收根完全发育后，根毛会消失。在离根冠很短的范围内，吸收根会发生栓化。在吸收根中已发现有内生菌。在栽培条件下，无论是

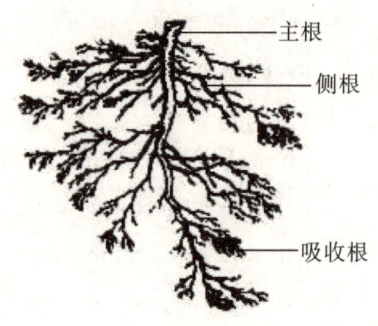

茶树根系

否进行耕作，吸收根都局限在较窄的土层中。根系除了具有吸收和传导水分和养分的作用外，当其直径达到 1~2 毫米时，根细胞中会贮存淀粉颗粒而成为重要的储存器官。贮存的这些碳水化合物在茶树修剪后（树势的恢复过程中）有非常重要的作用。

2. 叶

茶树地上部分是由实生苗和无性苗的主茎发育而成的。叶片互生，常绿，

呈倒卵形或披针形，渐尖。成叶边缘有锯齿，大小因品种不同。早期生长的或修剪后长出的叶子较后来的大。在品种和树龄混杂的茶园可以发现有 1～10 英寸（约 25～25 厘米）大小不等的叶片。除下表皮有稀疏的茸毛外，成叶通常无茸毛，而芽和节间上茸毛很多。老叶革质化，上表皮光亮，色泽深绿。

叶片的横截面显示：有高度角质化的表皮具有光泽，有 1～2 层栅栏细胞。其下是形状不规则的海绵组织和下表皮，气孔和保卫细胞在下表皮上。在叶内组织中，还有不常见的、木质化的石细胞。这些石细胞很典型，在加工过的茶叶中很容易识别，可以用于检测茶中是否掺有其他植物的叶片。在低倍显微镜下，能从细胞内含物中分辨出脂肪体和无机盐晶体。

芽头和叶片背面的茸毫

3. 花，果和种子

球状花芽生长在鳞片和叶的腋处，单生或丛生。在山茶属中，花蒂有长、短两种，茶树为短蒂类型。发育完全的茶花为宿存萼，有 5～7 个萼片。花瓣数量与萼片数相同，呈白色，表面有光滑的蜡质层，形状呈倒卵形，边缘有锯齿，内凹。花基和许多雄蕊（一般山茶有 20～200 条）连在一起，雄蕊较长，花药为黄色，由 2 个花粉囊组成，它们在基部连在一起，但在 2～3 毫米处分开。子房覆毛，单个子房内分 3～5 室。果实呈绿色、三室、厚壁，初期有光泽，后期无光泽且表皮粗糙。种子呈棕色，是典型的薄壳类型，约半英寸（约 1.2 厘米）大小，背面呈半球形或球形，前面呈楔形。内含两片大的子叶，分开子叶后，清晰可见胚根和胚芽。子叶的含油量高（占重量的 20%），其脂肪酸油脂的成分与橄榄油类似，可以用于烹饪。

茶花

茶果和茶籽

茶籽

4. 新梢的生长发育周期

茶树枝梢最为有趣的特性是具有明显的生长周期性,这点基本与气候或其他环境条件无关。这个节律早已为种茶的人所知晓,"旺盛生长"期产量最高,形成"驻芽"的休眠期产量最低。

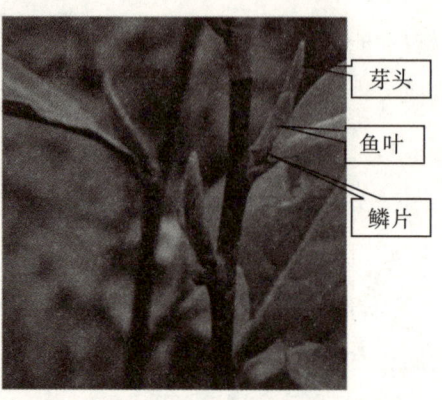

茶树新梢萌发期

处于旺盛生长的茶树新梢

进入驻芽期的茶树新梢

Unit 3 Tea Tree and Its Cultivation

在休眠期，枝梢的顶叶已经长到最大，并且露出一个长约 5 毫米的驻芽，比旺盛生长时期的活动芽（活动芽可以发育形成可采摘的新梢）短而瘦。驻芽好长一段时间只有膨大却没有发芽的迹象。然后最外一层终于萌动，长出鳞片而非正常叶。接着，展开第二个鳞片，第一批鳞片脱落。当第二个鳞片展开时，就可以看到里面新叶的叶尖了。在发育过程中可以看到这个新叶比鳞片大，但大小和形态都不像正常芽叶。它较小，较钝，叶缘无通常紧密的锯齿，这就是所谓的"鱼叶"。当考虑采摘标准时，鱼叶在新梢中的位置非常重要。随着芽的萌发，叶片不断产生，同时叶片面积增大至成叶大小，节间伸长，长出许多叶片后，枝梢顶端再次形成驻芽，从而结束了一个完整的周期，然后下一个同样的周期再次开始。这个周期与采摘无关。在一个时期，典型的生长过程会有 2 个鳞片，1 个鱼叶和 4 片真叶。当一个休眠芽开始萌动时，所有即将展开的都将会出现，它在下一个驻芽形成以前都已经分化形成了。换句话说，在两个驻芽之间形成的叶原基是预先决定和不可改变的，这可以通过驻芽的解剖结构观察到。表面上看，驻芽期茶农无事可做，但事实并非如此，因为正是这个时期决定了旺盛生长期的初始分化。从鳞片和叶片的生长顺序与时间的关系可以做出一系的函数曲线，结果表明：发育慢的是芽和鳞片，发育快的是叶。邦德认为：决定鳞片、鱼叶和正常叶是否发育的是生长发育速度，而生长发育速度又受到养分特别是氮素供应的影响。在茶树枝梢中氮素不足的情况下，新梢不会长出正常的叶子，而会长出一系列发育不完全的鳞片。当植株旺盛时就会出现相反的情况，主梢会连续不断地出现新叶。

一般生长节律模式受许多外部因素的影响，关于营养方面的影响已在上面说明，此外气候和人工采摘方式的影响也是显而易见的。虽然不会根据生长周期中细微影响因素来调节采摘，但是了解其自然特性后，可以提出经验性的解决方法。采摘工作必须适应生长周期的节奏，驻芽期不会影响采摘周期，同时也不耽误旺盛生长期，然后枝梢上不成熟的鳞片和鱼叶将回到缓慢的发育阶段。

Lesson 8
Optimal Environment of Growth of Tea Tree

Tea is native to subtropical areas. Though the growth has its own rules, the tea also has certain requirements to the environmental conditions. The following introduces them one by one mainly from four aspects: temperature, moisture, **illumination** and soil.

1. Temperature

Temperature is an important factor limiting the growth and development of tea tree, which decides the area of tea tree planting, growth speed, the length of tea production period and the yield and quality of tea.

According to the average temperature of the year, the area of tea planting can be divided into the most suitable area, more suitable area and suitable area. The average temperature of the most suitable region is 20 ℃ or higher, the suitable region, between 15 ℃ ~ 20 ℃, and the suitable region, less than 15 ℃ but more than 13 ℃. At the same time, only when the accumulated temperature is higher than 3000 ℃ · d, is it suitable for tea tree planting.

The growth of tea tree needs higher temperature. when the average temperature in spring is higher 10 ℃ stably, tea buds start to bloom; when it is between 14 ℃ ~ 16 ℃, tea leaves starts to expand; when it is between 17 ℃ ~ 30 ℃, the new shoots grow quickly. However, when the average temperature is higher than 30 ℃, new tips will grow slowly or just stop. If temperatures maintain more than 35 ℃ for a few days, new shoots will wither and be deciduous. On the basis of different varieties of tea, in general, the tea can live between 34 ℃ ~ 40 ℃, and the highest temperature that tea can survive is 45 ℃.

At the final of fall when the average daily temperature is below 10 ℃, tea trees start to enter the dormancy period. Tea tree is more sensitive to low temperature, on the basis of different characteristics, the extreme minimum temperature that tea tree can endure is －16 ℃～－5 ℃, and usually at －10 ℃, they are frozen heavily. In addition, the degree of tea tree suffered by frozen is related to the duration of low temperature. Generally, when the winter negative accumulated temperature is higher than －100 ℃·d, extreme minimum temperature is below －10 ℃ and the average daily temperature is lower than 0 ℃ for more than 14 days, tea tree is to be frozen easily in this winter.

When tea tree grows in the environment of larger **diurnal** temperature, it is **conducive** to the quality of tea, because in the day, tea trees have **photosynthesis** and accumulate the synthesis of organic matter while at the night, **respiration** is weak and then material consumption is low. All of these can accumulate effective substances in tea plant of high mountains or high-altitude areas, which are helpful to produce the tea with "strong aroma and thick taste".

2. Moisture

All activities of tea tree life must go with the cells containing sufficient moisture. The physiological activities such as photosynthesis, respiration, the absorption and transport of nutrients etc. must have the participation of moisture.

Precipitation: Most of the water for the growth of tea tree comes from natural precipitation. Tea tree prefers wet condition, but is afraid of water-logging. It is suitable for cultivation of the tea trees when the annual rainfall is above 1000 mm, and the most appropriate annual rainfall is about 1500 mm. In the growing season, the requirements of rainfall are greater than 100 mm. When the precipitation of several months is less than 50 mm and there are no artificial irrigation measures, the tea production would dramatically reduce. If in a month the rainfall is greater than 300 mm and there is a rainstorm once or more, it is still unfavorable to the growth of tea tree.

Humidity of the air: Air humidity can affect water evaporation of soil and transpiration of tea tree. Suitable air humidity for tea tree growth and development is 80%～90%. If it is less than 50%, the growth of new shoots will be subdued; and if less than 40%, tea tree will suffer from it. When the relative air humidity is high, it can reduce the moisture evaporation of soil, reduce the transpiration of tea plant and enhance the efficient use of water. When the relative humidity is higher than 90% at the same time, it often can form clouds so as to reduce the intensity of direct light, change the quality of light and increase the proportion of diffuse light,. It is conducive to the formation of the high quality of tea.

Soil moisture content: the soil moisture conditions in the tea garden can directly affect the growth of tea tree roots and also indirectly affect the growth of tea tree aboveground. When the relative water content is between 70%~80%, it is good for the growth of tea trees and every index of physiological and biochemical is better. When the relative water content of soil is deficient or excessive, it will restrict the growth of tea trees.

3. Illumination

Tea tree, like other crops, can use the light to produce the carbohydrate for itself. At the same time, it adjusts its growth and development according to the light quality, light intensity and light cycle.

Light intensity: tea tree prefers to bright light and shade, avoiding the strong and direct light. The light saturation point of tea tree is high of $2.1 \sim 3.0 \text{ J/cm}^2 \cdot \text{min}$ and the light compensation point is low, accounting for only about 1% of the total light intensity. Due to the high chlorophyll b in mature tea leaves, and the strong absorption of short wavelength spectrum, it makes tea prefer to growing under the diffuse light, and avoid direct light. The moderate shade of tea tree can increase the total content of amino acid in tea leaves and also make new shoots tender.

Light quality: light quality plays an important role in the regulation of carbon and the nitrogen metabolism pathway of tea tree. Compared with white light, red and orange light can promote the elongation of bud tip and the expansion of leaf area; Blue and purple lighe will inhibit the elongtion of bud tip, but blue and purple light can improve the supersession of nitrogen and the synthesis of protein. In addition, the purple light has a direct relationship with the formation of some nitrogen biochemical components attribute to tea quality such as: amino acids, vitamins, and a lot of aroma composition. In a certain altitude of tea area, because of plentiful rainfall, cloud and mist, the full air humidity, rich diffuse light, the proportion of blue and purple light increase. The amino acid, chlorophyll and nitrogen aromatic substances in tea are high while polyphenol content of tea is low. It is one of the reasons that the high mountains and many clouds make good tea.

Lighting time: the impact of lighting time of tea tree is mainly manifested in two aspects: the total radiation and photoperiodism. The longer the sunshine time is, the more the tea leaf accepts light energy, the more chlorophyll absorbs radiating energy, and the greater the accumulation of photosynthetic substance is. They are all beneficial to the improvement of the tea growth and yeild. Tea is a kind of short daylight plants, when the sunshine time is shorter in some seasons or regions, it is conducive to the breeding of tea tree in that it can bring forward the flowering time, increase the flower quantity and defer growth of new tips, at the same time, make them dormancy early. Instead, when the sunshine time is longer in some seasons or regions, the nutrition of tea tree growth will delay the dormancy and flower in new shoots, and it also will flower less or even no flowers. In winter when the time of light is less than 11 h per day for 6 weeks, the tea enters into the relative lull.

4. Soil

The soil of gravel and acidic sandy loam, which is loose and deep and has good drainage, is suitable for the growth of tea tree.

Tea is a kind of perennial deep root crop and the root system can extend to the 2 meters under the soil. So the depth of effective soil of tea garden reaches more than 1 m. At the same time, the level of underground water should be lower than the distribution of tea tree root in order to avoid tea tree roots being flooded and the root growth and development and the absorption of nutrients being influenced.

Tea tree prefers acid soil and despises the calcium. The suitable pH for the growth of tea is between 4.0 and 6.0, and the most suitable is between 5.0 and 5.5. When the pH is higher than 6.0, the nursery of tea is in poor condition, color of leaf is yellow and the loss of green is significant. More seriously, the buds will die and the roots will become reddish and then black. When the PH is lower than 4.0, there is poisoning disease of H^+. Leaf color turns from green to dark, then red. The root becomes red, then black, and even dead. At the same time, the demand for calcium of the tea tree crops is much lower than normal condition. Com-

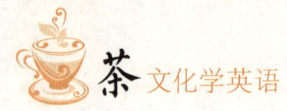

pared with mulberry and citrus growing in the same acidic soils, it is almost ten times or even dozens of times lower. When the active content of soil in the calcium content is more than 0.5% (CaO), the growth of tea tree is abnormal, and it can even cause death. So, tea tree is not suitable to be planted in calcareous purple soil and calcareous alluvial soil.

The organic matter of soils in tea garden is the material base for the microbial life and the sources of micronutrients of various kinds of tea. Its degree of content can reflect the degree of curing and level of garden soil fertility. The organic matter of tea garden of high yield and good quality is more than 2.0%.

To sum up, tea tree has the characteristics of "preferring warmth instead of coldness, wet condition instead of water-logging, light instead of sunshine, acid soil instead of alkali".

New words and expressions 生词和短语

illumination [ɪˌljuːmɪˈneɪʃən] *n.* 光照, 照度
diurnal [daɪˈɜːn(ə)ɪ] *adj.* 白天的, 每日的
conducive [kənˈdjuːsɪv] *adj.* 有益的, 有助于……的
photosynthesis [ˌfəʊtə(ʊ)ˈsɪnθɪsɪs] *n.* 光合作用
respiration [ˌrespɪˈreɪʃ(ə)n] *n.* 呼吸, 呼吸作用
precipitation [prɪˌsɪpɪˈteɪʃ(ə)n] *n.* 沉淀, 沉淀物
humidity [hjuːˈmɪdɪtɪ] *n.* 湿度, 湿气

Comprehension 理解

Give answers to the following questions in your own words and complete sentence as far as possible.

1. What are the suitable factors for the growth of tea tree?
2. When talks about moisture, what should we pay attention to?
3. What kind of soil is conducive to the growth of tea tree?
4. Tell the environmental characteristics of the growth of tea tree in your own words.
5. What's more do you know about the environmental requirements to the

growth of tea?

Notes on the text 课文注释

1. Active accumulated temperature：活动积温，它反映了一个地区气候对农作物所能提供的热量条件，是划分温度带的重要条件。

2. Light quality：光质，是影响植物光合作用的因素之一，光质会影响叶绿素 a、叶绿素 b 对于光的吸收，从而影响光合作用的光反应阶段。

Translation 参考译文

茶树的适生环境

茶树原产于亚热带，虽然其生长发育有自身的规律，但茶对其环境条件也有一定的要求。下面主要从温度、水分、光照和土壤四个方面逐一介绍。

1. 温度

温度是茶树生长发育的重要限制因子，决定着茶树种植区域的大小、生长发育速度的快慢、茶叶生产期长短以及茶叶产量的多少和品质的高低。

根据种茶区域年日平均温度的高低，可将其分为茶树最适宜区、适宜区和次适宜区。其中：最适宜区年日平均温度≥20℃，适宜区为15℃～20℃，次适宜区则小于15℃，但需≥13℃。同时只有当积温大于3000℃·d时才适宜种植茶树。

茶树生长发育需要较高温度。当春季日平均气温稳定超过10℃时茶芽才开始萌动，14℃～16℃时开始展叶，17℃～30℃时新梢生长迅速；但当日平均气温高于30℃，新梢生长就会缓慢或停止，如果气温持续几天超过35℃，新梢就会枯萎、落叶。因品种不同茶树一般能耐的最高温度是34℃～40℃之间，生存临界温度是45℃。

当秋季日平均气温低于10℃时，茶树开始进入休眠期；茶树是一种对低温比较敏感的植物，因品种不同能忍受的极限最低温度是－16℃～－5℃，一般在－10℃时受冻严重。此外，茶树受冻程度还与低温持续时间有关。通常认为：凡冬季负积温总值超过－100℃·d，极限最低气温低于－10℃，日均气温低于

0℃的连续超过14天，茶树在该年冬季即易受冻。

茶树在日较差较大的环境下生长，对茶叶品质非常有利。因为白天的光合作用强，合成有机物质多，晚上呼吸作用弱，消耗物质少，能使茶树体内有效物质积累多，从而形成高山茶或高纬度茶"香高、味浓"的品质特点。

2. 水分

茶树的一切正常生命活动都必须在细胞含有一定的水分状况下才能进行。茶树中光合、呼吸、营养物质的吸收和运输等生理活动的进行都必须有水分的参与。

降水量：茶树生长发育所需的水分多来自自然降水。茶树性喜湿润，喜湿怕涝，适宜栽培茶树的地区年降雨量要求在1000毫米以上，最适宜的年降雨量为1500毫米左右。在生长季节月降雨量要求大于100毫米以上。如连续几个月的降雨量低于50毫米，又未采取人工灌溉措施的，茶叶产量将大幅降低；若月降雨量大于300毫米且有一次以上暴雨，也不利于茶树生长。

空气湿度：空气湿度能影响土壤水分的蒸发和茶树的蒸腾作用。适宜茶树生长发育的空气湿度为80%～90%。若小于50%时，新梢生长将受到抑制，低于40%茶树将受害。当空气相对湿度高时，可以减少土壤水分蒸发，降低茶树蒸腾作用，提高水分利用率；同时相对湿度高于90%时，往往可形成云雾，降低直射光强度，改变光质，增加漫射光比例，有利于茶叶优良品质的形成。

土壤含水量：茶园土壤中的水分状况，直接影响茶树根系的生长，也间接影响茶树地上部分的生长。茶树在土壤相对含水量为70%～80%时生长良好，各项生理生化指标均较好，当土壤相对含水量亏缺或过量时都会使茶树生育受阻。

3. 光

茶树与其他作物一样，利用光能合成自身生长所需的碳水化合物，同时通过光质、光强和光周期调节其生长发育。

光照强度：茶树具有喜光耐荫、忌强光直射的特点。茶树的光饱和点较高，为 $2.1\sim3.0J/cm^2\cdot min$；茶树的光补偿点较低，仅占全光的1%左右。由于成熟茶树叶片中叶绿素b含量高，对较短波长的光谱有较强吸收，使得茶树适合在漫射光中生长，而忌强光直射。茶树适度遮阴可提高茶叶中氨基酸总量和新梢的持嫩性。

光质：光质对茶树体内碳、氮代谢途径有着重要的调节作用。与白光相比，红橙光能促进芽梢伸长、叶面积扩大；蓝、紫光抑制芽梢伸长，但蓝、紫光可促进氮代谢和蛋白质的合成，此外，紫光与一些含氮的品质生化成分如氨基酸、维生素和很多香气成分的形成有着直接的关系。在一定海拔高度的茶区，因雨量充沛，云雾多，空气湿度大，漫射光丰富，蓝、紫光比重增加，所以茶叶中的氨基酸、叶绿素和含氮芳香物质多，茶多酚含量低，这也是高山云雾出好茶的原因之一。

光照时间：光照时间对茶树的影响主要表现在两个方面，即辐射总量和光周期现象。日照时间越长，茶树叶片接受光能的时间越长，叶绿素吸收的辐射能量就越多，光合产物积累量就越大，有利于茶树生育和茶叶产量的提高。茶树是一种短日照植物，日照时数较短的季节或地区，利于茶树的繁殖生长，不仅能提早开花的时间，使花量增大，同时使新梢生长缓慢，提早休眠。相反，日照时数较长的季节或地区，茶树的营养生长期加强，推迟新梢休眠和开花时间，使花量减少，甚至不开花。当冬季连续6周每日光照少于11小时，茶树进入相对休眠期。

4. 土壤

土质疏松、土层深厚、排水良好的砾质、砂质酸性土壤适宜茶树生长。

茶树是一种多年生深根作物，根系分布可伸展到地表2米以下，所以要求茶园有效土层达1米以上；同时地下水位应低于茶树根系分布部位，以避免茶树根系被淹，影响根系生长发育和营养元素的吸收。

茶树是喜酸土壤和嫌钙的植物。适宜种茶的pH为4.0～6.0之间，最佳为5.0～5.5。当pH＞6.0时，茶苗生长不良，叶色发黄，有明显的失绿症；严重的则顶芽枯死，根系发红变黑。当pH＜4.0时，就会发生H^+中毒症，叶色由绿转暗再变红，根系变红、变黑，甚至死亡。茶树对钙的需求比一般作物低得多，如果与同时生长在酸性土壤中的桑树和橘树相比，几乎要低十几倍以至几十倍。当土壤中活性含量钙含量超过0.5%（CaO计）时，茶树生长就会不正常，严重时还会死亡。所以，茶树不适宜种植在石灰性紫色土和石灰性冲积土中。

茶园土壤的有机质是土壤微生物生活的物质基础和茶树多种微量营养元素的来源，其含量高低可反映茶园土壤熟化度和肥力水平。高产优质茶园土壤有机质含量要求达到2.0%以上。

综上所述，茶树具有"喜暖怕寒、喜湿怕涝、喜光怕晒、喜酸怕碱"的生态学特点。

Lesson 9
Tea Cultivars and Propagation

The construction of the new tea gardens and the replant of the old ones firstly need to solve the problems of tea species choosing and propagating.

1. Tea-tree Species and Their Selection

Tea tree species are the crucial factor that determine the quantity of the product, the quality of fresh leaves and processed tea. Being the original country of tea, China has a long history of **utilizing** and cultivating tea plants. Through long-term natural and artificial selection, it has formed abundant germplasm resources. There are more than 600 cultivated varieties in China, among which 96 varieties have been examined and approved by national and 120 varieties by provincial reviews respectively.

Different varieties have different characteristics. For instance, the blades can be large, medium and small; the bud colours have the distinction of being dark green, green, yellow green and purple; the sprout time can be early, middle and late. Meanwhile, quite large differences also lie in product quantity, stress resistance, process suitability and tea quality. As a result, when selecting the tea plant species, we should take the following aspects into consideration:

(1) To be fully aware of the ecological condition of garden, especially the status of soil, light, temperature, moisture, vegetation, natural enemies and disease pests and weeds, and choose the corresponding and strongly resistant plant varieties.

(2) On the basis of determining the appropriate tea species, choose the main

plant species with good processed suitability and quality and at the same time to match them with species that have different sprout times and complementary qualities. The practice shows that in terms of sprout time, the suitable match ratio of different species are 50%~60% for the early ones, 30%~40% for the middle and 10% for the late. This kind of collocation has the advantages of prolonging production season, relieving labor shortages and avoiding the economic loss caused by the rapid **diffusion** of plant diseases and insect pests and natural disasters resulted from the single plant species. In addition, through the reasonable collocation of different species with characteristics such as rich fragrance, fresh taste, the tea species can be mutually complemented so that the qualities improved and better products characteristics established.

2. Tea Plant Propagation

1) Propagation Classification and Characteristics

The propagation of tea plants can be classified into sexual and asexual propagation, the former of which propagate the descendent by breeds while the latter applies the ways of utilizing vegetative organs and somatic cells, such as cutting, layering, plant dividing and grafting, of which cutting plays a main role. Most of the tea plant varieties have the two reproductive capacity concurrently, but at present, the asexual propagation has been applied mostly due to its advantages of maintaining the characteristics of tea species, which can be beneficial to the management of the tea gardens, mechanized tea leaves pickup and processing, and can improve the tea quality in order to create the famous well-qualified tea. Its tea seedlings being root-strong and well-resistant, the sexual propagation are mainly applied in the high altitude areas where winter temperatures are quite low, or the relatively cold high mountain areas.

2) Propagation Methods

①Seed Propagation

The number of seed orchards which are specially set in our country is quite limited and the tea seeds are mainly collected in the bearing bushes during the ten days before and after the Frost's Descend Day (October, 22). The ripe tea seeds' shells are dark brown and shiny and their cotyledons are full and white. Before sown, the seeds need to be stored for a period. The suitable seeds for storage should have the moisture content of 30%, and the surrounding temperature is 5~

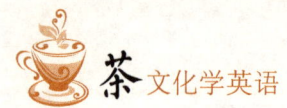

7 ℃, and humidity 60%～65%. Meanwhile, ventilation should be paid much attention to in order to adjust the temperature and humidity to ensure the needs of seeds' physiological activities. The methods of storage include piled storage, trench storage and patch storage. They all need a layer of fine sand at the bottom and then press tea seeds and sand in layers (each being 3～4 cm) or mix and place them by the ratio of 1∶1; the top layer should be covered by fine sands and straws with bamboo tubes for ventilation inserted in the pile. The height of the piles had better be controlled around 30 cm, the breadth within 1m, and length unlimited.

Most of the tea areas in China sowed tea plants from November to next March. After the processes of presoaking and pregermination, tea seeds can be sown when 40%～50% of them begin to reveal the radicles. During sowing, the soil should not be too thick, and the most suitable sowing depth is 3～5 cm. In direct sowing at large fields, the seeds can be sown according to the planned spaces of the tea gardens with each hole dibbling 3～5 seeds. After sowing, the holes should be covered with soil and pressed properly. In general, tea seeds won't sprout until May or June and the seedling emergence will be done in July.

Each seedling which is nurtured carefully will reach the height of over 25 cm, and the highest can be over 60 cm. To cultivate the seedlings propagated by the seeds, following works should be paid attention to in this year. Firstly, control the weeds in time to reduce the weeds which compete with plantings for water and nutrients. Secondly, fertilizers should be used multiply which should be done during June to September and commonly using the organic liquid fertilizers. Thirdly, plant diseases and insect pests should be prevented and controlled timely to ensure the normal growth of the tea plants.

②Clonal Propagation

To carry out the clonal propagation, parent fields for cutting should be established at first to provide the qualified cutting slips. The parent fields require that the grown plants must be the original clone seedlings with a varietal purity of 100%. At the same time, the management of water and fertilizer should be **enhanced**, plant diseases and insect pests should be prevented timely, and proper pruning and topping should be carried out in order to cultivate the strong branches.

Generally speaking, tea plant can be cutting sown all year round as long as there are cutting origins. However, in terms of the qualities of cuttings, they prefer to be sown in summers; and in terms of the **comprehensive** economic benefits, they'd better be sown in the early autumns, because in this way the qualities can be guaranteed and costs lowered so that the income of tea gardens can be increased.

In order to improve the cutting survival rate and seedling quality, the quality of cuttings and process technique must be grasped strictly. The shoots used as cuttings should be over 25 cm in length and 3~5 cm in stem diameter; 2/3 of their new tips will be lignification and presenting the colour of red or yellow green. It is best to shear the cuttings before 10 a.m. or after 3 p.m., and the cuttings should be put in the cool and moist places. Shearing and cutting should be done timely. The standard cuttings should be 3~4.5 cm in length with 1 or 2 matured leaves and a full axillary bud. After shearing, the cuttings can be processed using plant growth potion to prompt their roots. The cuttings are generally inserted on the seedling beds with row spaces of 7~10 cm; the plant distance depends on the leaves widths of different tea varieties and the blades had better be covered slightly. When inserted, the depth is appropriate to be two thirds of the cuttings and the distance which petioles could match the soil bed. What's more, the nearby soil should be pressed slightly to make a close contact of cuttings and soil, which is good for rooting.

In Japan, direct introduction of cuttings through paper pots with unclosed bottom becames popular. In this method, damage of vigorous root growth due to **transplanting** is lower than that of soil bed. The size of paper pot used for cutting depends on the size of plant at the time of transplanting. In Shizuoka, a convenient size for one-year-old cutting is 6 cm diameter and 15 cm in length. Even though the cutting grows than 30 cm in height, the paper pot can be moved from the nursery bed without any damage of roots.

After inserting, works such as water, light, fertilizer, weed control and disease, pest and cold prevention should be managed well. When the seedlings have reached over 20 cm in height and 1.8 mm in stem diameter, they can be transplanted.

New words and expressions 生词和短语

utilizing [ˈjutəlaɪz] *v.* 利用, 运用
diffusion [dɪˈfjuːʒ(ə)n] *n.* 扩散, 传播
enhance [ɪnˈhɑːns] *v.* 提高, 加强
comprehensive [kɒmprɪˈhensɪv] *adj.* 综合的, 广泛的
transplanting [trænspˈlɑːntɪŋ] *v.* 移植

Comprehension 理解

Give answers to the following questions in your own words and complete sentences as far as possible.

1. What are the advantages of sexual propagation?
2. Please summarize in short the factors that should be taken into consideration when selecting the tea seeds.
3. Summarize the process of breed propagation.
4. What should be paid attention to before, during and after the process of cutting respectively?

Notes on the text 课文注释

Frost's Descend Day：霜降是二十四节气中的第十八个节气，是秋季的最后一个节气，也是秋季到冬季的过渡节气。每年阳历10月23日前后，太阳到达黄经210度时为二十四节气中的霜降。

Translation 参考译文

茶树栽培品种及繁育

新茶园建设和老茶园改植换种时，首先要解决怎样选择茶树品种和如何繁育的问题。

78

1. 茶树品种及其选择

茶树品种是决定茶园产量、鲜叶和成品茶质量最重要的因素。我国是茶树的原产地，茶树开发和栽培的历史十分悠久，经过长期的自然选择和人工选择，形成了丰富的品种资源。现有茶树栽培品种600多个，经国家和省级审（认）定的品种分别为96个和120个。

不同的品种有不同的特性，如：叶片有大、中、小三类，芽叶色泽有深绿、绿、黄绿和紫色之分，萌芽有早、中、晚之别；同时，不同茶叶品种在产量高低、抗逆性强弱、茶类适制性和茶叶品质高低方面都存在较大的差异，所以，在选择茶树品种时，要着重考虑以下几个方面：

（1）要充分了解园地的生态条件，特别是土壤、光照、温度、水分、植被、天敌以及病虫草害的现状，选择与之相适应的、抗性强的茶树品种。

（2）在确定适宜发展的茶类基础上，选择适制性好、品质优异的主栽品种，同时选择搭配一些不同萌芽期和品质特色互补的茶树品种。实践表明：萌芽迟和早的品种最佳搭配比例为：早生种50％～60％，中生种30％～40％，晚生种10％，这样可以达到延长生产季节，缓解茶季劳动力不足的目的，也能避免因为品种单一造成病虫害等自然灾害的快速扩散而导致巨大经济损失；同时，将不同品质特色的产品进行合理搭配，比如香气浓郁的茶和滋味清淡的茶搭配，可以取长补短，提高茶叶品质，打造产品特色。

2. 茶树繁育

1）繁育类型及特点

茶树繁育包括有性繁育和无性繁育两大类。有性繁育是以种子的形式繁育后代的方式，无性繁育是利用营养器官或体细胞等繁育后代的方式，如扦插、压条、分株、嫁接等方法，其中以扦插为主。绝大多数茶树品种兼有有性繁育和无性繁育的双重繁育能力，但目前在生产中主要应用无性繁育的方式，因为这种繁育方式能很好地保持茶树良种的特性，有利于茶园管理、机械化采茶和茶叶加工，有利于提高茶叶品质，创制名优茶。有性繁育因其茶苗主根发达、抗逆性强的特点，目前主要在冬季气温低的高纬度茶区或一些较寒冷的高山茶区应用。

(2) 繁育方法

①种子繁育

我国目前设立的专用留种园很少，一般都在采叶园（bearing bushes）中采种。茶籽一般在霜降（10月22日）前后10天采摘。成熟的茶籽外壳为黑褐色，富有光泽，种内子叶饱满，呈乳白色。茶籽播种前需经过一段时间的贮藏，适宜茶籽贮藏的含水量为30%，环境温度为5℃～7℃，湿度为60%～65%，同时还要注意通风，以调节温度、湿度，满足茶籽生理活动的需要。茶籽贮藏的方式有堆藏法、沟藏法和畦藏法。无论哪种贮藏方式都需要在底部铺上一层细砂，然后把茶籽与砂分层放置（每层厚3～4厘米）或按1∶1拌匀后混合放置，上层盖上细砂和稻草，堆中插入通气竹管。堆的高度宜控制在30厘米左右，宽度宜在1米以内，长度不限。

我国大多数茶区在11月至翌年3月播种。播种前茶籽需要经过浸种、催芽处理，当有40%～50%的茶籽露出胚根时就可以进行播种。播种时盖土不宜太厚，最适宜的播种深度为3～5厘米。大田直播时按照茶园规划的株行距直接播种，每穴播种3～5粒。播种后覆土，并适当压紧。一般情况下，茶籽播种后要到5～6月份才开始出苗，7月份齐苗。

凡经过精心培育的茶苗，当年苗高可达25厘米以上，最高的可达60厘米以上。茶籽繁育的幼苗在当年应做好以下工作：第一，及时除草，防止杂草与茶苗争夺水分和养分；第二，多次追肥，追肥一般在6至9月份，以施有机液肥为主；第三，及时防治病虫害，确保茶树正常生长。

②扦插繁育

进行茶树扦插繁育，首先要建立采穗母本园，以提供优质插穗。母本园要求所栽苗木必须是原种无性系苗，保证品种纯度达到100%，同时加强水肥管理，及时防治病虫害，进行合理修剪和分期打顶，培养壮枝。

一般而言，只要有穗源，茶树一年四季都可以扦插，但从扦插苗木质量来看，以夏插为优，从综合经济效益来看，选择早秋扦插为理想，可保证质量又降低成本，增加茶园收入。

为了提高扦插茶树成活率和苗木质量，必须严格把握剪穗质量和扦插技术。用作穗条的枝梢长度要求在25厘米以上，茎粗3～5毫米，2/3的新梢木质化，呈红色或黄绿色。剪取时间以上午10时前或下午3时后为宜，剪下的穗条应放在阴凉、湿润处。穗条剪取后应及时剪穗和扦插。插穗的标准是：长度约3~4.5厘米，带有1~2个成熟叶和一个饱满的腋芽。插穗剪取后，可采用植物生长类药剂处理，促进生根。插穗一般插在苗畦上，其行距7~10厘米，株距依茶树品种叶片宽度而定，以叶片稍有遮叠为宜。扦插时，深度以插入插穗长度的2/3、至叶柄与畦面平齐为宜，并将插穗附近的土稍压实，使插穗与土壤紧密相接，以利生根。

在日本，通常将插穗插在未封底口的纸钵中，移苗时对根系的损伤小于土插。纸钵的大小取决于茶苗移栽时的大小。在静冈，生产的纸钵大小为直径6厘米，高度为156厘米。即使扦插苗的高度超过30厘米，纸钵也能与基质分离，且不损伤任何根系。

扦插后要做好水分、光照、施肥、除草、病虫防治以及防寒工作，当茶苗高度达到20厘米以上，茎粗达到1.8毫米以上时，可进行茶苗移栽。

Lesson 10
Tea Cultivation and Plucking

Tea is a labor-intensive crop, requiring tremendous human efforts at every stage of cultivation from propagation to plucking. This lesson mainly focuses on the relevant knowledge of how to build tea frame formation, fertilizing application, diseases and pest control, and tea plucking.

1. Frame Formation

Tea, left to its own natural devices will grow into a fairly **substantial** tree. For tea production, however, it is necessary to shorten the tea plants into bushes, and great care is taken to create a shape which lends itself to consistent picking, or plucking. This process, called *bringing into bearing* or *frame formation*, is achieved through pruning and, in some cases, pegging. Pegging is the practice of bending some branches down and pegging them into position. The relatively flat, consistent surface of the trained tea bushes is known as the *plucking table*.

Repeated plucking of the new growth on the plucking table eventually results in a growing surface that is heavily **congested** by old stems, and this must be cut out periodically, either by *skiffing*, a cut at only the highest levels, which allows new growth and thus new plucking to return quickly, or by *maintenance pruning* (trimming or pruning), a deeper cut, which also has the effect of lowering the plucking table down to a convenient height for the people doing the plucking. *Skiffing* is done generally either after every harvesting to keep the surface uniform for mechanical plucking and to increase the number of branches and plucking surface areas, or in autumn to remove the late-emerging shoot. Because of differences of effects between trimming and pruning, these treatments are done in different periods, the former every 2～3 years and the latter every 5 years. The aging tea plant needs tippy, after which the stem should be left 4～6 inches high. This process increases the number of branches which will produce fresh buds for plucking and help to produce a flat table for plucking.

2. Fertilizer Application

In every phase of the tea tree growth, a mineral nutrition from the soil is needed to support the crop. In order to meet this requirement and enhance the new branches, in the process of cultivation, a scientific fertilizer application is necessary, taking such principles into consideration as the characteristics of the tea tree nutrition, the law of fertilizing, nature of the soil nutrition and the effects of the fertilizers.

Compared with other plants, tea trees are characterized with the nature of "ammonium-loving, aluminum-collecting, manganese-containing, calcium-disgusting and chloride-avoiding". When a fertilizer is considered, it is better to choose an ammonium nitrogen fertilizer, eg. Ammonium sulfate, and Urea. As to a tea garden with high pH, a certain amount of Aluminium sulfate is better in order to provide tea trees with enough aluminium elements. When the fertilizing is done to the tender tea trees, it should avoid using those containing chloride or calcium.

The fertilizing also should consider such conditions as the kinds of the tea, the growth, the garden, the ecology and the other planting situations (irrigating, cultivating and plucking). For instance, different kinds will produce the bud at different times from 15 to 30 days, so the time to fertilize should be different. In some area, the spring is dry and cold, and the growth of the tea tree is restricted, while in the summer and fall, it is hot and rainy, and then the tea tree grows fast and needs more fertilizer, then it is the high time to fertilize and the amount of the fertilizer should be large. When the tea tree is tender, the fertilizer should be rich in Phosphorus and potassium in order to enhance the growth of the roots and build up a big system as well as a thick stem. In a garden of green tea, it is suitable to relatively increase the rate of nitrogenous fertilizer, while the one of black tea needs more phosphate fertilizer.

The established means of fertilizing are the following: "nutrition quota of abundance-or-lack", "the balance of soil nutrition", "the target yield" and "the function of the fertilizer effects", *etc*. At present, China mainly adopts a means of nitrogen-determining from experience, that is, a 100kg of dry tea will need 12~15kg of nitrogen, and the best **ratio** of these three elements (Nitrogen, Phosphorus and Potassium) is (2~4) : 1 : (1~2), so the amount of phosphorus and potassium can be clearly determined. When there is short of other nutritious elements, it is easy to determine and to provide. In other countries, "the balance of soil nutrition" is usually used. In Japan, plucking is generally done 2 or 3 times a year. 18,000kg/ha leaf is harvested annually, containing approximately 225kg N, 36kg P_2O_5 and 135kg K_2O. The absorption rates for nitrogen, phosphorus and potassium by tea plants are estimated to be 40%~50%, 20% and 45%, respectively. Generally, the standard amount of fertilizer is determined according to the total amount of tea flushes annually harvested and their contents of elements that is equal to 540kg N, 180kg P_2O_5 and 270kg K_2O per hectare.

3. Diseases and Pest Control in Tea Field

There are many insects and diseases attacking to tea mature or new leaves, twigs or roots. Pests are most notorious because they cause damages directly to the shoots. To protect tea plants from these pests and diseases, agricultural chemicals are used under very strict rules and conditions. Now, the area of organic cultivation is increasing and new techniques are being developed to reduce the amount of the agricultural chemicals. For instance, the cultivars with high resistance against pasts are selected for breeding. Light traps (in determined **optimum** spraying date for lepidopterans), sex pheromone dispensers disruption of communication, mild pesticides (**conserving** spontaneous natural enemies) and so on are recommended to use.

4. Tea Plucking

Generally, from April to October, tea shoots grow and harvest 2~4 times, first crop in late April to mid May, second crop in late June, third crop in late July to early August and fourth crop in mid September. The average yield of tea field is 8000 kg in the first harvest, 6000 kg in the second harvest and 4000 kg per hectare in the third harvest. First crop posses the highest quality and the highest price.

In Japan, the tea whose plucking is done by hand will be manufactured into the high-ranking one, where shears are widely used. The best teas are made from the youngest shoots of the plant, and pickers are taught to be very selective. 2 leaves with 1 bud **constitutes** a fine plucking, more than this is a coarse plucking. A practiced picker on a lower-grown or level estate can pluck about 90,000 shoots a day.

The freshly plucked tea must be carefully handled. If it is piled too high in the baskets used to collect it, the leaves at the bottom will be crushed, and bacterial is produced, potentially harming the quality. Generally, the fresh-plucked leaves are transported immediately to the factory, where processing begins, and the tea is on its way to becoming green, Oolong, or black tea, etc.

New words and expressions 生词和短语

ratio [ˈreɪʃɪəʊ] n. 比例，系数　　optimum [ˈɒptɪməm] adj. 最适宜的
conserving [kənˈsɜːv] v. 保存，保护　constitute [ˈkɒnstɪtjuːt] v. 构成，组成
substantial [səbˈstænʃ(ə)l] adj. 大量的；结实的，牢固的；重大的
congested [kənˈdʒestɪd] adj. 拥挤的；充满的

Comprehension 理解

Give answers to the following questions in your own words and complete sentences as far as possible.

1. Why is tea a labor-and-attention-intensive crop?
2. How to form a good tea tree?
3. What is a plucking table?
4. What facts should be kept in mind when fertilizing?
5. What is an organic cultivation of tea?

Translation 参考译文

茶树栽培与采收

茶树是一种劳动力密集型的作物，从育苗到采摘，每个阶段都需要花费大

量的人力。本文仅介绍茶树树冠培养、茶园施肥、病虫害控制和茶叶采收方面的相关知识。

1. 树冠培养

若是放任茶树自然生长，它们会长成参天大树。生产上，常需要通过修剪或压条的方法矮化茶树并形成一定的树形，从而有利于茶叶采摘，这个过程被称为树冠培养。压条就是把某些树枝压弯，使它们固定到某个位置。经过修剪形成相对平整一致的树冠表层就是所谓的"采摘面"。

采摘面上的新梢经反复采摘后会形成密聚的节结需要定期清除，一种方法是采用轻修剪的方式，可使茶树快速发芽，继续采摘；另一种是采用整形修剪的方式（包括深修剪和重修剪），它不仅能去除节结，同时还能降低采摘面的高度，方便采摘。轻修剪一般在每轮茶季后进行，其目的是为保持采摘面的一致，有利于机械采摘，同时也可增加发芽枝条数和扩大采摘面；轻修剪也可在秋天进行，其目的是剪去晚发的枝梢。由于深修剪和重修剪的作用不同，所以进行的周期不同，深修剪一般每2～3年进行一次，而重修剪每5年进行一次。当茶树衰老后应进行台刈，台刈过后的树干高度为4～6英寸（约10～15厘米）。台刈后树干会萌发新枝，通过定型修剪，会形成一个新的采摘面。

2. 茶园施肥

茶树整个生命周期的各个生育阶段，需要从土壤中吸收矿质营养，以保持其正常生长发育。为了满足茶树生长发育的需要，促进茶树新梢的正常生长，在茶树栽培过程中，需要根据茶树营养特点、需肥规律、土壤供肥性能与肥料效应运用科学施肥技术进行茶园施肥。

与其他植物相比，茶树具有"喜铵、聚铝、富锰、嫌钙、忌氯"的营养学特点。在肥料选择时，应优先选择铵态氮肥，如：硫酸铵、尿素等。对于pH偏高的茶园，应施用一定量的硫酸铝肥料，以满足茶树对铝元素的需求。在对茶园特别是幼年茶园施肥时，应尽量选择不含氯离子、钙离子的肥料。

茶园肥料还要根据茶树品种特点、生长情况、茶园类型、生态条件以及所采用的其他农艺措施（灌溉、耕作和采摘等）的实际情况进行合理施用。比如茶树品种不同（早芽种与迟芽种的发芽时间相差15～30天），施肥时间就应不同。有的茶区春天干旱，气温低，春茶生长受到一定的限制，而夏、秋季气温高，雨水多，茶树长势猛，吸肥量多，施肥效果好，所以可以适当提高夏、秋茶追肥比例。幼龄茶园应适当提高磷、钾肥用量比例，以促进茶树的根茎生长，培养庞大的根系和粗壮的骨干枝。生产绿茶的茶园，可适当提高氮肥的比例，而生产红茶的则应提高磷肥的比例。

茶园施肥量的确定方法有"养分丰缺指标法""地力平衡法""目标产量法"和"肥料效应函数法"等。目前，我国主要采用"以产定氮法"，即：每生产100千克干茶需要施用 12～15 千克纯氮，而氮、磷、钾的最佳配比为 (2～4)：1：(1～2)，从而可以确定磷和钾的含量，其他营养元素在缺乏时适量施用，以缺补缺。其他国家主要采用"地力平衡法"：在日本，每年采茶 2～3 轮，每公顷年采鲜叶 18 000 千克，大约含 225 千克 N、36 千克 P_2O_5 和 135 千克 K_2O，茶树吸收氮、磷、钾的效率分别为 40%～50%，20% 和 45%。通常茶园标准施肥量取决于鲜叶的年采收量，其营养元素的含量相当于每公顷施用 540 千克 N、180 千克 P_2O_5 和 270 千克 K_2O。

3. 茶园病虫控制

危害茶树新老叶芽和根茎枝叶的昆虫和病害有很多，最难缠的是危害叶芽的害虫。为了保护茶树和茶叶，在一定的规范管理和条件下会使用许多农用化学药剂。现在，有机种植的面积在不断扩大，降低化学药品残留的新技术不断发展。例如选育强抗病虫品种，使用诱光技术（准确测定鳞翅目昆虫的活动周期），利用散播性信息素进行干预，使用适量杀虫剂（保护害虫的自然天敌），等等。诸如此类的新措施越来越得以推广。

4. 茶叶采摘

一般情况下，4～10 月是茶芽生长期，可以收获 2～4 轮，第一轮在 4 月末到 5 月中旬，第二轮在 6 月末，第三轮在 7 月末到 8 月初，第四轮在 9 月中旬。每公顷茶园每轮的平均产量约为：第一轮 8000 千克，第二轮 6000 千克，第三轮 4000 千克。第一轮的茶叶品质最好，价格也最高。

在日本运用机械采摘的地方，手工采摘的茶都会加工成特级或高级别的茶。最好的茶来自最嫩的茶芽，采茶人必须善于挑选。采 1 芽 2 叶还属于嫩采，多于此就是粗采了。在地势低或平坦的茶园里，一个熟练的采茶工一天可以采摘 90 000 多个芽叶。

新采的茶必须小心处理。若是在采摘篮里堆得过高，底下的叶芽就会被压烂滋生细菌，影响新茶质量。通常新采下的叶芽会被立刻送往工厂，在那里被制成绿茶、乌龙或红茶。

Lesson 11
Tea and Its Processing

There are thousands of varieties of Chinese tea in the market, varying with different shapes, colors and Havors. How should we know and learn them? First, we have to keep their names in mind, then, come to know their characteristics. It will of course take a lot of time to remember them one by one. So it would be quick and efficient after we have some ideas of how the tea is named, processed and classified.

1. Labeling of the Tea

Each species of tea has to be labeled with a particular name. The naming of tea is based on a number of criteria:

(1) the shape of made tea: e. g. gunpowder tea, brick tea, silver needle tea.

(2) the color of dried tea and infusion e. g. Yellow Bud tea, Pekoe.

(3) the species of the tea trees e. g. Oolong tea, Ti Kuan Yin, .

(4) the time when the tea was picked and processed. e. g. Spring tea, Summer tea, Autumnal tea

(5) the method of processing e. g. fried green tea, baked green tea, steamed green tea.

(6) the market assigned for the specific type of tea e. g. tea for domestic, tea for export, tea for consumption in border region, tea for overseas .

(7) the regions of production and the species e. g. Wuyi rock-essence tea, West Lake Longjing tea, Mengding Yellow Bud tea, Keemun Black tea, Yunan Black tea.

In view of the different tea types, a uniform naming system is desirable to avoid confusion. In many cases, one species is given several names, or several tea species have the same name. Hence a reasonable system of classification and naming is indispensable to differentiate between the species for scientific researches, production, sale and consumption purposes.

2. Tea Processing

The fresh leaves picked from tea garden must be first manufactured before drinking. According to the materials, the processing of tea can be roughly divided into three types primary processing, fine processing and reprocessing.

The primary processing means to change the fresh tea leaves into the raw tea. It includes the following procedures: fixing, withering, rolling, rotating, yellowing, piling, fermenting and drying. Totally, these procedures consist of the following six fundamental parts:

(1) fresh leaf →fixing→rolling→drying(Green tea)

(2) fresh leaf →fixing→rolling→yellowing→drying(Yellow tea)

(3) fresh leaf →fixing→rolling→piling→drying(Dark tea)

(4) fresh leaf →withering→drying(White tea)

(5) fresh leaf →withering→rotating→fixing→rolling→drying(Qing tea or Oolong tea)

(6) fresh leaf →withering→rolling→fermenting→drying(Black tea)

During the primary processing, because of the different degree of **enzymes**-controlling in the fresh leaves, the biochemical elements of the fresh leaves have been transformed in different ways, and produced accordingly different teas with distinctive qualities and styles. The raw teas mainly can be classified into six basic categories, namely, Green tea, Yellow tea, Dark tea, White tea, Qing tea and Black tea.

In fine processing, physical methods —such as sifting, sorting, cutting and blending— are used, and the quality of the raw tea is **standardized**. The product is known as refined tea. Refined from Twisted fried green tea and Round Pan-dried green tea, there are Chunmee tea and Gunpowder tea which chiefly are aimed to output; while refined from baked-dried (cured) green tea, there is mainly Jasmine **scented** tea. Sun—dried green tea and the raw dark tea can be refined into the compressed tea。

During the reprocessing, the dark and green tea or black teas are shaped to brick, cake, bowl, and etc. by the application of pressure after the steaming and piling procedures. Also reprocessing involves the addition of other products by special processes resulting in teas with distinctive characteristics different from any of the basic teas as materials. At present, the reprocessed tea such as: scented tea, compressed tea, extracted tea, fruit flavored tea, healthy tea and *etc.* are produced.

3. The Criteria Used in the Classification of Tea

How to categorize the different types of tea is a controversial issue. Some people suggest that tea should be classified according to the degree of **fermentation** taking place in the leaves during processing, some advocate categorization on the basis of the extent of withering of the tea leaves. others suggestions are reference to the leaf shape, color, plant species or growth season. Opinions on the subject are so diverse that there seems to be no definite solution to the issue.

However relatively scientific method of classifying tea should satisfy two criteria, first, stating the quality of a particular tea type within the framework of a standardized grading system; second, reflecting the processing methods involved. Tea is a commodity. Various types of tea are qualitatively different. The differences in quality originate from the distinctive processing methods. Owing to different ways of processing, black tea and green tea differ utterly in terms of color, odor and taste. Fermentation is a necessary step in processing black tea which facilitates the activation of the enzymes in tea leaves and the relatively thorough **oxidation** of the **phenol** content. In contrast, green tea has to be exposed to intense heat to destroy the oxidation and activation of the enzymes, evaporate the water content in the tea leaves. As the processing techniques for green tea and these for black tea are different, the chemical changes which their contents undergo differently also lead to vast distinctions in their quality. Congou Black tea and Souchong are similar in quality and are processed in basically the same monner. Both require complete fermentation. Hence they fall under the same category. There is no significant difference between fried green tea and baked green tea. These two are treated in similar ways: intense heat is applied to **inhibit** the oxidation of the enzymes, preserve the original color of the leaves and soften the leaves. They are of the same category. Obviously, tea should be firstly classified according to the processing methods in order to establish a complete naming system.

Moreover, classification should be based on the shape and chemical content of the leaves. The most prominent indication of the qualitative difference between various spices of tea is the diversity of their colors. Green tea (including the fresh leaves, dried leaves and the beverage made from the leaves) is usually green, though differ types of green tea may show different shades of green. Some other types of tea like the Mengding Yellow Bud tea and the Silver Needle tea of Mountain Jun turn yellow after special treatment. They therefore belong to the category of yellow tea. Oolong tea, a type of qing tea, undergoes slight withering and partial fermentation during processing. Its color is between green and blue. If the color goes darker, it will look like and become the black tea. If processing procedures of tea vary greatly hence they fall under different categories.

The majority of tea experts agree that the traditional classification system used by the Chinese workers. That is the six basic tea types as follows: green tea, yellow tea, dark tea, white tea, qing tea and black tea.

New words and expressions
生词和短语

enzymes [ˌenzaɪˈmæs] n. 酶
oxidation [ˌɒdɪˈdeɪʃ(ə)n] n. 氧化(作用);氧化
phenol [ˈfiːnɒl] n. 酚;酚类
standardized [ˈstændəˌdaɪzd] adj. 标准的;标准化的
scented [ˈsentɪd] adj. 有香味的;有气味的;洒了香水的
fermentation [ˌfɜːmenˈteɪʃn] n. 发酵
inhibit [ɪnˈhɪbɪt] v. 抑制;阻止;

Comprehension
理 解

Give answers to the following questions in your own words and complete sentences as far as possible.

1. How many types the processing of tea has and what are they?
2. What is the product of the fixing progress?
3. What are the same principal processes undergone by all types of tea in the

final stage?

4. What is the difference between the fine processing and reprocessing?

5. Can you give some other examples of reprocessed tea?

Notes on the text 课文注释

1. Fixing：杀青，通过高温破坏和钝化鲜茶叶中的氧化酶活性，抑制鲜叶中的茶多酚等的酶促氧化，蒸发鲜叶部分水分，使茶叶变软，便于揉捻成形，同时散发青臭味，是促进良好香气形成的一种制茶步骤。

2. Rolling：揉捻，揉捻是绿茶塑造外形的一道工序。通过利用外力，使叶片揉破变轻，卷转成条，同时部分茶汁附着在叶表面，便于冲泡。

3. Pan-fired green tea：炒青绿茶，炒青是绿茶杀青的一种方式。

Translation 参考译文

茶叶和茶的加工

市场上有成百上千种茶叶，它们形态不一、颜色不同、味道各异。我们如何去认识这些茶叶产品呢？我们首先必须记住这些茶的名字，其次是要掌握这些茶叶的品质特点。如此众多的茶，如果我们一个一个去了解它的品质特点是一件非常耗时的事情。如果我们能首先了解茶叶的命名、加工和分类方法，则有助于我们快速有效地了解众多的茶叶产品。

1. 茶叶的命名方法

每一种茶叶都有一个特定的名字，茶叶的命名基于以下几点：

(1) 成茶的形状，如珠茶、砖茶、银针茶等；

(2) 干茶以及茶汤的色泽，如黄芽、白毫等；

(3) 茶树品种，如乌龙茶、铁观音等；

(4) 茶叶采摘和加工的时间，如春茶、夏茶、秋茶等；

(5) 茶叶加工方法，如炒青、烘青、蒸青绿茶等；

(6) 茶叶投放的市场，即内销、外销、边销和侨销等；

(7) 茶叶产地及种类，如武夷岩茶、西湖龙井、蒙顶黄芽茶、祁红、滇红等。

众多的茶叶种类需要一个统一的命名系统，以免发生混乱。有时一种茶可以有好几个名字，或者是不同的茶叶共有一个名字。因此，为了便于科研、生产、销售及消费等需要区分各种茶，而一个合理的茶叶分类和命名系统必不可少。

2. 茶叶加工

从茶园中采摘的鲜叶都需要加工才能成为可供饮用的产品。根据原料的不同，茶叶的加工方法可以分为初加工、精加工和再加工三种。

初加工是将鲜叶加工成毛茶的过程，主要工序有杀青、萎凋、揉捻、做青、闷黄、渥堆、发酵和干燥。各工序的有机组合形成了以下六个基本的工艺流程：

(1) 鲜叶→杀青→揉捻→干燥：绿茶

(2) 鲜叶→杀青→揉捻→闷黄→干燥：黄茶

(3) 鲜叶→杀青→揉捻→渥堆→干燥：黑茶

(4) 鲜叶→萎凋→揉捻：白茶

(5) 鲜叶→萎凋→做青→杀青→揉捻→干燥：青茶或乌龙茶

(6) 鲜叶→萎凋→揉捻→发酵→干燥：红茶

在初加工过程中，由于对鲜叶酶活性的控制不同，导致鲜叶中各种生化成分发生变化的途径不同，由此形成了品质风格各异的六大基本茶类，即：绿茶、黄茶、黑茶、白茶、青茶、红茶。

精加工主要使用物理加工方法，如筛分、风选、轧切、拼配等，毛茶的品质就标准化了。精加工后的产品称为精制茶。长炒青绿茶和圆炒青绿茶经精加工后有珍眉和珠茶产品，主要用于出口，而烘青绿茶的精制茶是茉莉花茶的主要原料，晒青绿茶和黑毛茶的精制茶还需再加工成紧压茶。

经过蒸汽、渥堆等加工过程，黑茶、绿茶或红茶在再加工过程被压制成砖、饼、碗等形状。另外，再加工还可以通过特殊方法，在茶叶中加入其他的一些产品，加工出的产品的品质特色明显不同于任何基本茶类。现在，生产的再加工茶主要有花茶、紧压茶、萃取茶、果味茶、保健茶等。

3. 茶叶分类的标准

如何将茶叶分类一直是一个有争论的话题。有人认为分类主要依据加工过程中茶叶发酵的程度，还有人提出分类要根据茶叶萎凋的程度来进行。其他的

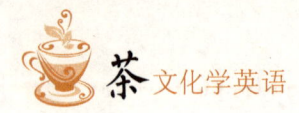

分类提议主要依据茶叶的形状、颜色、茶树品种或是生长季节等。关于茶叶的分类观点不一，似乎没有确定的结论。

但是相对来说，茶叶分类的科学方法首先需要满足两方面的标准：第一，在标准化的茶叶分级系统里确定某种茶叶的品种；第二，参考其所涉及的制茶方法。茶叶是一种日用品，不同茶类品质各异，而这种品质上的差异正是由于加工方法明显不同造成的。由于不同的加工工艺，红茶和绿茶在色泽、香气和滋味方面有很大的不同。发酵是红茶加工必不可少的工序，它能提高叶片中酶的活性，使多酚充分氧化。相反，绿茶需要利用高温杀青抑制氧化和钝化酶的活性，同时散失茶叶水分。由于绿茶和红茶的加工方法不同，茶叶中化学成分含量变化不同，从而导致这两类茶在品质上有很大的不同。工夫红茶和小种红茶品质相似，其加工方法也大致相同，都需要完全发酵，因此它们属于同一类茶。炒青绿茶和烘青绿茶也没有明显的差异，两者的加工方法类似：利用高温杀青钝化氧化酶的活性，保持叶片的绿色并使其柔软。它们都属同一类茶。很显然，为了建立一个完整的命名系统，茶叶首先应该根据加工过程来进行分类。

另外，分类还应参照茶叶的形状和化学成分。不同茶叶种类之间最显著的区别在于色泽。绿茶（包括鲜叶、干叶以及茶饮料等）通常是绿色，尽管不同种类的绿茶可能因遮阴而显现出深浅不同的绿色。其他一些茶类如蒙顶黄芽、君山银针等经过特殊处理会变为黄色，因此它们归属于黄茶。乌龙茶作为青茶的一种，在加工时有轻萎凋和部分发酵，它的色泽呈现出青色。如果颜色变深，看起来就会像是红茶。如果茶叶的加工方法发生大的改变，那么它便会变为另外的不同的品种。

大部分茶叶专家认同中国传统的茶叶分类法，即将茶叶分成以下六大基本茶类：绿茶、黄茶、黑茶、白茶、青茶、红茶。

Lesson 12
The Category of Tea

1. Green Tea

Green tea with its natural fragrance is very popular among many different people. It can be categorized according to the way of enzyme treatment, drying method as well as its appearance. A classification of green tea is given in Table 1.

Table 1 A Classification of Green Tea

Enzyme treatment	Drying method	Shape	Tea products
Pan—fixed	Pan—dried green tea	Twisted	Chunmee
		Round	Gunpowder
		Flat	Westlake longjing
		Needle shaped	Nangjing yuhuacha
		Crimpy	Biluochun
	baked—dried green tea	Twisted	Huangshan Maofeng, Raw material used to make **scented** tea
		Flaky	Liuanguapian
		Flat	Taipenghoukui
	Cured—roasted green tea	Twisted	Mengdingganlu
		Needle shaped	Anhuasongzhen
		Crimpy	Gaoqiaoyinfeng
		Flat	Jingtingluxue
	Sun—dried green tea	Twisted	raw material used to process puer
		Compressed	Puerfangcha
		Bowl shaped	Tuocha

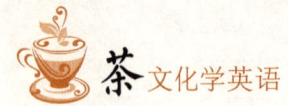

续 表

Enzyme treatment	Drying method	Shape	Tea products
2. Steam—fixed green tea		Twisted	Chinese sencha (Pan—dried)
		Needle shape	Enshiyolou

There are a lot of famous green tea in China, such as Longjing (Dragon Well) Tea around the West Lake in Hangzhou, Biluochun Tea from Mt. Donting in Jiangsu, Huangshan Maofeng Tea from Mt. Huangshan, Yunwu (Cloud and Mist) Tea from Mt. Lushan and etc.

2. Black Tea

Black tea is a kind of fermented tea which is the most popular tea in the world. According to the process method, black tea can be classified to three main groups: ① souchong black tea; ② congou black tea; ③ compressed black tea; ④ brokenblack tea. Souchong, congou and broken black tea can be further classified by place of origin or shape and quality.

Table 2　A Classification of Black Tea

Processing method	Place of origin	Processing method	shape	quality
Souchong black tea	Lapsong Souchong tea		Leaf tea	F. O. P
	Tarry Souchong tea			O. P
Congou black tea	Keemum Black	Broken black tea		P
	Yunnan Black		Broken tea	F. B. O. P
	Fukien Black			O. B. P
	Szechuan Black			B. O. P. F
	Ichang Black		Fanning	B. F
	Hunan Black			O. F
	Kwangtung Black		Dust	
Compressed black tea	Mizhuan			

F. B. O. P.: short for Flowery, Broken, Orange, Pekoe.
B. O. P. F.: short for Broken, Orange, Pekoe, Fanning

3. Qing Tea

Oolong tea is semi-fermented and is one of the special China tea prepared in Fujian, Taiwan and Guandong Provinces. It can further be classified according to cultivars of tea, processing methods and quality of tea into the following kinds:

Table 3 A Classification of Qing Tea

Place of origin	cultivar
Mingnan oolong tea	Tieh-kwan-yin
	Huangjingui
	Sechong
	Oolong
Mingbei oolong tea	Dahongbao
	Wuyi chi-chong
Taiwan oolong tea	Wenshanpouchong tea
	Dongding oolong tea
	Pekoe oolong (Penfeng tea)
Guangdong oolong tea	Fenghuang Dancong
	Fenghuang SueySian

4. White Tea

White tea is a specialty in China, mainly in such counties as Zhenghe, Jianyang and Fuding, Fujian Province, which is only slightly fermented. According to the types of tea tree and their leaves freshness, it is labeled as the following: Silver Needle Pekoe, White Peony, Kung-mee and Shou-mee.

5. Yellow Tea

Yellow tea, an unfermented tea, is a tea **peculiar** to China. It is produced mainly for domestic consumption. It remains yellow in infusion and has a mellow taste due to the procedure of yellowing (*Men Huang*). According to the **tenderness** of tea fresh leaves, yellow tea can be classified to three groups: yellow bud tea, small yellow tea and large yellow tea. Yellow bud tea is made from single bud, otherwise, it will become yellow junior tea or yellow brew when the tea material is composed of one bud with two leaves, and yellow senior tea when there is one bud with 4~5 leaves.

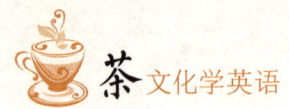

The main tea products of yellow tea showed in Table 4.

Table 4　A Classification of Yellow Tea

Tenderness of tea	Tea Products
Yellow bud tea(bud)	Junshan silver needle, Mending yellow bud tea
Small yellow tea (A bud and two leaves)	Huoshan yellow bud tea, Beigangmaojian, Luyuancha, Weishanmaojian, Pinyanghuangtang, Haimagongcha
Large yellow tea (A bud and four or five leaves)	Huoshan yellow big tea, Guandongdayeqing

6. Dark Tea And Compressed Tea

Dark tea, with its long history and rich variety, is a kind of peculiar tea in our country. The tea leaves are black-brown and tea soup is orange or orange-red. Since it goes through the process of fixing—a way of water-removing and enzymes-deactivation-at the initial stage of its production, dark tea has been regarded as one kind of unfermented teas. Its unique quality is the result of pile fermentation—a way of producing tea with the help of moist environment and microorganism, and thus it can also be called secondary fermentation tea. Provinces such as Hunan, Hubei, Sichuan, Yunnan, Guangxi, etc. are the main producing regions of dark tea.

Table 5　A Classification of Dark Tea

Pile fermentation	Place of origin	shape	product
Piled before first drying	Hunan dark tea	Basket-wrapped loose tea	Tianjian, Gongjian, Shenjian
		Basket—wrapped compressed tea	Qianliangtea
		Brick shape	Fubrick tea, Dark Brick, Hua Brick
	Guangxi dark tea	Basket—wrapped loose tea	Liubao tea
Piled after first drying	Hubei dark tea	Brick shape	Laoqingzhuan
	Szechwan dark tea	Basket—wrapped shape	Fangbao
Piled after final drying	Yunan puer tea	Round cake shape	Qizibingcha
		Small brick shape	Jincha
		Bowl shape	Puertuocha
		Twisted	Puer tea

7. Scented Tea

Scented tea is reprocessed tea produced only in China by scenting crude tea (or prime tea) with fragrant flowers in a closed cabin. It is classified according to the nature of crude tea and the flower used in scenting.

Table 6　A Classification of Scented Tea

Crude Tea	Flower＋Tea	Crude Tea	Flower＋Tea
Scented green tea	Jasmine tea	Scented Black	Rosy black scented
	Chloranthus tea		Litchi Black scented
	Magnolia tea	Scented Oolong	Osthmansus Tieh—Kwan—ying
	Dai Dai tea		Shu—lan Se—chong scented
	Pomelo tea		Jasmine Oolong
	Milan tea		
	Osthmansus tea		

8. Compressed Tea

Compressed tea is produced by reproduction of the raw tea into different kinds of tea, and also it is referred to as the "brick tea", which is China's oldest tea. According to the types of raw tea, it can be divided into dark tea, green tea and black tea. And also it can be divided according to its shapes.

In addition, according to the needs of tea market, in recent years, there are some new categories of tea, such as instant red and green tea, flavored instant tea, oolong tea juice concentration, step-down ingredients tea and health protection tea, etc.

New words and expressions
生词和短语

category [ˈkætɪg(ə)rɪ] n. 种类,分类;范畴
peculiar [pɪˈkjuːlɪə] adj. 特有的,特殊的
tender [ˈtendə] adj. 温柔的,柔弱的
scented [ˈsentɪd] adj. 有香味的
compressed [kəmˈprest] adj. 压缩的,扁长形的

Comprehension
课文理解

Give answers to the following questions in your own words and complete sentences as far as possible.

1. What are the basic tea categories in China?
2. Which kind of tea is most popular in China?
3. What is the main difference between Yellow tea and White tea?
4. Can you list out some scented tea?
5. Can you give some other examples of reprocessed tea?

Notes on the text 课文注释

1. Dark tea：黑茶，因其是全发酵茶，在发酵过程中形成了独有的有益微生物，色泽暗黑，故得名。黑茶已有超过四百年的悠久历史，是中国六大茶类之一，尤其是我国少数民族日常生活中不可缺少的饮料。黑茶的口感醇和、香气醇厚，这种香气能够很好地区别它与其他茶类，黑茶越陈越香越有价值。

Translation 参考译文

茶叶的种类

1. 绿茶

气味芳香自然的绿茶受到不同人群的喜爱。人们依据酶加工方式、干燥方式及外观形状，对绿茶进行分类。

表 1 绿茶的分类

酶处理方式	干燥方式	形状	茶叶产品
炒青绿茶	炒青绿茶	条形	眉茶
		圆形	珠茶
		扁形	西湖龙井
		松针形	南京雨花茶
		卷曲形	碧螺春
	烘青绿茶	条形	黄山毛峰茶，制作花茶的原料
		片状	六安瓜片
		扁形	太平猴魁

续　表

酶处理方式	干燥方式	形状	茶叶产品
	半烘炒绿茶	条形	蒙顶甘露
		松针形	安化松针
		卷曲形	高桥银凤
		扁形	敬亭绿雪
	晒青绿茶	条形	加工普洱茶的原料
		紧压形	普洱方砖
		碗状	沱茶
蒸青绿茶		卷曲形	中国煎茶
		针形	恩施玉露

中国有许多名贵绿茶，比如杭州西湖的龙井茶、江苏省洞庭山的碧螺春、黄山的毛峰茶、庐山的云雾茶等。

2．红茶

红茶是世界上最受欢迎的发酵茶之一。根据加工方法，红茶可以被分成三大类：①小种红茶；②工夫红茶；③紧压红茶；④红碎茶。小种红茶、工夫红茶和红碎茶可依据原产地、茶叶形状及茶叶品质进一步分类。

表2　红茶的分类

加工方法	产地
（1）小种红茶	正山小种
	烟小种
（2）工夫红茶	祁门红茶
	滇红
	闽红
	川红
	宜红
	湘红
	粤红
（3）紧压红茶	米砖

续 表

加工方法	形状	品质
（4）红碎茶	叶茶	F、O、P
		O、P
		P
	碎茶	F、B、O、P
		O、B、P
		B、O、P、F
	片茶	B、F
		O、F
	末茶	

F、B、O、P：指花、碎、橙黄、白毫。B、O、P、F：分别代指碎、橙黄、白毫、片。

3. 青茶

乌龙茶属于半发酵类，主要出产于中国福建省、台湾省和广东省。根据茶树品种、加工方法、茶叶品质以及产地的不同，还可进一步分类：

表 3　青茶的分类

产地	品种
闽南乌龙茶	铁观音
	黄金桂
	色种
	乌龙
闽北乌龙茶	大红袍
	武夷奇种
台湾乌龙茶	文山包种茶
	冻顶乌龙
	白毫乌龙（椪风茶）
广东乌龙茶	凤凰单枞
	凤凰水仙

4. 白茶

白茶为中国特产，属于微发酵茶类；主产于福建省的政和、建阳和福鼎等县。根据茶树品种和芽叶嫩度分为：白毫银针、白牡丹、贡眉和寿眉四种。

5. 黄茶

黄茶也是中国特产，属于不发酵类，主要用于国内消费。经过闷黄的加工过程，黄茶的茶水成黄色，并有一种芳醇味道。根据茶鲜叶嫩度的不同，黄茶可以被分为黄芽茶、黄小茶和黄大茶。黄芽茶是以单芽为原料加工的黄茶，以1芽2叶加工为黄小茶或黄汤，以1芽4～5叶加工的，称为黄大茶。黄茶的主要产品见表4：

表4　黄茶的分类

茶叶嫩度	产品名称
黄芽茶（单芽）	君山银针、蒙顶黄芽茶
黄小茶（1芽2叶）	霍山黄芽茶、北港毛尖、沩山毛尖 鹿苑茶、平阳黄汤、海马宫茶
黄大茶（1芽4～5叶）	霍山黄大茶、广东大叶青

6. 黑茶和紧压茶

黑茶历史悠久，种类丰富，是我国特有的一种茶叶。其颜色为黑棕色，茶汤成橘色或橘红色。黑茶被认为是一种不发酵的茶，因为在其生产初期需要去除水分、抑制酶的活化，这一过程被称为杀青。其独特的品质是渥堆的结果，即利用潮湿环境和微生物的影响来进行加工，因此人们又称其为次发酵茶。湖南、湖北、四川、云南、广西等省区是黑茶的主要出产地。

表5　黑茶的分类

渥堆方法	产地	形状	产品
初干前渥堆	湖南黑茶	篮装散茶	天尖、贡尖、舌尖
		篮装紧压茶	千两茶
		砖状	茯砖茶、黑砖、花砖
	广西黑茶	篮装散茶	六堡茶
初干后渥堆	湖北黑茶	砖状	老青砖
	四川黑茶	篮装	方包茶
最后干燥后渥堆	云南普洱茶	茶饼状	七子饼茶
		小砖状	金茶
		碗状	普洱沱茶
		螺纹状	普洱茶

7. 花茶

花茶亦为中国特产，属于再加工茶类，用茶坯（又称"素茶"）与香花窨制而成。按茶坯、香茶种类不同可分以下品类：

表6　黑茶的分类

茶坯	花＋茶
熏花绿茶	茉莉花茶
	珠兰花茶
	木兰花茶
	玳玳花茶
	柚子茶
	米兰茶
	桂花茶
熏花红茶	玫瑰红茶
	荔枝红茶
熏花乌龙	桂花铁观音
	树蓝色种茶
	茉莉乌龙茶

8. 紧压茶类

毛茶经再加工压制成不同形状的茶叶称紧压茶，亦简称为"砖茶"，是中国最古老的茶类。按毛茶种类可分为黑茶类、绿茶类和红茶类，分类又可按形状细分。

此外，根据茶叶市场的需要，近年来还创制了一些新的茶叶品类，如红速溶茶、绿速溶茶、调味速溶茶、乌龙茶汁浓缩、配料降压茶、保健茶等。

Unit 4
Tea Processing and Storage

Lesson 13
Green Tea Processing

Green tea, an unfermented tea, has been known in China from very early times. Even today it is the tea that is produced and consumed in the greatest quantities in China and Japan. There are many varieties of green tea but all share such common characteristics as greenness of the dry leaves, clarity, brightness, and when brewed, a distinct aroma and a deep, mellow taste. The appearance of the green tea products is various ranging from tiny pellets (gunpowder) to long, flat, or needle-like. Various processes **are required for** the manufacturing of green tea: fresh leaf→fixing (pan firing or steaming) →rolling→drying (in pan or basket, or in the dry machine, or in the sun).

First, a bud and the second or third leaf are plucked from a medium-or small-leaf tea plant. These are interspersed out thinly on clean bamboo trays for 3 to 6 hours. This step seems to improve the quality of the manufactured tea, by enzymatic reaction.

During the next step, which is called fixing, the freshly plucked leaves are steamed or pan fired to halt active enzyme which cause fermentation, or oxidation. It makes the leaves to be soft and **pliable**. This determines the quality of the final tea product. In China, the most commonly fixing method is pan firing, although a small amount of green tea is steam fixed. In addition, there are drum-fixing and microwave-fixing machines. In pan firing, the temperature must be high at first in order to stop the enzyme action then gradually decrease as the process progresses. If the temperature is too low, the green leaves turn red; but if the temperature is excessively high, the leaves turn **scorched**, with the result that **Chlorophyll** in the leaves is lost, so many other chemical compounds are affected, which makes leaves become yellow and not favored. Hand pan firing is done at a temperature of approximately 100℃ to 200℃. Drum-fixing machine temperatures are set about 220℃～300℃. Pan-fired tea is more **aromatic** and stronger in flavor than steam-fixed tea. However, when steam-processed leaves are brewed, it has a clearer green color.

After fixing, the next step in processing tea is rolling. During this procedure, leaf cells are broken, juices are liberated, and leaves are twisted tightly. Successful rolling **is dependent on** leaf temperature, method and amount of pressure applied, and rolling time. Today, leaves are rolled by machines. Tender leaves are rolled under light pressure for a short time after they are cooled, while the old leaves are reverse. This rolling procedure may be repeated for several times.

The last step is drying to remove **moisture** and to fix the quality for storage. Drying enhances flavor and improves appearance. Special attention is paid to the different appearance developed during drying. There are several methods for drying pan-fired green tea, such as drying in a basket, followed by final drying in a pan. Sun drying is also used, but this method **yields** a poorer quality tea, less aroma, and poorer appearance.

New words and expressions
生词和短语

pliable [ˈplaɪəb(ə)l] *adj.* 柔韧的；柔软的；圆滑的；易曲折的
are required for 需要
scorched [skɔːtʃt] *adj.* 烧焦的
chlorophyll [ˈklɔːrəfɪl] *n.* 叶绿素
aromatic [ærəˈmætɪk] *adj.* 芳香的，芬芳的；芳香族的
is dependent on 取决于，依赖于
moisture [ˈmɔɪstʃə] *n.* 水分；湿度；潮湿；降雨量
yield [jiːld] *v.* 出产；放弃

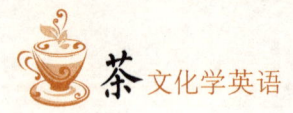

Comprehension 理 解

Give answers to the following questions in your own words and complete sentence as far as possible.

1. How many various processes are required for the manufacturing of green tea?
2. How to pluck fresh leaves to manufacture green tea?
3. What are the methods of green tea fixing?
4. Is the pan-fired tea same with the steam-fixed tea? Why or why not?
5. How to roll the tender leaves and the old leaves?
6. Why drying is needed to manufacture green tea?
7. What are the methods for drying?

Notes on the text 课文注释

1. unfermented tea：不发酵茶，又称绿茶。以采摘适宜茶树新梢为原料，不经发酵，直接杀青、揉捻、干燥等典型工艺过程，以区别经发酵制成的其他类型茶叶。

2. pan firing：锅式炒青，是指在制作茶叶的过程中利用微火在锅中使茶叶杀青的手法。

Translation 参考译文

绿茶加工

绿茶是一种不发酵茶，中国很早就有了。即使在今天，绿茶在中国和日本的生产和消费量也最大。绿茶产品花色很多，但有着共同的品质特点：干茶绿油润，汤色清澈明亮，泡出的茶清香浓郁，滋味醇厚。绿茶形状多样，从颗粒形（珠茶）到长条形、扁形、针形等。绿茶的加工制作要经过不同的工序：鲜叶→杀青（炒青或蒸青）→揉捻→干燥（在锅中炒干或在焙笼中烘干、干燥机中干燥或晒干）。

首先是鲜叶采摘与摊放。从中、小种的茶树上采摘 1 芽 2～3 叶，将其薄摊在干净竹盘中 3～6 小时，以便茶叶发生酶促反应，提高茶叶品质。

下一步即杀青。鲜叶经过蒸或炒，酶活性被钝化，从而抑制茶叶发酵或氧化。杀青也使叶片变得柔软。杀青是决定成品茶质量的关键工序。在中国，虽然有少量绿茶采用蒸青的方式杀青，但最常用的方法还是锅式杀青，此外，还有滚筒式杀青机杀青、微波杀青机杀青等机械杀青方法。采用锅式杀青机时，杀青温度应"先高后低"，先高温抑制酶促反应，再逐渐降温。如果温度太低，则茶叶会变红；如果温度过高，则茶叶会产生焦边焦叶，叶绿素损失，同时影响许多化学成分的反应，导致茶叶变黄，品质变差。手工锅式杀青，锅温掌握在 100℃～200℃；滚筒杀青温度设置在 220℃～300℃。与蒸青茶相比，炒青茶香高味更浓，但蒸青茶叶泡的茶，汤色和叶底色泽更绿亮。

杀青后，下一工序即揉捻。揉捻使叶细胞破损，茶汁溢来，茶叶卷转成条。决定揉捻质量的因素有叶温、加压方式、力度、揉捻时间等。目前，揉捻已实现机械化。嫩叶的揉捻宜摊凉后进行，注意要力轻、短时。而老叶则相反，揉捻可反复多次进行。

最后一步即干燥，达到去除水分，固定品质，以利贮藏的目的。干燥过程还能发展茶叶风味，进一步美化外形。在干燥时，可进行不同形状茶叶的塑造。炒青绿茶有以下几种干燥方法：烘干，随后炒干；晒干，但晒干绿茶品质较差，香味不浓，外形不美。

Lesson 14
Black Tea Processing

Black tea is a fully fermented tea. And It is the principal type of tea produced and consumed in the world. It can be further classified into broken black tea, Congou and Souchong black tea. The former is sold for its characteristics of **strength**, briskness, color and brightness while the others have fewer of these characteristics but have a more delicate aroma. Keemun black tea smells and tastes sweet and Soucheng black tea has a flavor of pine smoke, sometimes like aroma of litchi.

Primary processing of producing black tea consists of: picking fresh leaves→withering →rolling or cutting →fermenting →drying. Details of some of these procedures are as follows:

The fresh leaves, the buds and 1 or 2 leaves, are plucked from large or medium-leaf tea plants, and then brought to the tea factory, which is most often located on the estate, or very near to a collection of small farms.

Once it arrives, the tea is laid out in a withering house at 20℃～24℃ and relative humidity of 60%～70%. The leaves are spread about 15～20cm deep on **screens** fitted to long wooden boxes called **withering troughs**, and turned lightly at 1～2 hour intervals. Here the tea leaves are allowed to withered by air passing through and over the **intact** leaves, to remove moisture. The rate at which air passes through the leaves, the temperature of the air, and even the depth of the tea piled in the troughs will impact the final quality of the tea. For great tea, tremendous care must be taken at this stage. How dry the tea is allowed to become is determined by what process will be used to make the black tea from this stage. The withering process is complete when the leaves emit a clean aroma. Red and dead leaves are eliminated. The average moisture content is about 60%; 58%~61% in spring and 61%~64% in summer and autumn teas.

The withered tea is then rolled, usually by mechanical rollers, although this can be accomplished by hand. This rolling disrupts the **cellular** structure of the tea leaves, making **oxidase** in the leaf combine with polyphenols and other constituents in the leaf to form the unique **molecular** structures, which give black tea its **distinctive** flavor and aroma. In the manufacturing process of Congou black tea, the withered leaves are rolled until more than 80% of the leaf cells are broken and twisted more than 90%. The twisted leaf should be wiry and uniform. For black broken tea, there are two available processes-**orthodox** manufacture and CTC (for crush, tear, and curl), a more highly mechanized process primarily used for the production of tea-bag grades. From the orthodox roller, the processed leaves will pass through vibrating sifters that take out and separate clumps or balls of wet, crushed tea leaves, and then move on to the fermentation stage.

Fermentation is actually the oxidation of the tea constituents. Chemical interaction between the various components of the tea leaf in the presence of oxygen will cause the tea to turn from a green to a coppery red to deep brown and, finally, a nearly black color. Fermentation is usually carried out at 24℃~28℃ at relative humidity over 90%. The length of time and degree of oxidation will determine the final flavor and aroma characteristics of the tea. Congou black tea is fermented for 3~5 hours in spring, and for 2~3 hours in summer and autumn. When fermentation is completed, more than 85% of the leaves have turned red and emit a heavy, fruity aroma.

After fermentation, the tea is dried, or fired. The first drying for Congou is carried out at 110℃~120℃ for 10~15 minutes. The leaves are spread about 1~2 cm deep. At the end of this first drying, the moisture content is reduced to 20%~25%. After spreading for 45~60 minutes, the leaves are dried again at 80℃~100℃ to reduce the moisture content around 3%.

The orthodox black tea is then sifted to various sizes, and the stalk and fiber are removed. Sifting is accomplished by using a variety of **sieves**, each succeeding one finer than the previous; the pieces which do not pass through any given sieve are **conveyed** to a **designated** container. This is the rough grading of the leaf,

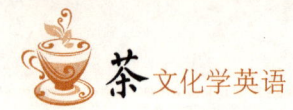

which will determine whether it is a leaf grade or one of many smaller broken grades. Stems, stalk, and fiber are removed by passing the tea over or under electro-**statically** charged rollers prior to entering the sieves. The charged rollers attract the fibers, which are then **brushed off** and collected.

New words and expressions
生词和短语

strength [streŋθ] *n.* 力量；优点，文中指滋味刺激性强
trough [trɒf] *n.* 水槽，食槽
withering troughs 萎凋槽
screen [skriːn] *n.* 屏幕；屏风；*vt.* 筛（煤、矿石等）
intact [inˈtækt] *adj.* 未受损伤的
cellular [ˈseljʊlə] *adj.* 细胞的；多孔的
oxidase [ˈɒksɪdeɪz] *n.* [生化] 氧化酶
molecular [məˈlekjʊlə] *adj.* [化学] 分子的
distinctive [dɪˈstɪŋ(k)tɪv] *adj.* 有特色的，与众不同的
designated [ˈdezɪɡˌneɪtɪd] *adj.* 指定的；特指的
orthodox [ˈɔːθədɒks] *adj.* 正统的；传统的
sieve [sɪv] *n.* 筛子；滤网
convey [kənˈveɪ] *v.* 传达；运输
statically [ˈstatɪcalɪ] *adv.* 静态地；静止地
brushed off 拂去

Comprehension
理 解

Give answers to the following questions in your own words and complete sentence as far as possible.

1. What is the purpose of withering?

2. In order to get the good results of fermentation what condition should be paid attention to?

3. How does the color of the leaf change as fermentation proceeds?

4. What does C. T. C means?

5. What is the purpose of drying of black tea?

Notes on the text 课文注释

1. broken black tea：红碎茶，红茶的一种。
2. Congou black tea：工夫红茶，工夫红茶是中国特有的红茶，比如祁红、滇红等。
3. Souchong black tea：小种红茶，是最古老的红茶，同时也是其他红茶的鼻祖，其他红茶都是从小种红茶演变而来的。它分为正山小种和外山小种，均原产于武夷山地区。

Translation 参考译文

红茶加工

红茶属于全发酵茶类，是世界上生产和消费的主要茶叶产品。红茶又可细分为红碎茶、工夫红茶和小种红茶。红碎茶与其他红茶相比，滋味浓强、鲜爽，汤色红艳明亮，而工夫红茶和小种红茶的香气更好。祁红的香气和滋味都甜如蜜，小种红茶则有松烟香，有时具桂圆味。

红茶加工的主要工序包括：采摘鲜叶 → 萎凋 → 揉捻或切断 → 发酵 → 干燥。各工序的具体要求如下：

从大叶或中叶种茶树上采摘1芽1叶或1芽2叶鲜叶后，将其运送到茶厂加工。茶厂一般位于大型茶场内或临近有小型茶场的地方。

鲜叶运到茶厂后，摊放在萎凋室中。萎凋室的温度宜保持在20℃～24℃，相对湿度60%～70%。鲜叶摊放在萎凋槽上底部有网孔的木盒中，摊叶厚度为15～20cm，每隔1～2小时翻拌一次。风透过叶片带走水分，茶叶发生萎凋。风速、风温甚至萎凋槽上的摊叶厚度都能影响成茶品质。要想茶叶品质好，这一过程需要特别注意。萎凋叶含水量（即干度）的高低与下一步工序有关。当茶叶散发出清香时，萎凋即可完成。其中的红叶和枯叶需拣除。萎凋叶平均含水量控制在60%左右，春茶为58%～61%，夏秋茶为61%～64%。

萎凋叶接下来进行揉捻。揉捻虽可手工完成，但通常采用机器机来进行。

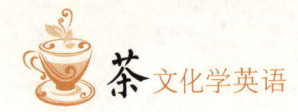

揉捻能破坏叶细胞结构，使叶内的多酚氧化酶与多酚类化合物和其他化合物接触，形成红茶所特有品质风格的化合物。工夫红茶加工时，萎凋叶适宜的揉捻程度指标是：细胞破损率超过80%，成条率超过90%，条索必须紧卷且均匀一致。红碎茶有两种制法，即：传统法和CTC法（CTC即Crush碾碎、Tear撕裂、Curl卷起）。CTC法更为先进，主要用来加工袋泡茶。采用传统揉捻机揉捻时，揉捻叶要经过解块筛分机进行筛分，将团块解散分开，进转子机揉切，然后再进入发酵阶段。

发酵实际是茶叶中的化学物质的氧化。茶叶中各种化合物质在有氧条件下发生的化学反应将导致叶片色泽由绿到橙红、棕褐到乌。发酵时温度宜在24℃～28℃，相对湿度为90%以上。发酵时间和氧化程度也将影响成茶的滋味和香气特点。工夫红茶春季发酵需3～5小时，夏秋季发酵需2～3小时。发酵后，85%以上的叶片色泽变红，并散发出浓郁的果香。

发酵后茶叶应进行干燥。工夫红茶第一次干燥（即毛火）温度宜设置在110℃～120℃，时间10～15分钟，摊叶厚度1～2厘米。毛火后，茶叶含水量降至20%～25%。摊晾45～60分钟，再在80℃～100℃的温度下再次干燥（即足火），使含水量降至3%左右。

传统红茶随后要进行筛分规格、拣剔茶梗和筋毛的作业。筛分是由一组筛网来完成的，下层筛网孔径小于上层筛网，各筛网上的茶叶将放入指定的容器。这即茶叶的粗分，它将决定茶叶是归为叶茶还是碎茶。茶叶在筛分之前，需经过静电拣梗机，将梗、茎和筋毛去除。静电拣梗机的辊子能吸住茶叶的筋毛，然后将筋毛刷除并收集起来。

Lesson 15
Oolong Tea Processing

Oolong tea, which **is peculiar to** China, originated in the 18th century and is produced mainly in Fujian, Guangdong and Taiwan province. It is a semi-fermented tea which has strong aroma and is made only with particular varieties of tea.

1. The Basic Processing of Oolong Tea

The raw material for oolong tea is a dormant bud with 2 or 3 leaves picked from tea bushes with leaves of medium size. Processing of produce oolong tea consists of: picking fresh leaves→ withering →rotating →fixing →rolling →drying →sifting and cutting, **winnowing**, **sorting** →Fe-firing →blending →packing. Details of these procedures are as follows:

(1) Withering: The best way is withering fresh leaves in the sun (Shai Qing), followed by a period indoors (Liang Qing), with ideal weather conditions including a north wind. During cold weather or rainydays, withering is done indoors in heated rooms, but the results are not as good as withering outdoors. For outdoor withering, fresh leaves are spread out on a flat bamboo mats or basket and exposed to weak sunlight around noon. Leaves should not be overlapped and there should not be any spaces between them. Usually the leaves are exposed to sunlight for 10~60 minutes, which depend intensity of sunlight and on the thickness of the leaves. Usually Shai Qing is done only once, but if the leaves are very **turgid** or contain a high level of moisture, the procedure may be repeated. When Shai Qing is considered to be adequate, the leaves become soft, lose their **gloss** and **grassy odor**, give off a light fragrance, and have a moisture content loss of

10%～20%. The acceptable degree of Sai Qing varies according to the type of oolong tea being processed as Baochong Tea＜Southern Fujian Oolong Tea ＜North Fujian Oolong Tea ＜Pekoe Oolong. After Shai Qing, the tea is transferred indoors and withered at room temperature for six to eight hours, with the leaves being gently stirred by hand or by rotating machine which is called rotating.

(2) Rotating: Rotating is a special operation unique to the processing of oolong tea. Rotating can cause friction between leaves, disrupt the cellular organization at the edge of the leaves, and bring about a limited degree of fermentation. Rotation is done indoors at a temperature of 20℃～25℃ and at a relative humidity of 75%～85%. A special machine is used for rotating the leaves, and after rotating, the leaves are spread out on a bamboo mat. This sequence of rotating and spreading are repeated 5 to 10 times in a period of 7～13 hours, which depends on the type of oolong tea being produced. The period and number of rotations, as well as the time of spreading, increase **progressively** as the process is continued. Fermentation begins at the edge of the leaf, and then gradually spreads to the leaf veins. Fermentation is judged to be complete when the leaf edge turns red, the green part of the leaf becomes lighter in color, the veins become transparent, and the whole leaf is best described as "red-rimmed green leaf" and has a fragrance. At this stage, the leaf contains 60%～65% moisture. The degrees of oxidation of **catechins** in different types of oolong tea as follows: Boachong tea, 12±5%; Southern Fujian Oolong Tea, 20±3%; Northern Fujian Oolong Tea, 30±3%; Pekoe Oolong, 58±5%.

(3) Fixing: Fixing reguires heating the leaves for 3～7 minutes at 160℃～240℃ in a pan. The exact time of fixing varies slightly for different types of oolong tea.

(4) Rolling: Rolling is carried out 2 or 3 times under pressure while the leaves are hot, followed by alternate periods of drying; the exact procedure varies with the type of oolong tea being produced. Northern oolong tea is rolled twice, whereas southern oolong tea, because of emphasis of appearance, is rolled three times. In the latter case, the leaves are packed in cloth and passed through a ball rolling mill before the second and third rolling to impart curl in the leaves. Rolling is done for 4～6 minutes under alternating light and heavy pressure at a speed of 60 **revolutions** per minute. The degree of cell destruction is about 30%, which is

less than that in black or green tea and so Polong tea repeated brewing.

(5) Drying: Drying is usually done in two stages. In the first stage, leaves are spread thinly and dried quickly at high temperatures. For the second drying, the temperature is lowered. A certain amount of moisture, necessary for re-rolling, is retained during the first drying. However, there are variations in the procedure for different types of oolong tea. For example, in the case of northern Fujian oolong tea, because of emphasis on aroma, slow drying at a low temperature is practiced.

(6) Blending: During blending, the original appearance of the tea is retained as much as possible, and sifting and cutting are **minimized**. Every **endeavor** is made to preserve fragrance and taste, and the tea blend is finally dried at a low temperature.

2. Northern Fujian Oolong Tea

Fresh leaves are withered in the sun at 30℃~40℃ for 30~90 minutes and turned over 1~2 times during this period. Weight loss is 12%~15%. Leaves are then kept indoors at 20℃~26℃ for 30~60 minutes, **alternately** rotated and spread out 7~8 times. Time of rotation varies from 0.5 to 4 minutes, and time spread out is about 30~150 minutes. The total time for this step is 7~8 hours, and weight loss is 25%~28%. The leaves are rolled for 6~7 minutes at 55~65 rpm. Then the leaves are dried at 95℃~100℃ for about 12 minutes, spread, and allowed to cool. Yellow leaves and stalks are picked out at this stage. Leaves are again dried at 60℃~89℃ for 2~4 hours with the leaves being turned over every 15 minutes until the moisture content is 4%~5%. The processed tea leaves are **refined** and blended.

3. Southern Fujian Oolong Tea

Fresh leaves are withered in the sun at 30℃~40℃ for 20~50 minutes and turned over 2~3 times during this period. Weight loss is 7%~10%. Leaves are then kept indoors at 20℃~26℃ for 20~30 minutes, alternately rotated and spread out 4~5 times. Time of rotation varies from 3 to 20 minutes, and time spread out is about 1.5~5 hours. The total time for this step is 11~13 hours, and weight loss is 10%~15%. The leaves are dried at 200℃~240℃ for 7~10 minutes, and then rolled for 3~5 minutes. Leaf **lumps** are broken into pieces and dried at 90℃~100℃ for 10~20 minutes while being turned over 2~3 times.

文化学英语

Leaves are packed in cloth and rolled for 5～10 minutes or passed through a ball roller. Leaf lumps are broken and dried at 70℃ for 10～15 minutes. Leaves are again packed in cloth and rerolled for 2～3 minutes or passed through a ball roller. The leaves are then packed tightly in cloth and set aside for 20～30 minutes. The leaves are dried at 60℃ until the balls loosen naturally. Then drying is continued until the moisture content is about 10%～20%. The leaves are then spread out to cool for 60 minutes and then dried at 50～60℃ for 30～60 minutes until the moisture is reduced to 4%～6%. The processed leaves are then refined and blended.

New words and expressions
生词和短语

be pecliar to   特有的
sort [sɔːt] vt. vi. 分类 vt. 挑选
gloss [glɒs] n. 光彩，光泽
revolution [ˌrevəˈluːʃən] n. 转数
endeavor [enˈdevə] v. 努力；尽力
subjectively [səbˈdʒektɪvlɪ] adv. 主观地
progressively [prəˈgresɪvlɪ] adv. 逐步；日益增加地
catechin [ˈkætɪtʃɪn] n. 儿茶素
alternately [ɔːlˈtɜːnɪtlɪ] adv. 交替地；轮流地；间隔地
minimized [ˈmɪnəˌmaɪz] adj. 最小化的；使达到最低限度的

winnow [ˈwɪnəʊ] vt. 选择；除去
turgid [ˈtɜːdʒɪd] adj. 肿胀的；浮夸的
grassy odor 青草气
lump [lʌmp] n. 块，块状；肿块
refined [rɪˈfaɪnd] adj. 精炼的；微妙的

Comprehension
理 解

Give answers to the following questions in your own words and complete sentences as far as possible.

1. Where is the original place of oolong tea and in which provinces they are produced?
2. What are the standards of fresh leaf for oolong tea?
3. What are the general standards of withering end?
4. What are the results of rotating and how is it carried out?
5. How to judge the fermentation during rotating processing?
6. How is the Southern Oolong Tea rolled and dried?

乌龙茶加工

乌龙茶起源于18世纪，是中国的特种茶，主要产于福建、广东和台湾省。乌龙茶是半发酵茶，重香味，需用特殊品种加工。

1. 乌龙茶基本加工工艺

乌龙茶以中叶种茶树已形成驻芽的2或3叶新梢为原料。工艺流程包括：采摘鲜叶→萎凋→做青→杀青→揉捻→干燥→筛分和轧切、拣剔、风选→复焙→拼配→包装。各工序具体说明如下：

（1）萎凋：最好的萎凋是有北风的理想天气条件，将鲜叶在太阳下萎凋（即晒青），随后进行室内晾干（晾青）。当天气寒冷或下雨时，萎凋在加热的室内进行，但效果不如室外萎凋好。室外萎凋是将鲜叶摊放在水筛或竹席上，在中午前后阳光较弱时接受照射。茶叶摊放时，叶与叶之间既不相互重叠也不留有空隙，晒青时间长短根据光照强度和摊叶厚度而定，通常为10～60分钟。晒青一般一次完成，但若摊叶太厚或茶叶水分过高，则可重复一次。萎凋适度时，茶叶变软，失去光泽和青草气，并散发出清香，水分含量减重10%～20%。不同的乌龙茶产品，其晒青程度不同，由轻及重依次为：包种茶、闽南乌龙、闽北乌龙、白毫乌龙。晒青后将茶叶转入室内，再在室温下萎凋6～8小时。同时要手轻轻翻动叶子或用摇青机摇青。

（2）做青：做青是加工乌龙茶制作的独特工艺。摇青可使叶片相互摩擦，破坏叶缘细胞组织，导致部分发酵。做青时室内以温度20℃～25℃、相对湿度75%～85%为宜。有专门做青的机械设备。茶叶做青后摊放在竹席上，根据产品不同，在7～13小时的做青过程中，摇青和静置要重复5～10次。摇青的时间和次数、静置的时间逐渐延长或增加。发酵自叶缘开始，随后逐渐到叶脉。当叶边转红，绿色部分变淡，叶脉透明，整个叶片"绿叶红镶边"，并散发花香时，发酵就完成了。此时，茶叶含水量为60%～65%。不同乌龙茶产品的儿茶素氧化程度如下：包种茶12±5%、闽南乌龙20±3%、闽北乌龙30±3%、白

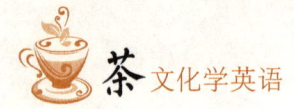

毫乌龙58±5%。

(3) 杀青：杀青是在160℃～240℃的锅里加热3～7分钟完成的。杀青的准确时间因产品不同而有轻微的变化。

(4) 揉捻：揉捻进行2～3次，采用热揉方式，并与干燥交替进行。具体过程随所加工的产品不同而不同。闽北乌龙揉捻两次，而闽南乌龙茶因为重其形状，需揉捻三次。在第二、三次揉捻之前，先用布将茶叶包起来，并用速包机包揉成球形，使茶叶卷紧。揉捻时轻压、重压交替进行，转速为每分钟60转，时间4～6分钟。其细胞破损率约30%，小于绿茶和红茶，因而乌龙茶可以反复冲泡。

(5) 干燥：干燥通常分两步进行。第一次干燥时，茶叶薄摊，用高温快速干燥。而第二次干燥则降低温度。第一次干燥后要保持一定的茶叶含水量，这是复揉所必要的。但不同的乌龙茶制作要求不同。如：闽北乌龙茶由于重其香气，因而采用文火烘焙。

(6) 拼配：拼配时，应尽量保持茶叶原来外形，很少拣剔和轧切。要努力保持其香味。拼配好的茶叶最后需文火干燥。

2. 闽北乌龙茶

将鲜叶在30～40℃的阳光下晾晒萎凋30～90分钟，并翻转1～2次，减重12%～15%。再在温度为20℃～26℃的室内晾青30～60分钟，做青（摇青和静置交替）7～8次。摇青时间为0.5～4分钟，静置时间30～150分钟。做青总时长7～8小时，减重25%～28%。茶叶以55～65转/分钟的速度揉捻6～7分钟。随后，在95℃～100℃的温度下干燥12分钟，摊晾，并捡出黄片和茶梗。捡剔后再在60℃～89℃的温度下干燥2～4小时，并每隔15分钟翻转一次，直到茶叶含水量为4%～5%。加工的成茶需精制和拼配处理。

3. 闽南乌龙茶

将鲜叶在30℃～40℃的阳光下晾晒萎凋20～50分钟，并翻转2～3次，减重7%～10%。再在20℃～26℃的室内晾青20～30分钟，做青4～8次。摇青时间3～20分钟，静置时间为1.5～5小时。做青总时长11～13小时，减重10%～15%。做青叶在200℃～240℃温度下炒青7～10分钟，再揉捻3～5分钟。

解块后于 90℃～100℃ 温度下干燥 10～20 分钟，翻转 2～3 次。茶叶用布包裹，揉捻 5～10 分钟，或用球茶揉捻机揉捻（速包机和平板机）。解块后于 70℃ 的温度下干燥 10～15 分钟，再重新打包复揉 2～3 分钟或用球茶揉捻机揉捻，定型 20～30 分钟。再在 60℃ 下干燥直至茶球自然散开，继续干燥至含水量 10%～20%。然后摊晾 60 分钟，再在 50℃～60℃ 温度下干燥 30～60 分钟，将含水量减至 4%～5%。加工的成茶再经精制和拼配处理。

Lesson 16
Dark Tea Processing

Dark tea, one of Chinese aneient types of tea, originated in the 11th century and is produced only in the southwestern and middle-southern districts of China. Dark teas are **consumed** chiefly by people belonging to minority groups in China, such as Tibetans, Mongols, etc. Only a small portion of dark tea is exported to the other countries.

1. Quality of Dark Tea

Dark tea is post-fermented and is brownish-yellow or brownish-red in infusion. The leaves are coarse and large, and aroma is stale, **piney**, smoke-like, and a mellow taste. It is processed into a variety of shapes, such as brick, pillow, cake, bowl, etc., each piece weighing from a few grams to several kilograms. Only a small amount is processed as loose tea leaves.

2. Primary Processing

The material of dark tea is maturestall over the 6 pinds of tea, and it's common to pluck bud with 4 or 6 leaves, stems and twigs from tea plants. The sequence of manufacturing is as follows: fresh tea leaves→ fixing→ rolling→ piling→ first drying→ final drying→raw dark tea → shaped by steam and pressure→finished tea.

Fixing: Mature raw leaves used to make dark tea must be sprinkled with water during fixing because their moisture content is low. The fixing pan temperature is about 280℃~320℃. More ever, steaming and boiling the leaves are another two good methods.

Rolling: The leaves must be rolled twice. The fixed leaves need to be rolled while they are still warm. This first rolling would squeeze out the juices and **twist** the leaves to make them suitable for piling. The second rolling after piling must further twist the leaves, tightly and evenly.

Piling: Piling is an important step in the making of dark tea, similar to the yellowing process in manufacturing yellow tea. Piling may be carried out at different stages. In general, piling is carried out after rolling and is called damp piling. If it is after the first drying, it is called dry piling, and if done during the final processing, it is called processed tea piling. Some dark tea must be piled several times. Fu brick tea, is processed as raw dark tea and then piled again during the finishing process. The piling time can vary from several hours to several weeks, depending on the types of dark tea being manufactured. For optimum piling, the room temperature should be over 25℃, relative humidity over 85%, and the location must be a clean floor away from windows to avoid direct sunshine. Since room temperature and humidity in the piling process are kept high for a long time, **microorganism**, such as aspergillus glaucus, saccharomyces, and others are produced naturally. Polyphenols are oxidized because of the dampness, heat, and the action of the **microorganism**. The level of catechins in dark tea is lower than that found in yellow tea. Dark tea contains no chlorophyll, and the free amino acid concentration is lower in dark tea than in yellow tea. These chemical reaction bring about a mellow flavor of dark tea and changes in the color of infusion as well as in the infused leaves. The infused leaves and dry tea leaves turn to dull auburn, and the brew becomes brownish→yellow and a little reddish.

Drying: Leaves are dried at low temperature for a long time.

Shaping: By piling and steaming, the raw dark leaves can be compressed into various shapes in the final process.

3. Examples of Dark Tea Processing

The processes for different types of dark tea are as follows:

1) Fu brick tea

Primary process: Fresh leaves→ pan fixing→ rolling →piling (1meter high for 12 to 24 hours, with leaf temperatures of 50℃ to 60℃ and moisture content of 67% to 68%)→ rerolling→leafy lumps breaking →firing→ made tea.

Fine process and re-process: raw tea→blending →sifting, winnowing, orting → steaming→ piling (2~3m high for 3~4 hours with leaf temperature of 45℃ to

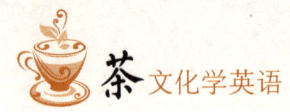

78℃ and moisture content of 18％ to 20％, heat is **evolved**)→steaming→pressing and shaping it into bricks → piling (for 16~20 days, with 25％ to 30％ moisture)→re-firing →packing→ made tea.

2) Hei brick tea and Hua brick tea

Primary process: Fresh leaves→ raw tea. Process similarly as above.

Fine process and re-process: raw tea→blending →sifting, winnowing, sorting → steaming → pressing and shaping it into bricks → re-firing → packing→ made tea.

3) Qing brick tea

Sun-dried raw green tea→piling (2~3m high for 30~60 days with water sprayed on to maintain 18％ to 20％ moisture at a temperature of 50℃ to 60℃, heat evolved) → raw tea blending → sifting, cutting, winnowing, sorting → steaming →steaming, pressing and shaping it into bricks → firing → packing→ made tea.

4) Pu'er tea

Sun-dried raw green tea→piling (2~3m high for 30~60 days with water sprayed on to maintain 18％ to 20％ moisture at a temperature of 50℃ to 60℃, heat evolved)→raw tea blending →sifting, cutting, winnowing, sorting →steaming →steaming, pressing and shaping into bricks →firing →packing→ made tea.

New words and expressions
生词和短语

consume [kənˈsjuːm] v. 消耗
piney [ˈpaɪnɪ] adj. 松树般茂盛的；似松的
microbial [maɪˈkrəʊbɪəl] adj. 微生物的
twist [twɪst] vt. 捻；拧；扭伤；编织；使苦恼 vi. 扭动；弯曲
evolve [ɪˈvɒlv] v. 发展；进化

Comprehension
理 解

Give answers to the following questions in your own words and complete sentence as far as possible.

1. What are the characteristics of dark tea?

2. Tell the major progressing stages of manufacturing dark tea.

3. What happens during the piling of dark tea and what is the result?

4. State the difference between dark tea and yellow tea.

5. State the surroundings for optimum piling of dark tea.

6. What is the most important process in manufacturing dark tea and what it is?

Translation 参考译文

黑茶加工

黑茶起源于 11 世纪，是中国最古老的茶叶产品之一。黑茶仅产于中国西南和中南地区，主要消费群体为少数民族，如藏族，蒙古族等，仅有少量销往外国。

1. 黑茶品质

黑茶是后发酵茶，茶汤呈棕黄或棕红色。压制黑茶茶叶大而粗糙，香气平淡，如松香，似烟香，味道醇厚。黑茶具有各种形状：砖形，枕形，饼状，碗形等。重量轻则几克，重则几千克，只少部分制成松散茶叶。

2. 黑茶加工

用于加工黑茶的原料是六大茶类中成熟度最高的，一般采摘 1 芽 4 叶至 6 叶以及嫩枝和茎梗。其工艺流程为：鲜叶→杀青→揉捻→渥堆→初焙→复焙→毛茶→汽蒸定形→成品茶。

杀青：由于原料成熟度高，含水量低，所以，杀青时通常需要洒水灌浆。杀青时锅温为 280℃～320℃。也可采用蒸汽杀青和泡青的方式进行杀青。

揉捻：茶叶需揉捻两次。杀青叶需趁热揉捻，初揉时揉出茶汁并转曲叶片，适于渥堆；复揉时要进一步卷紧叶片。

渥堆：是黑茶加工中尤为重要的工序，就如闷黄对于黄茶加工一样重要。渥堆可在不同的阶段进行。一般而言，揉捻后的渥堆称之为"湿渥"，初干后渥堆称之为"干渥"。此外，也可在再加工时渥堆，称之为成茶后渥堆。一些黑茶需渥堆几次，如茯砖茶，在黑毛茶加工时渥堆，在再加工时也渥堆。渥堆时间长短取决于生产的黑茶种类，从几小时至几星期。适宜的渥堆条件是：室温

25℃以上，相对湿度85%以上，渥堆地点必须是干净的地面，并远离窗户，避免太阳直晒。因为渥堆时的温度和湿度都高且持续时间长，自然会产生大量像灰绿曲霉、酵母菌这样的微生物，同时，这种湿热环境和微生物作用也会导致多酚类物质的氧化，儿茶素含量比黄茶低。黑茶中无叶绿素残留，游离氨基酸含量也较黄茶低。这些化学变化使黑茶的滋味醇厚，并使叶底和干茶色泽变成棕褐色，茶汤成棕黄或棕红色。

干燥：茶叶在低温下长时间干燥。

成型：通过渥堆和汽蒸，黑毛茶被压制成各种形状的紧压茶。

3. 黑茶加工实例

不同黑茶的制作工序如下：

1) 茯砖茶

主要工序：鲜叶→炒青→初揉→渥堆（堆叶1米高，持续渥堆12～24小时，叶温50℃～60℃，含水量67%～68%,）→复揉→解块→干燥→毛茶。

精加工和深加工：毛茶→拼配→筛分、风选拣剔→汽蒸→渥堆（叶堆2～3米高。持续3～4小时，叶温45℃～78℃，含水量18%～20%，并不断加热）→汽蒸→紧压定形→渥堆（持续16～20天，含水量25%～30%）→复焙→包装→成品茶。

2) 黑砖茶和花砖茶

主要工序：鲜叶→毛茶。主要步骤与上面相似。

精加工和深加工：毛茶→拼配→筛分、风选拣剔→汽蒸→紧压定形→复焙→包装→成品茶。

3) 青砖茶

晒青绿茶→渥堆（叶堆2～3米高，持续30～60天，洒水保持含水量18%～20%，温度50℃～60℃，持续加热）→毛茶拼配→筛分、剪切、风选拣剔→汽蒸→汽蒸并紧压定形→烘焙→包装→成品茶。

4) 普洱茶

晒青绿茶→渥堆（叶堆2～3米高，持续30～60天，洒水保持含水量18%～20%,温度50℃～60℃，持续加热）→毛茶拼配→筛分、剪切、风选拣剔→汽蒸→汽蒸并紧压定形→烘焙→包装→成品茶。

Lesson 17
Processing of Other Teas

In the world black fer and greer tea are most productive. While iu china, oolong tea, dark tea, yellow tea, while tea and scenfed tea are also produced in great quantity. This lesson mainly focuses on the latfer part.

1. Yellow Tea

Yellow tea is a tea peculiar to China and it **originated** before the 16th century. The main growing areas are Hunan, Anhui and Hubei provinces.

The manufacture of yellow tea is similar to green tea, from the plucking of the fresh leaves to the final drying. The process begins when the fresh leaves are plucked and spread out for a short time. The next step must be carried out on the same day that the leaves are picked. Pan fixing is done at a temperature about 150℃, which is lower than the temperature at which green tea is fixed. This lower temperature may help in the yellowing of the leaves.

Over 50% of chlorophyll is destroyed in the processing of yellow tea, more than in the processing of green tea. The amounts of polyphenols in yellow tea are lower than that of green tea, this maybe **account for** non-enzymatic oxidation occurring in the processing of yellow tea.

During the men-huang, or yellowing process, the leaves are stacked, and the polyphenols in the leaves are oxidized because the stacks become warm and damp. While the leaves are hot, they are placed in container or covered with a wet cloth, so the leaves turn yellow by **thermal**, not enzymatic, reactions. This yellowing which takes place after fixing is called damp leaf yellowing. The yellowing time

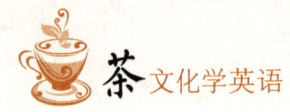

varies from several hours to 5~10 days, depending on the method used. Dry leaf yellowing requires more time than damp leaf yellowing and, as expected, a more yellow tea is obtained. The yellow infusion color is a characteristic of yellow tea.

2. White Tea

White tea is produced in Fujian Province. It is a fermented tea peculiar to China and originated before the 16th century. Material comes from fresh leaves from the first plucking of spring tea, with a moderate content of polyphenols; these are large and medium leaves with profuse hairs. Sprouting buds are used for to process Silver Needle Pekoe, and the sprouting bud with two to three fresh leaves for White Peony and other white tea groups. The outline for the process is as follows: fresh leaves→withering→firing→raw tea→sorting→packing→made tea.

1) Withering

Leaves are spread on a bamboo mat. The leaves are over-lapped so that there are no spaces between them. On cloudless days, the leaves are dried in the sun for several hours before 11 a.m. and after 2 p.m., and then moved indoors. This procedure is repeated for 2 to 3 days. The leaves can also be withered by spreading the leaves out in a well-**ventilated** room, temperature of 29℃~30℃, relative humidity of 65%~70%, until the buds contain about 30% moisture and the leaves about 13% moisture. During withering, no fanning or stirring. The edge of the leaves curl, hairs whiten, and leaves become fragrant.

2) Firing

Bud tea: fire at a temperature of 40℃~45℃ for 20~30 minutes.

Leaf tea: fire at a temperature of 70℃~80℃ for 10 to 15 minutes until the leaves contain about 6% moisture. Stir gently as little as possible.

3. Scented Tea

Scented tea is reprocessed tea, and it possess the fragrance of fresh flowers. Jasmine tea, a scented green tea, is the main product. Scented teas are made with green, oolong, black and other teas. The fragrance is determined by the flowers added, such as jasmine, prynne (*michelia* alba DC), rose, pomelo (*Citrus grandis*), Daidai (*Citru aurantium var. amara*), *Chloranthus*, *Osmanthus*, etc.

The processes for jasmine tea are as follows:

Preparation of flowers is as follows: white buds are picked and immediately spread out in a **well-ventilated**, **hygienic** room, away from direct sunlight. Flowers are piled 20～30 cm deep at about 34℃. If the temperature is higher, the pile is made less deep, and if the temperature is lower, the pile is made deeper. Care must be taken to not injure the flower buds. When the flowers are opened 60％～70％, they are sifted to remove unripe buds and **impurities**. Vibrating during sifting helps the flowers to open. When 90％ of the flowers bloom, the flowers are mixed gently, but quickly, with tea leaves. Care is taken not to injure the flowers and to prevent them from turning red and losing their fragrance. The mixture of tea leaves and flowers is set aside to allow the tea leaves to absorb the fragrance of the flowers. This is piled 30～50 cm deep for 8～12 hours at 38℃～44℃. If the temperature becomes too high, the mixture is turned over for cooling to prevent the flowers from withering too quickly. When the tea leaves have fully absorbed the fragrance, the mixture is **sifted** and the flowers, which have withered and turned yellow, are separated from the tea leaves.

The tea leaves, after the fragrance has been added, are dried at about 100℃, 2 cm deep, for 8～10 minutes, until moisture content become 7％～8％. The leaves are spread out to cool dowm until the leaf temperature is below 25℃ and then immediately stored in boxes before blending. In traditional processing, the moisture content was maintained below 9％, which required firing and drying. However, recent research has shown that tea leaves not dried before willadd fragrance, and contain over 9％ moisture, produce a better-quality tea. **Elimination** of the extra drying step lowered the costs, simplified the procedure, and yielded a better product. Both the final drying after fragance and the preserving of the fraganle are necessary. The final product is a produced by blending 1％～2％ of high quality flowers to the tea leaves processed with added fragrance.

New words and expressions
生词和短语

originate [əˈrɪdʒɪneɪt] v. 发源；发生；起航
account for 对……负有责任；对……做出解释
thermal [ˈθɜːm(ə)l] adj. 热的；热量的
ventilate [ˈventɪleɪt] v. 使通风
well-ventilated adj. 通风好的
hygienic [haɪˈdʒiːnɪk] adj. 卫生的；保健的

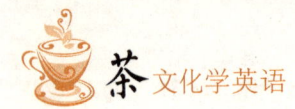

impurities [ɪmˈpjʊərətɪz] *n.* 杂质
elimination [ɪˌlɪmɪˈneɪʃən] *n.* 消除；淘汰；除去
sift [sɪft] *v.* 筛方；筛下

Comprehension 理 解

Give answers to the following questions in your own words and complete sentence as far as possible.

1. What is the most important processing stage in making yellow tea?
2. State the major processing stage in manufacturing white tea.
3. What is the scented tea?
4. State briefly the processing of scented tea?
5. Discuss the differences between traditional processing and present processing of scented tea.

Translation 参考译文

其他茶类加工

世界上许多产茶区主要生产红茶和绿茶。而中国还生产乌龙茶、黑茶、黄茶、白茶和花茶等。本课主要讨论以下几种茶的加工方法。

1. 黄茶

黄茶起源于 16 世纪，是中国的特产。主要产地为湖南、安徽和湖北省。

从鲜叶采摘到最后干燥，黄茶的加工工艺近似于绿茶。首先采摘鲜叶并将其摊晾一会，两步必须在同一天完成。锅式杀青要求温度在 150℃ 左右，稍低于绿茶杀青，这个相对较低的温度易于闷黄茶叶。

黄茶加工过程中，超过 50% 的叶绿素被破坏，其破坏程度高于绿茶。黄茶中的多酚含量低于绿茶，这可能由于黄茶加工过程中发生非酶酶促氧化所致。

闷黄时，将茶叶堆起来，由于茶堆的湿热作用，茶叶中的多酚类物质被氧化。趁茶叶还热时，将茶叶置于容器内或用湿布盖起来，这时，茶叶就会在高温作用下变黄。杀青后即闷黄称之为"湿坯闷黄",闷黄时间由于所用方法不同需要时间不同。与湿坯闷黄相比,干坯闷黄需要更长时间,但能使茶叶颜色更黄。黄汤是黄茶的显著特点之一。

2. 白茶

白茶产于福建,是一种发酵茶,起源于 16 世纪,是中国的特产。原料采自春茶的第一轮新梢,这种新梢的多酚含量中等,叶形较大或中等,叶背多白色的茸毫。茶芽被用来加工白毫银针,而 1 芽 2 或 3 叶则用来加工白牡丹或其他白茶。白茶加工工艺流程如下:鲜叶→萎凋→干燥→毛茶→分类→包装→成品茶。

1) 萎凋

茶叶摊于竹帘上,叶叶层叠不留空隙。天气晴好时,在上午 11 点前和下午 2 点后将茶叶晾晒几小时,然后移至室内。这个步骤需持续 2～3 天。茶叶也可选择在通风良好的室内干燥,室温在 29℃～30℃,相对湿度在 65%～70%。萎凋至茶芽含水量 30% 左右,叶片含水量 13% 左右。萎凋时无须风扇扇风或翻动。当叶缘卷起、茸毛变白和茶叶散发芳香时即萎凋适度。

2) 干燥

芽茶:在 40℃～45℃下干燥 20～30 分钟。

叶茶:在 70℃～80℃下干燥 10～15 分钟,直到含水量在 6% 左右。干燥过程中,尽可能轻翻或少翻动茶叶。

3. 花茶

花茶是再加工茶,添加了鲜花的香味。茉莉花茶是花茶的主要产品之一。花茶可由绿茶、乌龙茶、红茶和其他茶类加工而成。茶香取决于所加鲜花的种类,如茉莉花、白兰花、玫瑰花、柚花、玳玳花、珠兰花、桂花等。

茉莉花的加工方法如下:

鲜花准备:采摘白色花蕾后,即刻摊放于通风良好、干净卫生的室内,避免阳光直晒。花朵摊放厚度为 20～30 厘米,室温 34℃ 左右。若温度高,则花堆薄;若温度低,花堆则厚。摊放时要格外小心,以免碰伤花蕾。当 60%～70% 的花朵绽放时,要筛去未绽放的花蕾和夹杂物。筛选过程中筛子的振动有利于花朵的开放。当 90% 的花朵开放时,将花朵与茶叶轻柔而迅速地拼和。操作时应

小心避免弄伤花朵，以免变红或散失香气。将拼和的茶堆静置，让茶叶充分吸收花的香味，堆的厚度为30～50厘米，在38℃～44℃温度下静置8～12小时。若堆温过高，则需翻堆摊凉，以防花朵过早萎蔫。茶叶充分吸收花香后，再将茶花拼和物筛分，将已枯萎的花朵与茶叶分开。

吸收花香后的茶叶摊成2厘米厚，在100℃的温度下干燥8～10分钟，至含水量为7％～8％。将干燥后的茶叶摊开冷却至叶温低于25℃时装箱，以后再拼配。传统加工中，茶叶含水量低于9％时就需要烘焙和干燥。但近来的研究表明，在增香之前不干燥且含水量高于9％的茶叶，加工后质量更佳。这不仅省去了多余的干燥步骤，降低了成本，简化了工序，而且提高了茶叶产品品质。需注意的是，增香后的干燥步骤不是多余的，它能确保香气不散失。最后，将1％～2％高质量的花朵拼配到窨制的茶叶中，成品花茶就生产出来了。

Lesson 18
Storage of Tea

The tea can take in moisture, oxygen and the other smell, so it is liable to change in the storage, even to staling, smelling or being chesty. As to the majority of the tea products, they should be kept to the largest extent to their original quality during the time of storage, only but Pu'er tea, which should complete the process of transferring the raw tea into the mature one with the help of storage.

Factors Affecting the Tea Qualities in Storage

There are two factors which affect the tea qualities during the storage: one is related to tea itself, eg. the amount of water; the other concerns such environmental elements as the temperature, moisture and the amount of oxygen.

1. Amount of Water in the Tea

Water is an important media for all kinds of biochemical changes in the tea, and an essential condition for the growth and reproduction of themicroorganisms. Usually, the higher the amount of water in the tea, the sooner the staling is. When the amount of water mounts to 3%~6%, the chemical changes will slow down and the microorganisms could not reproduce; when the amount rises to 6.5%, the staling will need six months; while the amount surpasses 7%, the flavor will **deteriorate**; and **mycosis** will be enriched and the tea will smell chesty if the amount roars up to 12%.

What controls the amount of water is that the degree of tea's dryness, the relative moisture of the air and **permeability** of the package materials.

2. The Temperature

The quality changes in the stored tea are the results of the changes occurring in the contents. The higher temperature of the environment, the faster the changes will be, and the more obvious will the quality changes be. Researches prove that the tea could retain its original color in a long time if the temperature is kept 0℃~5℃; the color will change slowly when 10℃~15℃. Similarly, one rise of 10℃, 3~5 times the speed of the browning of the color. In the end when the temperature mounts to higher than 30℃, the browning speed will quicken greatly and obviously.

3. The Relative Moisture of Air

Since the tea is quite **fallible** to moisture, the higher the moisture of the storage environment is, the sooner will the tea absorb the water and being damp; the lower the amount of water in the tea is, the quicker will the tea absorb the moisture. When the relative amount of moisture in the air is 40%, the average amount of water in tea is about 8%; but the amount will increase more than 10% a day in the tea, till to the highest, 21%, if the relative amount of the air moisture gets 80%. It is studied that the tea should be stored in an environment with the relative moisture of 30%~50%, or in a well shut package with no air or water being touched.

4. The Light

In storage, there will be some enhanced oxygenization of phytochromes or that of lipid materials in the tea, if it is shined continually by the light. Especially, when it is shined by ultraviolet rays, the tea will smell of the sun and degrade its flavor and the color.

5. Oxygen

Tea Polyphenols, Vitamin C and the lipoid will be easily and automatically oxygenized and will result in the bad quality of the tea. For instance, the color of the green tea will change from the green to the brown, from the fresh to the withered; and the brewing water will turn to yellow, even worse to red; losing the original flavor. Except Pu'er tea, all the other teas should be stored on a condition with lower degree of oxygen. The good and famous tea should be packed in a container with the oxygen amount less than 0.1%, then, the quality may be guaranteed.

What's more, the storage environment should be clean enough without any bad smell.

In conclusion, the suitable condition of tea storage should be: less than 6% of the water amount in the tea leaves, low temperature (under 5℃), low moisture (under 50%), avoiding of light, being deoxygenized(lower than 0.1% in the container) and no other bad smell.

Methods of the Storage of the Tea

1. Being Completely Dried Before Storing

As for those high priced refined tea, it is better to keep 3%~5% of water in the tea leaves, no more than 6%, and never higher than 7%. For the other teas, the specified water content mustn't be exceeded.

2. Well Packed

In order to prevent from moisture and avoid oxygen and light, the tea should be packed with proof-light and layers of well shutmacromolecular composite materials, eg. Aluminum foil compound bags. At the same time, the opening should be shut absolutely and closely.

3. Deoxygenized Package

Put some deoxygenizing materials (mainly Active iron powder) into the well shut container in which the tea is packed, to consume the oxygen. Usually, 24 hours later, the oxygen amount will cut down to less than 0.1%. This method is especially suitable to green tea, best to the refined tea.

4. Vacuum Package

With help of the vacuum machine, extract the air out of the tea container. This method is widely used in storing the Oolong tea powder.

5. Storage in the Low Temperature

With help of refrigerator or cold storage, tea can be saved in a low temperature. Keep the temperature to $-18℃\sim 2℃$ to meet the need of retaining the fresh quality of the tea. As to green tea, the quality will remain the same after 8~12 months being stored under 5℃; and it will last 2~3 years if the temperature is under $-10℃$.

New words and expressions
生词和短语

fallible ['fælɪb(ə)l] *adj.* 易犯错误的

permeability [pɜːmɪəˈbɪlɪtɪ] n. 渗透性，弥漫
deteriorate [dɪˈtɪərɪəreɪt] v. 恶化；变坏
mycosis [maɪˈkəʊsɪs] n. 霉病菌
vacuum [ˈvækjʊəm] adj. 真空的

Comprehension 理 解

Give answers to the following questions in your own words and complete sentence as far as possible.

1. What are the factors that affect the tea qualities in storage?
2. What can we do to control the amount of water well?
3. What is the appropriate moisture of air to storage the tea?
4. How to storage the tea perfectly?
5. Tell what else measures do you know to storage the tea fully?

Notes on the text 课文注释

1. deoxygenized package：脱氧包装是在密封的包装容器中，使用能与氧气起化学作用的脱氧剂与之反应，从而除去包装容器中的氧气，以达到保护内装物的目的。

2. vacuum package：也称减压包装，是将包装容器内的空气全部抽出密封，维持袋内处于高度减压状态，空气稀少相当于低氧效果，使微生物没有生存条件，以达到果品新鲜、无病腐发生的目的。目前应用的有塑料袋内真空包装、铝箔包装、玻璃器皿及其复合材料包装等。

Translation 参考译文

茶叶的贮藏

茶叶具有很强的吸湿性、氧化性以及吸收异味的特性，因此茶叶在贮藏过程中容易发生品质的变化，甚至出现陈化、霉变、串味等变质现象。对于大部分茶叶产品而言，加工好的茶叶需要在贮藏过程中最大限度地保持其原有的品质，只有普洱生茶需要在贮藏过程中完成其向普洱熟茶的转化。

贮藏过程中影响茶叶品质变化的因素

茶叶在贮藏过程中的品质变化主要受两个方面因素的影响：一是茶叶本身的因素，如含水量高低；二是茶叶贮藏的温度、湿度、光照和氧气浓度等环境因素的影响。

1. 茶叶含水量

水分是茶叶内各种生化成分反应必需的介质，也是微生物生长繁殖的必要条件。通常情况下，茶叶含水量越高，陈化越快。当茶叶含水量为3%～6%时，茶叶化学反应缓慢，微生物无法滋生；当含水量超过6.5%时，存放6个月茶叶就会产生陈气；含水量超过7%时，滋味就会逐渐变差；含水量超过12%时，霉菌大量滋生，霉味产生。

影响茶叶含水量高低的因素有：茶叶的干燥程度、空气相对湿度和包装材料的透气性。

2. 温度

茶叶在贮藏过程中的品质变化是茶叶内含成分变化的结果，环境温度越高，反应速度越快，品质变化越明显。研究结果表明：在0℃～5℃范围内，茶叶可在较长时间内保持原有色泽；在10℃～15℃时，色泽变化较慢。随后温度每升高10℃，茶叶色泽褐变的速度要加快3～5倍。当温度超过30℃，茶叶色泽褐化速度很快且明显。

3. 空气相对湿度

茶叶具有很强的吸湿性，贮藏环境的空气湿度越高，茶叶吸湿返潮越快；茶叶含水量越低，吸湿越快。当在空气相对湿度为40%的环境贮藏时，茶叶的平均含水量仅为8%左右；当在空气相对湿度为80%的环境中贮藏时，茶叶含水量一天可增加10%以上。据研究：茶叶应贮藏在空气相对湿度为30%～50%的环境中，或采用密封性好的包装材料以阻隔茶叶与空气中水分的接触才能保证茶叶的品质。

4. 光照

茶叶在贮藏过程中若受到光线的作用，会促进植物色素或脂类物质发生光氧化反应，产生令人不快的异味。特别是受到紫外线的照射，会导致茶叶香气和色泽的劣变。

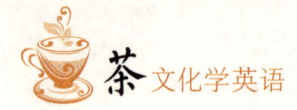

5．氧气

茶叶中的茶多酚、维生素C、类脂等化合物都易发生自动氧化，氧化后的产物大多对茶叶品质不利。如绿茶在贮藏过程中外形色泽由绿变褐，由润变枯，就会导致茶汤色泽变黄，甚至变红，滋味失去鲜爽的风味。除普洱茶外，其他茶最好在低氧的条件下贮藏。名优茶包装容器内的氧气含量需控制在0.1％以下，其品质才有保证。

此外，贮藏环境应清洁无异味。

综上所述，茶叶保鲜的适宜条件为：茶叶含水量低于6％，低温（5℃以下）、低湿（50％以下）、避光、脱氧（容器内含氧量低于0.1％）以及无异味的贮藏环境。

茶叶贮藏方法

1．贮藏前茶叶充分干燥

对于价格高的名优茶，茶叶含水量以3％～5％为佳，尽量控制在6％以内，最高不超过7％。其他茶叶不得超过产品标准中规定的含水量要求。

2．密封包装

为了起到很好的防潮、隔氧和避光的作用，茶叶包装时必须选用不透光、密封性好的多层高分子复合材料，如铝箔复合袋。同时，包装袋封口一定要严密。

3．脱氧包装贮藏

在装有茶叶的密封容器内，放入袋装脱氧剂（活性铁粉为基材），以消耗容器内的氧气。一般封入脱氧剂24小时后，容器内的氧气浓度可降低到0.1％以下。此法适宜在绿茶，尤其是名优绿茶包装中使用。

4．真空包装

采用真空包装机械，将茶叶容器中的空气去除。此法在颗粒型的乌龙茶中广泛使用。

5．低温贮藏

采用冷库或冰箱等设备对茶叶进行低温贮藏。将温度保持在－18℃～2℃范围内能达到茶叶品质保鲜的目的。就绿茶而言，在5℃以下贮藏，经8～12个月的贮藏，绿茶品质能保持基本不变；若在－10℃以下贮藏，可保持2～3年品质基本不变。

Unit 5
Evaluation of Tea Quality

Lesson 19
Sensory Evaluation of Tea Quality

Special examination and inspection are applied to estimate tea quality, tea processing level and differentiate each kind of tea. There are two kinds of tea examinations: sensory and scientific. The former is handled by experienced tea masters through seeing, smelling, tasting and feeling to **verdict** whether the color, scent, taste and shape of tea match certain standard or its quality characteristics. Kinds of instruments and equipments are used in scientific examination, through which the quality of tea is estimated by physical and chemical analysis. To reduce error, maximum identity of both subjective and objective condition should be created in practice because sensory examination, relative to scientific one, is inevitably influenced by human sense and environmental factors. Since it is difficult to get full experimental data in scientific examination because the excessive use of instruments and complex analysis, sensory examination is still a chief method for tea appraisal at present.

Tea Connoisseur

A tea connoisseur, like a poet, is born to be, not made to be. Of course he must be trained, he will never be an expert judging of teas unless he has a delicate **palate** and an exquisite sense of smell to begin with. A talented connoisseur is like a **maestro**, who will know how it will sound by the look of a score, or a great chef, who will know what the taste of a dish will be by an expert knowledge about its constituents. The connoisseur not only has to estimate the value of thousands of pounds worth of tea by merely tasting a sample, but also is expected to know how the various samples of different teas will blend together. It is evident, therefore, besides high talent, he also needs years of practice and study to be a successful connoisseur of tea.

As a tea connoisseur, he is supposed to pay attention to the life habits, some bad habits should be avoided. Smoking and drinking, the pungent food such as garlic and onion as well as the food with too much sweet and fried should be forbidden. Antibiotics and Chinese herbal medicine should be cautiously taken, and fragrant cosmetics should not be used before testing.

Conditions for Tea Sensory

Light plays an important part in tea tasting. The ideal testing room has windows on the north side only. The counter or table for testing is placed where the light is steady and no shade, and surrounds each cup equally. If the light on each is not equal, the colors of the liquors cannot be compared. Direct sunlight or **artificial** light must be avoided. Therefore, the screens or shades on the windows can be adjusted to keep the proper light.

Temperature in the room should be maintained at the range of 20℃～25℃ in order to avoid the tea liquor being cool quickly.

Besides, the room should be kept clean and dry, the fresh air smoothly cycling and free from of any odor; the surroundings are quiet and no noise maker.

Methods of Tea Sensory Examination

The technique of tea sensory examination should conform to a standard procedure and special equipments should to ensure that comparisons made between various samples are affective. The general equipments and procedure for tea testing are as follows:

In the room, there must are shelves on which rest various samples. A kettle rests on a stove. Long counters about four feet high are used for tea to be tested. Samples of dry tea are ranged on the counter to be examined for their color, uniformity, twist, tip and etc. Before them are placed a line of small, covered china pots or mugs. Usually they have no spouts, although sometimes Europe pots with spouts are used. In front of each sample and pot is a thin china bowl.

After assessing the characteristics of dry tea, about 3 or 5 grams of tea is weighed out from each sample on a small **handnever balance scale**. Then the tea is placed in the pots. When ten, twenty, or thirty teas have been "weighed," the

batch is ready for watering, that has just reached the boiling point, always used. It is never brought to a boiling point the second time. The water is poured over the tea and the covers placed on the pots. The tea is then allowed to stand for a period of four, five, or six minutes. Tasters used a **sand-glass** to tell the time in the past, but today usually use an alarm clock. The clock is set for a proper period, and the bell rings at the expiration of the time set. The pots are turned sideways in the bowls, permitting the brew to drain off the leaves and to flow into the bowls. A batch, as a rule, is arranged from left to right.

After the liquor is drawn off, the inner quality of tea (including aroma of **infused leaf** and the color, taste of infusion) can be examined. In tasting, Instead of sipping it, the liquors should be drown into mouth by an in ward breath. This brings them into intimate contact with the tongue, palate and walls of the **buccal cavity**, which are physiologically sensitive to the flavor, strength and **astringency** of the liquid. The liquor is not swallowed, but is **expectorated** in a **spittoon**.

At last, the infused leaf is shaken on to the lid, by inverting pot. then the reversed lid is replaced on the pot and pressed free of excess moisture in infused leaf for inspecting their color, uniformity, soft, brightness and etc

There are certain rules which should be strictly followed in a testing room. The pots and bowls should be of exactly the same cubic content. The scale must be kept exactly true so that the leaves can be weighed out accurately. The kettle must be kept perfectly clean and free from odor of any kind. The tea cups and spoons should be thoroughly washed and wiped dry with a clean cloth.

New words and expressions
生词和短语

connoisseur [ˌkɒnəˈsɜː] n. 鉴赏家
maestro [ˈmaɪstrəʊ] n. 大师；名家
handnever balance scale 扭力天平
infused leaf（茶叶专业术语）叶底
buccal [ˈbʌk(ə)l] adj. 脸颊的；口的
astringency [əˈstrɪndʒənsɪ] n. 收敛性
expectorate [ɪkˈspektəreɪt] v. 吐出；吐痰
verdict [ˈvɜːdɪkt] n.（经过试验、检验或体验发表的）决定；意见

palate [ˈpælət] n. 味觉；上颚
artificial [ˌɑːtɪˈfɪʃ(ə)l] adj. 人造的
sand-glass 沙漏；一种计时器
spittoon [spɪˈtuːn] n. 痰盂；痰桶
cavity [ˈkævɪtɪ] n. 腔

Comprehension

Give answers to the following questions in your own words and complete sentence as far as possible.

1. What are the difference and relation between two kinds of tea examination?
2. Why is a tea connoisseur born?
3. Draw a picture to demonstrate the right procedure of sensory method.

Translation

茶叶品质的感官评价

对茶叶品质、加工水平进行评估以及区分各种茶叶的特点时，会运用到一些专用检查与检测方法。通常有两种方法：感官审评方法和理化分析方法。前一种方法由有经验的茶叶专家来完成，通过看、嗅、尝和感觉来评判茶叶的色泽、滋味以及形状是否达到特定的标准或符合茶叶的品质特点。理化分析方法中要应用多种仪器设备，运用物理与化学分析手段来检验茶叶的品质。为减少误差，在实际工作中，主观与客观分析条件都应尽量具备，因为相对于理化方法，感官评价法不可避免地受到人的感觉和环境因素的影响。理化法需要大量的仪器设备和复杂的数据分析才能获得理想的实验数据，所以，感官审评法仍是目前茶叶品质评审的主要方法。

评茶师

据说评茶师如同诗人一般，其天赋与生俱来而非后天培养。当然，评茶师必须进行培训，但是如若没有灵敏的味觉和一流的嗅觉，是绝对无法成为专业评茶师的。优秀的评茶师，就像音乐大师一看到乐谱就知道是什么样的旋律，就像厨师长只凭菜肴的成分就知道味道一样。专业的评茶师不仅靠品尝茶样就能估计出上千英镑的茶叶价值，而且还要知道如何将各种不同的茶叶拼配在一起。很显然，要成为一位成功的评茶师，需要具备很高的天赋，同时还需经过

多年的实践和学习。

作为评茶师,在日常生活中还应注意一些生活细节,避免一些不良的爱好。平时不吸烟,不喝酒,少吃葱蒜类辛辣食品以及过甜、油炸等食品;生病时慎用抗生素类药物,慎服中成药;评茶前不涂擦芳香气味的化妆品等。

评茶的条件

光线对评茶起着至关重要的作用,只有北边开窗的房间是最理想的。评茶的长桌或圆桌应放置在光线稳定且无影的地方,保证每杯茶的光线一致。如果光线不一致,就无法对茶汤色泽进行比较。要避免阳光直射和使用人造光。所以,可以调节窗户上的遮光板以保证合适的光线。

为保证茶水不会迅速降温,房间的温度应保持在20℃~25℃之间。

此外,还应保持室内清洁,干燥,空气新鲜流通,无异味干扰;四周环境安静,无噪音源。

感官审评方法

为保证不同茶样之间的比对是有效的,评茶应遵循标准化的程序和使用专门的用具。大致的用具和步骤如下:

房间里要有用来放置不同茶叶样品的样茶架,配有烧水壶的炉子。评茶用的长桌应有4英尺(约1.2米)高。干茶样置于长桌上,以便评茶师对其色泽、匀度、卷曲度、嫩度等进行评价。样茶前放置一排审评杯,通常为无嘴的小瓷壶或瓷杯,有时也会用到带嘴的欧式壶。每份样本和审评杯前放一个薄瓷的审评碗。

审评完干茶特征后,每份茶样用扭力天平称取3~5克茶叶,放入审评杯中。每称取10份、20份或30份为一批,加水冲泡,通常使用刚达到沸点的水,但从来不用第二次沸腾的水。将水倒在茶叶上之后,盖好盖子。静置4~6分钟。过去人们用沙漏计时,如今通常用闹钟,将闹钟设定了适合的时间之后,当时间一到,铃声响起。按照从左到右的规定,将审评杯依次斜搁在审评碗的碗沿上,让茶汤全部流入审评碗中。

待茶汤倒完后,就可以进行茶叶内质(包括叶底的香气,茶汤的色泽、滋味)的审评了。在品尝滋味时,应该用吸气的方式将茶汤吸入口中,而不应该采用呷（小口喝）的方式，这样可以保证茶汤与舌头、上腭以及口腔壁等紧密接触，这些部位对风味、强度和收敛性（刺激性）有敏锐的感知。尝完茶汤后不应将其吞咽而应吐在吐茶桶中。

最后，将审评杯翻转，将叶底摇至审评杯盖子的反面。然后将倒过来的盖子放在审评杯上，压掉盖上多余的水分，评定叶底的色泽、匀度、柔软度和亮度等。

在评茶室中，有些细致的规定必须遵守。审评杯和审评碗的容积必须一样，天平要精确才能保证茶叶称量准确。烧水壶要绝对干净且无任何异味。茶杯和茶匙必须彻底清洗后，再用干净的布擦干。

Lesson 20
Description of Tea Quality

The recognized features of tea quality relate to shape, color, taste and **aroma**, and all these are described in specialized terms. There are many **synonyms**, but the following represent those in common use and are listed as terms of the characteristics when tea testing is in progress. **Self-explanatory** terms are omitted except when it is desirable to indicate the cause of the characteristic they describe.

1. Terms Describing Dry Leaf

Black: a black appearance is desirable preferably with "bloom".

Blackish: a satisfactory appearance for CTC type teas.

Bloom: a sign of well manufacture and sorting.

Bold: particles of leaf are larger than the particular grade.

Brown: a brown appearance in CTC type teas that normally indicates overly harsh treatment of leaf.

Chunky: a very large broken-leaf tea.

Clean: leaf that is free from fibre, dirt and all extraneous matters.

Crepy: leaf with a crepied appearance common to larger grade broken-leaf teas such as BOP.

Curly: leaf appearance of whole leaf grade teas such as O. P., as distinct from "wiry".

Even: teas true to their grade, consisting of pieces of leaf of fairly even size.

Flaky: flat open pieces of leaf often light in texture.

Grey: caused by too much **abrasion** during refine processing.

Grainy: describes primary grades of well-made CTC teas such as Pekoe dust.

Leafy: the tea tends to be on the large or longish size.

Light: tea light in weight, of poor density, and sometimes flaky.

Make: a term used to describe tea manufacture, in tea-taster's terms a make that means a well-made tea or not true to its grade.

Mushy: tea that has been packed or stored with a highly moisture content.

Neat: a grade of tea without impurities and having good uniformity size.

Powdery: fine light tea dust.

Ragged: an uneven badly manufactured in size and thickness.

Stalk and Fibre: bits of tea bush other than the leaf which should be minimal in superior grades but are unavoidable in lower-grade tea.

Tip: apparents in top grades of tea that suggests afine plueking.

Uneven and Mixed: "uneven" pieces of leaf particles indicating poor sorting and resulting in a tea unmatch a particular grade.

Well Twisted: used to describe whole-leaf Orthodox tea grades, often referred to as well "made" or "rolled".

Wiry: leaf appearance of a well-twisted, thin, long leaf.

2. Terms Describing Infused Tea Leaf

Aroma: smell or scent denoting 'inherent character' usually in tea grown at high altitudes.

Biscuity: a pleasant aroma often found in well-dried Assam.

Bright: a lively bright appearance, which usually indicates that the tea will produce a bright liquor.

Coppery: bright leaf that indicates a well manufactured of tea.

Dark: a dark or dull color that usually indicates poor quality of the tea.

Dull: lacks brightness and usually denotes poor tea. It can be due to faulty tea manufacture or a high moisture content of tea in storage.

Green: when referring to black tea it means the leaf has been under-**fermented**, it can also be caused by inadequate rolling during manufacture.

Mixed or Uneven: leaf of varying color.

Tarry: a smoky aroma of Lapsang Souchong black tea.

3. Terms Describing Tea Liquor

Bakey: anaroma of an over-fired tea that too much moisture has been driven

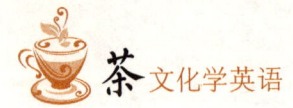

off the leaf while drying.

Bitter: an unpleasant taste associated with raw teas.

Body: a liquor has enough both substance and **pungent** as opposed to being thin.

Bright: denotes a lively fresh tea with good quality.

Brisk: the most "live" characteristic resulted in good manufacture.

Burned: taint was caused by extreme over-drying during manufacture.

Character: an attractive taste, specific to describ teas grown at high altitude.

Coarse: a tea producing a harsh undesirable taste.

Coloury: indicates useful depth of color and strength.

Common: a very plain and thin liquor with no distinct flavor.

Cream: a natural precipitate obtained as the liquor cools down.

Dry: indicates slight over-firing or drying during manufacture.

Dull: not clear, lacking any brightness or briskness.

Earthy: normally caused by damp storage of tea but can also be used to describe a taste that is sometimes "climatically inherent" in teas from certain regions.

Empty: a liquor lacking fullness. No substance.

Flat: not fresh, usually due to age. Tea tends to lose its characteristics and taste with age, unlike some wines which become mature with age.

Flavor: a most desirable extension of character caused by slow growth at high altitudes. Relatively rare.

Fruity: can be due to over-fermenting during manufacture and/ or **bacterial** infection before firing or drying, which gives the tea an over ripe taste. Unlike wines, this is not a desirable taste in tea.

Gone off: a flat or old tea. Often denotes a high moisture content.

Grassy: unpleasant metallic quality similar to brass. It is usually associated with un-withered tea.

Green: It used to refer to black tea liquor denotes an immature "raw" character. This is mostly due to under fermenting and sometimes to under withering during manufacture.

Hard: a very pungent liquor, a desirable quality in tea.

Harsh: a very rough taste which generally due to the leaf was under withered during manufacture.

Heavy: a thick, strong and colored liquor with limited briskness.

High—fired: over fired or dried, but not bakey or burned.

Lacking: describes a neutral liquor with no enough substance or pronounced characteristics.

Light: lacking strength and depth of color.

Malty: desirable character in some Assam teas.

Muddy: a dull, opaque liquor.

Muscatel: desirable character in Darjeeling teas with a grapey taste.

Musty: a **suspicion** of mould.

Plain: a liquor that is 'clean' but lacking of desirable characteristics.

Point: a bright, acidic and penetrating characteristic.

Pungent: **astringent** with a good combination of briskness, brightness and strength.

Rasping: a very coarse and harsh liquor.

Raw: a bitter, unpleasant taste.

Soft: the opposite of briskness. Tea lacks any 'live' characteristics and is caused by inefficient **fermentation** and/ or drying.

Stewed: a soft liquor with undesirable taste that lacks pungent that caused by drying at low temperatures or not sending out moisture in time.

Strength: substance in a cup.

Sweaty: unpleasant taste. Poor tea.

Taint: characteristic or taste that is foreign to tea such as oil, garlic etc. often due to the tea being stored next to other commodities with strong characteristics of their own.

Thick: liquor with good color.

Thin: an **insipid** light liquor that lacks desirable characteristics.

Weedy: a grass or hay taste associated with teas that have been under withered during manufacture and sometimes referred to as "woody".

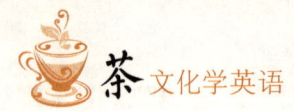 文化学英语

New words and expressions
生词和短语

synonym [ˈsɪnənɪm] n. 同义词
self-explanatory [ˌselfɪkˈsplænətrɪ] adj. 不解自明的，明显的
chunky [ˈtʃʌŋkɪ] adj. 矮胖的；粗短的；厚实的
flaky [ˈfleɪkɪ] adj. 薄片的
abrasion [əˈbreɪʒn] n. 磨损
ragged [ˈrægɪd] adj. 参差不齐的，凹凸不平的
aroma [əˈrəumə] n. 芳香
tarry [ˈtɑːrɪ] v. 等待；逗留；耽搁；adj. 涂了焦油的
ferment [fəˈment, ˌfəːment] n. 发酵
fermentation [ˌfəːmenˈteɪʃən] n. 发酵
pungent [ˈpʌndʒənt] adj. 辛辣的；刺激性的
bacterial [bækˈtɪrɪəl] adj. 细菌的
malty [ˈmɔːltɪ] adj. 麦芽的；含麦芽的
muddy [ˈmʌdɪ] adj. 泥泞的；模糊的；混乱的
muscatel [ˌmʌskəˈtel] n. 麝香葡萄酒；麝香葡萄
musty [ˈmʌstɪ] adj. 发霉的
suspicion [səˈspɪʃən] n. 怀疑；嫌疑；疑心；一点儿 vt. 怀疑
astringent [əˈstrɪndʒənt] adj. 涩的；n. [医] 收敛剂
insipid [ɪnˈsɪpɪd] adj. 清淡的

Comprehension
理 解

Give answers to the following questions in your own words and complete sentence as far as possible.

1. In your opinion, what does a cup of quality tea mean in color?
2. In your opinion, what does a cup of quality tea mean in shape?
3. In your opinion, what does a cup of quality tea mean in taste?
4. In your opinion, what does a cup of quality tea mean in aroma?
5. Can you list in China ten major well-known teas?

Notes on the text
课文注释

1. Assam teas：阿萨姆茶，是出产于印度东北部的阿萨姆邦的红茶。阿萨姆位于东喜马拉雅山南麓，与不丹相邻。这种茶以茶汤浓稠，滋味浓烈，有麦芽香，色泽清透鲜亮而出名。在历史上，阿萨姆是继中国以后第二个商业茶叶生产地区。

2. Darjeeling teas：大吉岭红茶，产于印度西孟加拉邦北部喜马拉雅山麓的大吉岭高原一带。当地年均温15℃左右，白天日照充足，但日夜温差大，谷地里常年弥漫云雾，是孕育此茶独特芳香的一大因素。以5月至6月的二号茶品质最优，被誉为"红茶中的香槟"。大吉岭红茶拥有高昂的身价。3月至4月的一号茶多为青绿色，二号茶为金黄，其汤色橙黄，气味芬芳高雅，尤其上品带有葡萄香，口感细致柔和。大吉岭红茶最适合清饮，但因为茶叶较大，需稍久焖（约5分钟）使茶叶尽舒，才能得其味。下午茶及进食口味生的盛餐后，最宜饮此茶。

3. C.T.C 分别指压碎（Crush）、撕裂（Tear）、揉卷（Curl）三个英文单词的第一个字母，也叫红碎茶，指茶条在加工过程中，通过两个不同转速的滚筒挤压、撕切、卷曲而成的颗粒状的碎茶。C.T.C 一般制成茶包饮用，如立顿红茶。近年来，除了红碎茶以外，云南也有 C.T.C 绿茶生产。

4. 红茶名称中的缩写词含义：

P：Pekoe，带有白毫的嫩芽。

O：Orange，橙黄色嫩芽。

B：Broken，碎茶。

F：Fanning，片茶，指BOP筛选下来的小片茶叶。

D：Dust，粉尘状般的细末茶，筛选到最后的粉末状碎屑。多以茶包形式出现。

G：Golden，黄金色的光辉。

T：Tip，含有大量新芽。

S：Souchong，小种红茶。

OP：Orange Pekoe，常见的等级指的是叶片较长较大而完整的茶叶。

BOP：Broken Orange Pekoe，制成较细碎的OP，叶片较小。滋味较浓重，一般适合用来冲泡奶茶。

FOP：Flowery Orange Pekoe，有较多芽叶的红茶。

TGFOP：Tippy Golden Flowery Orange Pekoe，含有较多金黄芽叶的红茶。

FTGFOP：Fine Tippy Golden Flowery Orange Pekoe，经过精细地揉捻精制而成的高品质茶叶。

茶叶品质术语

茶叶可识别的品质特征包括外形、色泽、滋味和香气，所有这些都有专门的术语描述。下面列出的常用术语有许多的同义词，这里按评审顺序排列。一些浅显易懂的术语被省略，除非需要用它们来描述品质成因时才出现。

1. 干茶审评术语

乌（Black）：红茶外观要求乌润。

带乌（Blackish）：CTC 红茶较好的外观色泽。

油润（Bloom）：加工和分类好的标志。

粗实（Bold）：叶子的大小规格大于特定等级的要求。

棕褐（Brown）：呈现棕褐色的 CTC 茶通常表明加工过度。

粗短（Chunky）：粗大而断碎的茶叶。

净（Clean）：茶叶中没有筋毛、泥土及其他杂质。

皱折（Crepy）：皱折的叶子，通常在形体较大的切细叶茶中出现，例如 BOP。

卷曲（Curly）：叶形完整的叶茶外观，例如 OP，与细紧不同。

匀整（Even）：完全符合等级要求，茶叶叶片大小一致。

轻薄（Flaky）：扁平的叶子通常质地轻。

灰色（Grey）：由于在精制过程中太多的磨损造成的。

多颗粒（Grainy）：描述加工优异的 CTC 茶的低档茶，例如白毫末茶。

叶茶（Leafy）：茶叶形体规格大而长的。

轻飘（Light）：茶叶密度小重量轻，有时为扁片形。

加工（Make）：这个术语用来描述茶叶加工，在评茶术语中，意味着加工质量好的茶叶或与其等级不相符的茶叶。

潮湿的（Mushy）：包装或储存的茶叶含水量很高。

匀净（Neat）：无杂质，大小匀齐的级别茶。

粉末状（Powdery）：细轻的末。

粗糙（Ragged）：形状大小粗细不匀的茶叶。

茎梗和筋毛（Stalk and Fibre）：除叶片外的新梢部分，在高等级的茶叶中要尽量少，但在低等级的茶中却不可避免地存在。

锋苗（Tip）：在上等茶中存在，是采摘原料好的表现。

花杂不匀（Uneven and Mixed）："不匀"表明分级不合理，将导致茶叶与级别不符。

紧卷（Well Twisted）：通常用来描述传统茶中的叶茶等级，通常也指加工或揉捻好。

细紧（Wiry）：指茶条紧卷、细而长。

2．叶底审评术语

香气幽雅（Aroma）：香气幽雅芬芳是高海拔地区茶叶的内在品质表现。

烘烤香（Biscuity）：宜人的香气，常存在于干燥好的阿萨姆茶中。

明亮（Bright）：鲜艳明亮的外观，通常也表明茶叶会有产生明亮的汤色。

紫铜色（Coppery）：明亮的叶底意味着茶叶的加工好。

暗色（Dark）：深或暗的色泽通常表明茶叶品质差。

暗（Dull）：缺少光泽，通常表明茶叶的品质差。可能是由于茶叶加工不当或茶叶贮藏时含水量高所致。

花青（Green）：描述红茶时，花青意味着叶片发酵不足，也有可能由于加工时揉捻不充分所致。

花杂不匀（Mixed and Uneven）：叶片色泽多样。

松烟香（Tarry）：小种红茶的一种烟熏味。

3．茶汤审评术语

老火味（Bakey）：干燥过度导致茶叶过度失水而形成的一种香气。

苦（Bitter）：口味不佳，与生青有关。

浓厚（Body）：茶汤内含物丰富且刺激性强，与淡薄相反。

明亮（Bright）：表明茶叶新鲜，品质好。

鲜爽（Brisk）：因茶叶加工好，茶叶具鲜爽的特性。

焦味（Burned）：加工过程中因过度干燥导致的。

韵味（Character）：滋味独特，尤其是生长在高海拔地区的茶叶。

粗涩（Coarse）：茶叶刺鼻，味道不纯正。

鲜艳（Coloury）：色泽及力度上乘。

正常（Common）：滋味平淡且无特殊风味。

凝乳（Cream）：茶汤冷却后出现浑浊的现象。

枯燥（Dry）：加工过程中，火温稍高或干燥稍过。

浑暗（Dull）：汤色不清，缺乏亮度和鲜活度。

土腥味（Earthy）：通常由储藏过程中受潮引起，也可用来描述某一地区因气候原因而产生的一种茶叶的味道。

淡薄（Empty）：茶汤中缺少内含物。

平淡（Flat）：不新鲜。通常随着贮藏时间的延长，茶叶品质特色及口感变差，不同于酒，愈久愈醇。

风味（Flavor）：由于在高海拔地区缓慢生长而形成的独特品质，非常少有。

熟味（Fruity）：加工过程中发酵过度或干燥前因细菌感染致使茶叶产生熟味过重。不同于酒类，茶不需此类滋味。

变质（Gone off）：通常表明因茶叶含水量高导致茶叶品质变差。

青味（Grassy）：口味不佳，有青草味。通常与没萎凋或摊放茶叶有关。

生青（Green）：以此描述红茶茶汤时指生青的特点。大多由于加工时发酵不足，有时也因萎凋不足所致。

强（Hard）：茶汤的刺激性强，是茶叶品质好的表现。

粗（Harsh）：茶叶滋味粗涩，通常由于加工时萎凋不足导致的。

浓（Heavy）：茶汤滋味浓，强，色泽深，鲜爽度稍欠。

高火（High-fired）：火温过大，但没有达到老火或焦的程度。

贫乏（Lacking）：茶汤纯正，但内含物不丰富或无显著特色。

轻淡（Light）：缺少强度，色泽较浅。

麦芽糖味（Malty）：一些阿萨姆红茶所具有的特性。

泥色（Muddy）：暗而浑浊的茶汤颜色。

麝香葡萄味（Muscatel）：一般指大吉岭茶带有葡萄味道。

霉味（Musty）：有发霉的味道。

平淡（Plain）：茶汤虽然清亮，却无特色。

尖锐（Point）：明亮、略酸和具穿透力的特性。

刺激性（Pungent）：集鲜爽度、亮度和强度于一体的收敛性。

粗涩（Rasping）：粗涩的茶汤。

生（Raw）：苦而不佳的味道。

纯和（Soft）：与鲜爽相反。茶叶缺乏新鲜特性，是由于发酵或干燥不充分造成的。

熟闷味（Stewed）：茶汤纯和缺乏刺激性。由于在低温下干燥或不及时散发水分所致。

强度（Strength）：杯中的实体。

馊味（Sweaty）：难闻的味道。低劣茶的味道。

串味（Taint）：与茶无关的特质或味道，如油、洋葱等。通常是因为储藏茶时，靠近其他具有强烈气味的物品所致。

浓厚（Thick）：茶汤色泽鲜亮而深。

清淡（Thin）：茶汤平淡而无特色。

杂草味（Weedy）：加工时萎凋不足导致的青草味或干草味，有时也指木质气味。

Lesson 21
How to Estimate the Quality of Black Tea

Tea is judged by three factors: ① the appearance, twist, and smell of the dry tea leaf, which are judged by sight and smell; ② the color, brightness, and odor of the infused leaf, also judged by sight and smell; ③ and the color, thickness, strength, **pungency**, and flavor of the liquor which are, judged by sight and taste.

1. Dry Leaf

Well-twisted leaf of the black tea denotes a good wither. Brown, flaky leaf denotes a poor wither. However, a leaf with a brown shade can make the best liquoring tea; black, pretty leaf generally gives poor liquor. Open, flat leaf infuses very quickly, and all the essence of the tea is extracted with the first water poured thereon. The leaf which is closely twisted generally gives a better second cup. In general, the leaf of black tea should be small, well-rolled and uniform. Tip is not always necessary for the black tea, but in the United States, where perhaps undue attention has been given to buying for style, many buyers give too much consideration to Pekoe tips as an indication of quality in black teas, whereas the best drawings of all varieties of blacks are oftentimes without any indication of tip. For example in Taiwan, the tea in a fine Formosa, small, black, well twisted, uniform leaf is a surer indication of quality than rough, uneven leaf with an abundance of tip, and this is also true of the choicest Darjeelings sold at the fanciest prices, the best of which are entirely black. If the tea is tippy, the tips should be golden, long, and well twisted.

Black teas in Ceylon, Java, and India are much alike in appearance of the dry leaf. Actually, Java tea is grown from an Assam seed, so it is **well-nigh** impossible to distinguish between them. China black tea is quite distinct from the others. Each growth, however, has a distinct aroma. It is thus possible after some practice to distinguish between them "by the nose".

A fair value may sometimes be placed on the teas by an expert using merely this test of the dry leaf.

2. Infused Leaf

The color of the infused leaf is very important. In the case of black teas, a bright infusion with some greenish leaf showing in it usually goes with a brisk tea, and also indicates under-fermentation. Such teas, when over brisk, are often called "raw" or "green". A dark green infused leaf goes with a flat leaf often denotes under-withering, accompanied by over-fermentation. Yellow leaf with a greenish shade generally denotes pungency. Rich-golden leaf invariably denotes high quality. Reddish leaf denotes rich, full liquor. Dark leaf is a sure indication of low-grade and common tea. The color should always be even. In the case of green teas, a clear, greenish — yellow or greenish-golden color, bright and **lustrous** to the bottom of the cup, denotes a young, early picked leaf; a dull, lifeless, dark or brownish yellow color denotes an old or low-grade leaf.

The lighter the liquor of light-liquoring teas is, the younger the leaf is, and as a rule, the better the tea is. A very high grade of Chinese green tea such as An-ji Bai tea, has a remarkably light colored liquor, that it would naturally suggest a lack of body and strength, but this is not the case. Extremely light colored liquor, must not be taken as evidence of a lack of other cup qualities.

By smelling the infused leaf, one may distinguish variations in character of the teas and detect point, thickness, richness, and burnt or over fermented teas. To an extent, some buyers rely on the banking qualities of the infused leaf. After the liquor has been well drained off, good banking leaf will still retain a considerable quantity, so that by pressing it like a **sponge**, quite a lot of liquor may be squeezed out.

3. Tea Liquor

However helpful is the inspection of the dry leaf and the infused leaf, the final test of quality and flavor lies in the liquor. The ideal liguor is the brisk, full, rich, flavor, thick or **syrupy**, not dark, but rich in color. The liquor of a good tea has a bright sparkling appearance immediately after it is poured out, but it sometimes will "cream down" rapidly as it cools.

It is difficult to describe the different terms used in tasting tea. For instance, the tea may be brisk, rich, thick, insipid, grassy, fishy, smoky, flavor, harsh, metallic acrid; it may have body, strength, pungency; it may cream down. Pungency is a sensation of the gums. It is a roughness or astringency feeling in the mouth, but not a taste. Rawness or greenness is a bitter taste. Briskness is a live, as opposed to a flat taste; comparable to a fresh soda water against a stale one. Flavor is a sweetish taste, a honey—like smell. and it also has been described as a **bouquet** which can be tasted. "Creaming down" means that the tea gets quite thick and looks as if a quantity of rich cream had been stirred into it, making a milky film rises to the surface of the cup. It cannot be taken as an invariable test of good tea, but, when present, it may be assumed that the tea is at least strong and rich in quality. It is no indication of flavor.

Chemically speaking, tea polyphenols have a strong **astringent** or pungent taste. It is this taste which gives the characteristic of bite to the liquor. Tea polyphenol oxides also are responsible for the golden, red, and brown color of the liquor, and partly responsible for the creaming down. Caffeine provides the stimulant; the essential oil, the aroma, is the greater part of the flavor. The total soluble solids give the thickness.

In addition to the qualities mentioned above, the taster looks for "character"; i. e., something distinctive. He wants a tea that can be put into blend or ordinary leaf and force its character into that blend. A tea may lack most of the desirable individual qualities, but if it has one distinctive outstanding quality or character, it will bring a good price.

Next, the color of the liquor is examined. Here is a sample that is "standing up"; i. e., holding its original color, better than the others. Another may be quite darkening. The color is compared with the cup containing the tea to be matched standing on the comparison shelf, the **desideratum** being a dead match; i. e., a tea that shows equal qualities all around.

The tea cools rapidly and the tester comes now to the actual sipping of the liquor. He sees that the liquor is not too hot, for to scald the mouth greatly interferes with the sense of taste. A spoonful is taken into the mouth by drawing it with a quick inward breath between the lips. The liquid is kept in continuous contact with the palate by rolling it around in the mouth, in the same manner that a wine connoisseur tastes wine. The liquor will not be swallowed, for to do so would impair the sense of taste for the time being. Having fully tasted it, the taster ejects it from the mouth into a tall wide mouthed **cuspidor**, usually placed on the floor between his knees. These cuspidors are specially made for this purpose. In the United States, they reach almost to the table top, in other countries they are sometimes much higher. They resemble an hourglass in shape. The object of tasting is, of course, to learn the true quality of the tea with a view to utilizing it either straight or in a blend.

New words and expressions 生词和短语

well-nigh *ad*. 几乎
lustrous [ˈlʌstrəs] *adj*. 有光泽的；光亮的
syrupy [ˈsɪrəpɪ] *adj*. 似蜜糖的
bouquet [buˈkeɪ] *n*. 韵味
astringent [əˈstrɪndʒənt] *adj*. 止血的；收敛性的
sponge [spʌndʒ] *n*. 海绵
desideratum [dɪˌzɪdəˈrɑːtəm] *n*. 想要得到的事物
pungency [ˈpʌndʒənsɪ] *n*. （气味等的）刺激性；辣；（言语等的）辛辣；尖刻
cuspidor [ˈkʌspɪdɔː] *n*. 痰盂

Comprehension 理 解

Give answers to the following questions in your own words and complete sentences as far as possible.

1. What is the main idea of this passage?
2. From the aspect of dry leaf, how to estimate a kind of tea is good or bad?
3. What a tea with a good quality looks like from its liquor?
4. How does the taster in the passage taste the tea?
5. How to use the sight and smell in examining a tea?

如何品评红茶

茶叶品评有三个要素：①干茶的外形、紧卷度和香味，可以通过看和嗅来辨别；②叶底的色泽、亮度和香气，也可以通过看和嗅来辨别；③茶汤的色泽、滋味的浓强度和香甜度，可以通过看和尝来辨别。

1. 干茶

色泽乌、紧卷度高的红茶表明其萎凋好。色泽棕褐、叶片扁碎的红茶萎凋较差。但色泽带褐的红茶泡出的茶汤最好；色乌、形状好的红茶往往茶汤不好。开张、扁平的红茶冲泡速度非常快，第一泡就可将全部精华泡出，而紧卷度高的红茶，第二泡更好。一般而言，红茶外形宜小、紧卷且大小均匀。锋苗对红茶并不是必要的，在美国，消费者也许太看重华而不实的东西，许多消费者太过于把毫尖视作衡量红茶品质的指标，其实最好的红茶产品外观通常没有毫尖。例如在台湾，外形小、乌润、紧细、匀度高的红茶一定比条索粗松不匀但有很多毫尖的红茶品质好。售价高昂的大吉岭茶也同样如此，品质最好的茶是全乌润的。如果茶叶多毫尖，则毫尖应是金色、条索长而紧细的。

斯里兰卡、印尼爪哇和印度的红茶在外形上很相似。实际上，爪哇红茶用的是印度阿萨姆茶种，所以几乎难以区分两种红茶。中国红茶与其他红茶的区别很明显，各个地区的红茶都有自己独特的香气。通过一些练习（训练）可以以"嗅闻"的方式将它们区分。

专家仅通过评定干茶便能估出茶叶的价格。

2. 叶底

叶底色泽至关重要。对于红茶而言，泡出的茶汤明亮，同时叶底色泽带绿，这种茶如果过于收敛，我们通常称为"生青"。暗绿而扁片形的叶底通常表明萎凋不足或发酵过度。叶底黄且略显绿，通常表明茶汤滋味浓强鲜。叶底呈深金黄色，表明茶叶质量上乘。叶底显红色说明茶汤口感浓厚。叶底发暗说明茶叶品质较低或一般。对于绿茶而言，叶底明亮、呈黄绿色或绿黄色，在杯底有光亮，说明是早期采摘的嫩叶。如果色泽暗而不活、呈暗色或棕黄色则表明是陈茶或低档绿茶。茶汤亮度越高，茶叶越嫩，茶的品质也越好。高品质的中国绿茶如安吉白茶，汤色很浅，有时会误被认为缺乏内含物和滋味不够厚，但实际情况却不是这样。茶汤色泽深浅不能作为判定茶叶品质的依据。

通过嗅闻叶底香气，可以辨别出各种茶的不同特点，审评其香气的高锐、浓郁、饱满度以及判断是否有焦味或过度发酵的气味。一般来说，消费者会依据叶底的品质来判断茶叶的好坏，如当茶汤倒出后，好茶会较好地叠在一起，保持相当多的水分，甚至挤压时像海绵一样能挤出很多的茶汤来。

3. 茶汤

尽管可以通过审评干茶和叶底来判断茶叶的品质，但最终决定茶叶品质和风味的却是茶汤。理想的茶汤应是滋味鲜爽、浓厚，有浓郁的甜香或蜜香且汤色艳丽。好茶的茶汤刚泡好时其色泽明亮，有时当茶汤快速冷却时会出现"冷后浑"。

评茶所用的各种术语的确很难描述。例如：茶汤可能鲜爽、浓、厚、平淡、生青、腥味、烟味、浓郁、粗涩、金属味；它也可能为厚、强、浓强鲜；它也可能产生"冷后浑"。浓强鲜（Pungency）是牙龈产生的一种感觉，它在口腔中产生强烈刺激或收敛的感觉，而非一种滋味。"生"或"青"是一种苦味。"鲜爽"是一种新鲜而具活力的味道，与"平淡"相对，就好像新鲜的苏打水和过期的苏打水一样。"风味"是一种甘甜的滋味，闻起来有蜂蜜一样浓郁的甜香。也有人将其描述为可以感知的花香。"冷后浑"意味着茶汤相当浓，看起来好像有大量的凝乳搅拌在里面，一层乳白色的薄膜浮在茶汤的表面。"冷后浑"不能用做评判好茶的恒定标准，如果出现"冷后浑"，还是至少可以认定这个茶具有浓厚的品质，但不能反映茶的香味特点。

从化学角度来说，茶多酚有很强的收敛性和浓强鲜的滋味特点，也正是这种刺激性使得茶汤略显苦涩。茶多酚氧化产物使茶汤呈现金黄色、红色或棕色，而且与"冷后浑"的形成有关。咖啡因有兴奋剂的作用。香精油即香气在很大程度上决定了茶汤的风味。可溶性物质总量决定茶汤浓度。

除了上述品质外，评茶者一般还会期待品质独特的茶。将优质茶拼配或将其放入普通茶中，能使拼配茶具有独特的品质。一种茶可能缺少很多理想的品质，但如果它能有一种与众不同的品质或特色，就能卖个好价钱。

在评定茶汤的色泽方面，有一个"高标准样"，即选定一款优质茶的茶汤作

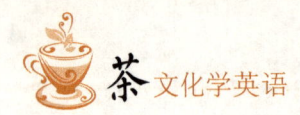

为终极对比物,在评定茶汤色泽时,所有的茶都与这一款茶的品质进行比较。

茶汤很快凉了下来,评茶师开始正式评茶。他知道茶汤温度不高,不会烫伤口腔而影响味觉。张嘴喝进一勺茶水,同时快速吸气,像品酒师品酒那样,把茶水在嘴里来回转,让茶水和上颚不断接触。茶水不能咽下,否则会使味觉的灵敏度迅速降低。充分品尝之后,品茶者将茶汤吐进宽口吐茶筒中,这些吐茶筒通常立于评茶者的膝间,是专用的。当然,评茶的目的是为了评定茶的品质,以便决定某种茶叶是用于直接销售还是拼配销售。

Unit 6
Benefits of Tea Drinking

Lesson 22
Tea and Health Care

Tea is a natural and healthy drink. People have enjoyed drinking it for thousand years. This tradition has developed and remained popular to this very day. Nowadays, more than half of the people in the world drink tea. Modern researches indicate that tea contains a lot of nutrients that help to build up good health.

1. Tea is Refreshing and Helps you Work Efficiently

Tea is a true stimulant, because of the caffeine it contains. Caffeine stimulates the central nervous system and blood circulation. It helps muscles to relax and influences the metabolic process of all body cells. Tea also effect of blood vessel dilation and prevents from the cardiovascular and coronary diseases. Tea is used to cure angina pectoris and myocardial infarction. In clinics, tea is used to cure cold and headache with no adverse side-effects. Caffeine is also contained in **Aspirine** tablets.

2. Tea is a Thirst Quencher and Aids Digestion of Food

In summer time, when tea is drunk, the comforting quality is felt at once. This is because of the **polyphenols**, carbohydrates, amino acid and etc. contained in tea reacts chemically with the saliva to result in dispersing the excessive body heat and purging **toxin**, promoting the waste disposal of the body. Metabolism keeps balance after drinking tea.

Tea could be used as a mouth cleaner. One might feel thirsty and bitter taste when get up early in the morning. A cup of morning tea will clear mouth odor and slime and promote appetite.

Tea also provides iodine and fluoride. Iodine plays an important role in preventing hyperthyroidism. Fluoride is an ingredient of bone, teeth, hair and nails. Ten grams of tea used for making tea beverage every day are enough to meet the need of fluoride for human being and to prevent tooth decay.

After a heavy meal, a cup of strong tea will stimulate the secretion of gastric juice and help digestion of food. The vitamin groups such as **inositol**, folio acid, **pantothenic** acid etc. and compounds as **methionine**, thenylcyoteine, **choline**, etc. contained in tea contribute to promote the fat metabolism.

Aromatic substances contained in tea also aid todigestion of food and disperse unpleasant mouth odor since fat can be dissolved in aromatic substances. That's why tea is indispensable to our brethren nationalities who take meat and butter as their staple food.

3. Tea Helps to Disinfect and Alleviate Inflammation as well as Urinary Output and Purge Toxine

Polyphenols contained in tea can kill the colon bacillus, typhoid and cholera, etc. by solidifying their protein contained in those bacteria. Folk remedies prevailing in China showrd that a cup of strong tea is good for curing the bacillary dysentery, applying for external wounds; dispersing toxine and inflammation. The patent drugs used tea as raw materials are good for dysentery and cold. Polyphenols contained in tea can be used to purify water by decomposing the **aluminium**, zinc and alkaloid contained in water.

Tea is known for its efficaciousness in combating alcoholism and nicotism. When one is heavily drunken, one or two cups of strong tea will help to dispose all the unnecessary things out by neutralizing alcohol with caffeine and polyphenols. Nicotine contained in cigarettes enters into human body when one smokes. Most heavy smokers use tea to alleviate the harm. That's why most cigarrets smokers savor tea.

4. Tea Makes Nutrition Sense and is Good for Health

Tea, green tea in particular, is rich in vitamin C, which collaborates with vitamin P, could be easily absorbed by human body. It is helpful to depress cerebral haemorrhage. Catechine contained in polyphenols, like vitamin P, makes blood vessels more flexible and permeable and helps to depress arteriosclerosis and apoplexy. Pantothenic acid helps to moisten skins. Vitamin B1 is capable of promo-

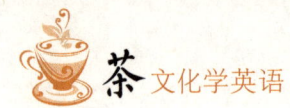

ting the growth of blood cells. In addition, vitamin B2 helps to alleviate inflammation, such as keratitis and pneumonia, etc. Black tea is rich in vitamin K, five cups of black tea a day give sufficient vitamin K to the body requirement.

5. Tea Helps Fitness and Against Cardiovascular Diseases

Pu'er tea produced in Yunnan Province is renowned for its pharmacological functions. Research shows that Tuocha, a kind of Pu'er tea, is excellent for diets and helps against cardiovascular diseases. Clinical experiments show that drinking Tuocha from time to time helps to reduce weight significantly and decreases the contents of antilipoidic compounds. People suffering from over-weight, hypertension and cardiovascular diseases could be helped by drinking Tuocha.

Oolong tea can be used as diets. It is functional in dissolving fat, and helps in digestion of food and discharge of urine and constipation.

People suffering from radioactive pollution can benefit from drinking tea. Polyphenols contained in tea acted combinatively with **oligosaccharose** and vitamin C in absorbing the radioactive element SR90. Therefore, tea merits as "Beverage of Atomic Age." Being cultivated, so-called "black tea germs" or "Hai Bao" in Chinese can be developed in black tea liquid. It can be used as a beverage and is helpful to promote the metabolism and discharge of customary constipation and eliminate the bacteria existed in large and small intestines and duodenum.

New words and expressions
生词和短语

aspirin [ˈæsprɪn] n. 阿司匹林

polyphenol [ˌpɒlɪˈfiːnɒl] n. 茶多酚

toxin [ˈtɒksɪn] n. 毒素

inositol [ɪˈnəʊsətəʊl] n. 肌醇

pantothenic [ˌpæntəˈθenɪk] adj. 泛酸的

methionine [meˈθaɪəniːn] n. 蛋氨酸

oligosaccharose [ˌɒlɪɡəˈsækərəʊz] n. 脂多糖

choline [ˈkəʊliːn] n. 胆碱

disinfect [ˌdɪsɪnˈfekt] v. 消炎

aluminum [əˈljuːmɪnəm] n. 铝

Unit 6 Benefits of Tea Drinking

Comprehension 理 解

Give answers to the following questions in your own words and complete sentence as far as possible.

1. In what aspects can tea do good to body health?

2. Why is tea indispensable to our brethren nationalities who take meat and butter as their staple food?

3. Can tea be used to purify water?

4. How many cups a of black tea should one drink a day in order to get sufficient vitamin K?

5. Why is the tea called as "Beverage of Atomic Age"?

Notes on the text 课文注释

Black tea germs: Black tea germs are also called Hai-bo or Wei-bo. The germs are produced from sugar, tea and water with help of ferment. Such germs can benefit human health, especially good for stomach disease. And it can help to regulate the blood pressure, better the sleep quality as well as prevent kinds of other diseases. 红茶菌又名"海宝""胃宝",是用糖、茶、水加菌种经发酵后生成的对人体有益的物质,尤其对各种胃病有很好的治疗作用,而且还有调节血压、改善睡眠、预防各种疾病的效果。

Translation 参考译文

茶叶与保健

茶叶是一种天然、健康的传统饮料,数千年来为人们所乐饮。如今,饮茶的传统与时俱进,广为普及,现在全世界约有半数以上的人饮茶。现代研究表明茶叶含有许多营养成分,饮茶有益于人体健康。

1. 提神益思,提高工效

饮茶能提神益思、消除疲劳,原因是茶叶中的咖啡碱能刺激中枢神经系统,清醒头脑，活跃思维，又能加快血液循环，舒展筋肉，促进新陈代谢。茶叶还有扩张血管、预防心血管和冠状动脉疾病的作用。茶叶还被用来治疗心绞痛和心肌梗死。在临床上，用它治疗伤风头痛，没有副作用。西药中的阿司匹林也含有咖啡因的成分。

2. 止渴生津，消食除腻

盛夏酷暑，饮上清茶一杯，会让人感到满口生津，遍体凉爽，这是因为茶汤中的多酚类、醣尖、果胶、氨基酸等与口中涎液发生了化学反应，使大肠得以滋润，产生清凉的感觉，使体内大量热量和污物得以排除，加快新陈代谢使人体取得新的生理平衡。

茶叶还是一种口腔卫生剂。每天起床后，感到口干舌苦，喝一杯早茶，可除去口中黏液，消除口臭，增进食欲。

茶叶含有碘和氟化物，碘有防治甲状腺功能亢进的作用。氟化物是人体骨骼、牙齿、毛发、指甲的构成成分，每天饮用10克茶叶冲泡的茶汤，就可以满足人体对氟素的需要，预防龋齿（蛀牙）。

在丰餐盛宴以后，泡饮一杯浓茶促进胃液分泌和食物的消化。茶汤中的肌醇、叶酸、泛酸等维生素物质，以及蛋氨酸、半胱氨酸、胆碱等多种化合物，都有调节脂肪代谢的功能。

茶中的芳香物质有溶解脂肪、帮助消化和消除口中腥膻的作用，所以，一些以肉类、乳酪为主食的少数民族，都把茶叶视为生活必需品。

3. 杀菌消炎、利尿解毒

茶中的多酚类物质，能使蛋白质凝固沉淀，杀死细菌，民间常用浓茶汤治疗细菌性痢疾，或用来敷涂伤口，消炎解毒，促使伤口愈合；茶多酚还能使铝、锌和生物碱等物质分解沉淀，净化水质。

茶还有醒酒戒烟的效用。当滥饮烈性酒以后，喝几杯浓茶，借茶中的多酚类物质和咖啡因中和酒精，使酒精及时排出体外，得以醒酒。人们连续吸烟时，尼古丁会随着烟雾进入体内，而茶叶中的咖啡因对尼古丁有抵制作用，这就是生活中吸烟者都爱喝茶的原因。

4. 补充营养，增强体质

绿茶含维生素C较多，维生素P与维生素C有协同作用，能帮助机体吸收维生素C，有减少脑溢血发生的作用。茶多酚中的儿茶素和维生素P也具有协同作用，能增强血管弹性和血管壁的渗透能力，预防动脉硬化和中风。泛酸有润泽皮肤的作用。维生素 B_1 还能帮助血细胞生长，维生素 B_2 对防治各类炎症，如角膜炎、肺炎等都有一定作用。红茶中的维生素 K（叶缘醌）含量较多，如果每天饮五杯红茶，即可满足人体对维生素 K 的需要。

5. 减肥健美、强心防病

云南普洱茶历来以药效显著而闻名于世，普洱茶中的沱茶，有减肥健美和防治心血管疾病的作用。临床试验结果表明：常饮沱茶，能明显减轻体重，降低人体中三酸甘油酯的含量，对过度肥胖者及高血压和心血管疾病患者，都有一定的治疗作用。

乌龙茶也有减肥健美的作用。乌龙茶有很强的分解脂肪的作用，常饮能助消化、利尿，对治疗便秘也有一定的效果。

茶叶还能防止某些放射性物质对人体的危害。茶叶中的多酚类物质脂多糖和维生素 C 综合作用，能吸收放射性物质锶 90（SR90）。人们又称茶叶为"原子时代的饮料"，茶叶冲泡成茶汤后，经过菌种培养，还可以制成一种名叫"红茶菌"的饮料。"红茶菌"原称"海宝"，又称"红茶菇"。"红茶菌"含有多种代谢产物，对人体新陈代谢起促进作用。饮用"红茶菌"对治疗习惯性便秘、消减十二指肠、小肠、大肠内部各种有害细菌，都有明显效果。

Lesson 23
A Cup of Tea a Day Keeps the Doctor Away

Drinking tea may help keep the doctor away. A new study finds that tea **boosts** the body's defenses against infection and contains a substance that might be turned into a drug to protect against disease, US researchers said, and Coffee does not have the same effect.

A component in tea was found in laboratory experiments to **prime** the **immune system** to attack invading bacteria, viruses and fungi, according to a study in the **Proceedings** of the US National Academy of Sciences.

A second experiment, using human volunteers, showed that immune system blood cells from tea drinkers responded five times faster to **germs** than did the blood cells of coffee drinkers.

"We worked out the molecular aspects of this tea component in the test tube and then tested it on a small number of people to see if it actually worked in human beings," said Dr Jack F. Bukowski, a researcher at Brigham and Women's Hospital in Boston and Harvard Medical School. The results, he said, gave clear proof that five cups of tea a day can **sharpened** the body's disease defenses.

Kris-Etherton, a nutrition specialist at Penny State University, said Bukowski's study adds to growing evidences that tea is an effective disease fighter. "This is potentially a very significant finding," she said. "We're seeing multiple benefits from tea." But she said the work needs to be confirmed in a much larger study, involving more people.

In the study, Bukowski and his co-authors isolated from ordinary black tea a substance called **L-theanine**. Bukowski said L-theanine is broken down in the liver to ethylamine, a molecule that primes the response of an immune system element called the gamma-delta T cell. "We know from other studies that these gamma-delta T cells in the blood are the first line of defense against many types of bacteria, viral, fungal and parasitic infections," he said. "They even have some anti-tumor activities."

The T cells prompt the secretion of **interferon**, a key part of the body's chemical defense against infection. Bukowski said, "We know from mouse studies that if you boost this part of the immune system it can protect against infection,".

To further test the finding, the researchers had 11 volunteers drink five cups of tea a day, and 10 others drink coffee. Before the test began, they drew blood samples from all 21 test subjects. After four weeks, they took more blood samples from the tea drinkers and then exposed that blood to the bacteria called **E-coli**. Bukowski said the immune cells in the specimens secreted five times more interferon than did blood cells from the same subjects before the weeks of tea drinking. Blood tests and bacteria challenges showed there was no change in the interferon levels of the coffee drinkers, he said.

Bukowski said it may be possible to further isolate and refine L-theanine from tea and use that as a drug to boost the infection defense of the body.

New words and expressions
生词和短语

boost [buːst] *v.* 增加；改进
immune system [ɪˈmjuːnˈsɪstəm] *n.* 免疫系统
proceeding [prəˈsiːdɪŋ] *n.* 会议记录
germ [dʒɜːm] *n.* 病菌
sharpen [ˈʃɑːpən] *v.* 使变的敏锐、灵活
prime [praɪm] *v.* 启动；发动
E-coli [iːˈkəʊlaɪ] *n.* 大肠杆菌
L-theanine [elˈθiːənɪn] *n.* L—茶氨酸
interferon [ˌɪntə(ː)ˈfɪərɔn] *n.* 干扰素

Comprehension 理解

Give answers to the following questions in your own words and complete sentence as far as possible.

1. What is the benefit from drinking tea?
2. What is the affection of tea to human's T cells?
3. What was discovered by Dr Jack·F·Bukowsk?
4. How did Kris·Etherton comment on Dr Jack·F·Bukowsk's discovering?
5. In what way is tea better than coffee to man's health?

Notes on the text 课文注释

gamma-delta T cell: Gamma-delta T lymphocytes are the most represented cell populations in mucosal associated lymphoid tissue. They share several characteristics of innate and adaptive immune responses. Gamma-delta T cells have attracted more and more interest for tumor immunotherapy. γ－δ型T细胞大量分布于黏膜中相关的淋巴组织中，其作用介于固有免疫和适应性免疫之间，在抗肿瘤免疫中具有重要作用。

Translation 参考译文

每天一杯茶，无须医生开药方

喝茶可有助于预防疾病。美国研究人员研究发现，喝茶能改善人体的防御系统，茶叶种的一种化合物可以在人体内可以转化成一种药物，起到防治疾病的作用。

根据美国国家科学院公布的一项研究结果，发现茶叶中含有一种化学成分，能促进免疫系统攻击入侵的细菌、病毒和真菌。

以人类志愿者为对象的第二个实验结果表明：饮茶者免疫系统的血细胞对

病菌的反应速度比喝咖啡者的快5倍。

"我们在试管中确定了茶叶中这种化学成分的分子特性，然后用小部分人来做实验，以确定它是否对人类确实有效。"在波士顿和哈佛医学院的布里格姆妇女医院（Brigham and Women's Hospital in Boston and Harvard Medical School.）的研究者杰克·F·布考斯基说。实验结果清楚地表明：每天（饮用）五杯茶，可以激活身体的疾病防御机能。

宾夕法尼亚州立大学的营养学专家克里斯·埃瑟顿说，布考斯基的研究提供了新的证据，证明茶可以作为一种有效的抗病药物。"这可能是一个极其重要的发现，"她说，"这让我们看到了茶叶的多种功效。"但她表示仍需进行更大规模和更多的人参与的实验。

在这项研究中，布考斯基和他的合作者从普通红茶中分离出一种名为L-茶氨酸的化合物。布考斯基说L-茶氨酸在肝脏中降解为乙胺，这种产物能引起γ-δT细胞免疫系统反应。"从其他研究中发现，血液中的这些γ-δT细胞是防御多种细菌、病毒、真菌和寄生虫侵害的第一道防线，"布考斯基表示，"他们甚至有一些抗肿瘤的活性。"

T细胞能促使干扰素的分泌，而干扰素是人体抗感染和化学防御的重要组成部分。布考斯基说："我们从小鼠实验知道，如果你提高这部分的免疫能力，它就能有效预防感染"。

为了进一步证实（上述研究）发现，研究人员让11名志愿者每天喝5杯茶，另外的10人喝咖啡。实验前，他们采集了21位实验对象的血液样本。4周后，他们又从喝茶者身上抽取了更多的血液样本，然后将血液样本置于含有大肠杆菌的菌液中。布考斯基说，样本中免疫细胞分泌的干扰素是几个星期前没有喝茶者的5倍多。血液检验和细菌诱导实验结果表明：饮用咖啡者的干扰素水平没有发生变化。

布考斯基说，有可能会进一步提取和纯化茶叶中的L-茶氨酸，并把它作为一种提高人体抗感染能力的药品使用。

Lesson 24
Drink Tea Correctly

Tea contains more than 5,000 biochemistry ingredients closely correlated to human body. Tea not only can refresh the mind and help people lose weight, but also has certain pharmacology effects on some diseases, like radiation sickness, cancer, heart disease, and blood sickness. In fact, drinking tea also should be the error-free as the following in order to avoid negative effects.

1. Choose Suitable Tea for Different Occasions

Doctor of traditional Chinese medicine believes that people should drink different teas according to the different seasons. Black tea can warm the stomach, refresh the mind, and accelerate digestion. Therefore, drinking warm black tea in the cold winter is the most suitable choice. Flower-tea (mainly **jasmine tea**) can help people to get rid of coolness of body accumulated in winter and to bring about vigor, so it is suitable for people to drink in spring. Green tea, bitter and cold, can give off heat, detoxify the body, increase **gastrointestinal** function, promote digestion and prevent **diarrhea** and skin infections such as sore boils, so it is suitable for summer. Oolong tea, quite mellow, not cold or hot, can eliminate the waste heat completely in the human body and **exhilarate** their activities, so people like to drink oolong tea in autumn.

People who always work in places with air conditioning may face skin problems such as easily dry skin and the growth of small wrinkles. Therefore, the moisture content of their bodies need to be supplemented. Among all the drinks, green tea is the best choice, because there are four primary polyphenols (natural chemicals that are beneficial to health) in green tea and they are often collectively referred to as **catechins** (types of flavored chemical compounds). Also, green tea, like makeup, can prevent computer radiation, thus green tea is the best choice for office workers.

2. Do Not Drink Tea Too Strong and Much

However, tea of certain strength is drinkable. Such strong tea is good for heart and lung, helps **sober up** and digest fatness, and sometimes is used as **prescription** of **hypothermia**, detoxification, **diuresis** and clearing out **phlegm**. It may surely benefit people with **inflammation** or those who drink, smoke and eat too much. Otherwise, strong tea, which is made by putting more than 3 or 4 grams of tea in one cup of water, is not suitable for many people. For instance, drinking strong tea at night causes **insomnia**, **tachycardiac** heart trouble, **gastric ulcer** and **neurasthenic**, etc. So those who are weak or have a chill stomach should not drink strong tea, and the illness could be **aggravated**. In addition, strong tea leads to distress of stomach when it is empty, even results in heart-**throb** and **queasiness**, symptoms called Tea **Inebriation** which could be eliminated by taking some water or sweets.

Drinking too much tea or strong thick tea, especially on the occasion of eating, may affect the absorption of many constant elements (like calcium) and trace elements (like iron and zinc). Also, people should not drink tea with milk or other milk products because the caffeine and **tannin** (a kind of complex organic compound) in the tea may reduce the nutritional value of milk products. Therefore, do not drink too much tea when you are eating.

3. Don't Drink Tea on Certain Occasions

Don't drink tea with an empty stomach: Tea can dilute gastric juice, reduce digestion and absorption rate of food, let large number of components in tea into the blood, and thus cause person to feel dizzy, flustered and powerless of hands and feet.

Don't drink tea in the menstrual period: Drinking tea (especial strong or thick tea) in the menstrual period, can induce or increase menstrual syndrome. Medical experts studies found that compared with those not drinking tea, tea habits menstrual risk 2.4 times higher, with more than 4 cups of tea a day, 3 times an increase of risk.

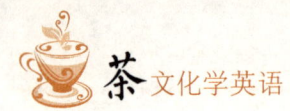

Gastric ulcer patients are not suitable to drink tea: The caffeine in tea may promote the gastric acid secretion, increase acid concentration, or even induce ulcer perforation.

New words and expressions
生词和短语

diarrhea [ˌdaɪəˈrɪə] n. 腹泻
catechin [ˈkætɪtʃɪn] n. 儿茶素
sober up [ˈsəʊbə ʌp] v. 使清醒
diuresis [ˌdaɪjʊəˈriːsɪs] n. 利尿
phlegm [flem] n. 痰
throb [θrɒb] v. 搏动;跳动
insomnia [ɪnˈsɒmnɪə] n. 失眠
gastrointestinal [ˌgæstrəʊɪnˈtestɪnlnl] adj. 胃肠的
prescription [prɪˈskrɪpʃn] n. 处方
tachycardiac [ˌtækɪˈkɑːdɪæk] adj. 心动过速的
gastric ulcer [ˌgæstrɪk ˌʌlsə] n. 胃溃疡
neurasthenic [ˌnjʊərəsˈθenɪk] n. 神经衰弱
inebriation [ɪˌniːbrɪˈeɪʃn] n. 酩酊;醉

exhilarate [ɪgˈzɪləreɪt] v. 激活
tannin [ˈtænɪn] n. 单宁
hypothermia [ˌhaɪpəˈθɜːmɪə] n. 体温过低
inflammation [ˌɪnfləˈmeɪʃn] n. 炎症
aggravate [ˈægrəveɪt] v. 加重;恶化
queasiness [ˈkwiːzɪnəs] n. 恶心
jasmine tea [ˈdʒæzmɪn tiː] n. 茉莉花茶

Comprehension
理 解

Give answers to the following questions in your own words and complete sentences as far as possible.

1. What tea is suitable respectively in four seasons a year?
2. What tea is helpful for those people working in an air-conditioning room?
3. Is it good for people to drink strong tea while eating?
4. What will happen if a strong tea is served to somebody with empty stomach?
5. What is a scientific tea drinking habit?

Unit 6 Benefits of Tea Drinking

Notes on the text 课文注释

Chinese medicine: It is usually called Traditional Chinese Medicine (TCM) which refers to a broad range of medicine practices sharing common theoretical concepts which have been developed in China and look back on a tradition of more than 2000 years, including various forms of herbal medicine, acupuncture, massage therapy, and dietary therapy. The doctrines of Chinese medicine are rooted in books such as the *Yellow Emperor's Inner Canon* and the *Treatise on Cold Damage*, as well as in cosmological notions like yin-yang and the Five Phases. 中国医学是指中国传统医学，通常简称为中医，是中国2000年来发展起来的医学实践，包括各种草药疗法、针灸疗法、按摩疗法和食疗。中医理学植根于《黄帝内经》和《伤寒杂病论》以及阴阳五行概念等。

Translation 参考译文

你会科学饮茶吗？

茶叶含有与人体密切相关的5000多种生化成分，茶叶不仅具有醒脑、减肥的功能，同时还对一些疾病如癌症、心血管病等具有药理作用，但在饮用时也需注意以下方面，避免因饮茶不当而引起的副作用。

选择合适的茶

中医认为：人们应当根据季节喝不同特性的茶。红茶能暖胃、醒脑、促进消化，适合在寒冷的冬季饮用。花茶（主要为茉莉花茶）可以帮助散发人体冬季淤积体内的寒邪，促进人体阳气生发，适宜春季饮用。绿茶性味苦寒，能清热解毒，增强肠胃功能，促进消化，防止腹泻和皮肤疮疖感染等，适宜在夏季饮用。乌龙茶属温性茶，不寒不燥，能清除体内余热，令人神清气爽，人们喜爱在秋季饮用。

整天都处在空调环境里的上班族，皮肤较其他人更容易出现问题，干涩、容易长皱纹，必须补充体内水分。在所有的饮料中，绿茶是最好的选择。因为它含有四种主要的茶多酚类化合物（天然保健化合物），通常统称为儿茶素。像某些化妆品一样，绿茶还可阻挡计算机的辐射。所以，绿茶是办公人员的最佳选择。

喝茶不宜过浓或过量

一定浓度的茶是可饮用的，它对心脏和肺有益，能帮助消耗脂肪，有时可作为退烧、解毒、利尿和去痰的药剂使用，对喝酒、吸烟以及饱腹的人有益。但是过浓的茶（每杯超过3～4克茶）不适合大多数人。如很多人晚上饮用过浓的茶会导致失眠、心脏搏动过速、胃溃疡、神经衰弱等。胃弱或胃寒的人不宜饮用浓茶。患者饮用浓茶也会加剧病情。此外，空腹饮浓茶会引起胃痛，甚至导致心搏过快和恶心，出现茶醉，可通过饮水和吃糖来消除。

大量饮茶或饮用过浓的茶，特别是就餐时，会影响人体对很多常量元素（如钙等）和微量元素（如铁、锌等）的吸收。同时，人们最好不要在喝牛奶或其他奶类制品时同时饮茶。茶叶中的咖啡因和单宁（一种复杂的有机化合物）会降低奶类制品的营养价值。所以，不要在用餐时饮用过量的茶。

不宜饮茶的几种情况

空腹不宜喝茶。空腹喝茶可稀释胃液，降低对食物的消化和吸收能力，致使茶叶中大量成分进入血液，引发头晕、心慌、手脚无力等症状。

月经期不宜饮茶。在月经期间喝茶，尤其是喝浓茶，可诱发或加重经期综合征。医学专家研究发现：与不喝茶者相比，习惯喝茶者发生经期紧张症的概率高出2.4倍，每天喝茶超过4杯者，增加3倍。

胃溃疡病人不宜饮茶。茶叶中的咖啡因可促进胃酸分泌，升高胃酸浓度，诱发胃溃疡甚至穿孔。

Unit 7
Essentials in Tea Drinking

Lesson 25
Chinese Teahouse

Receiving intimate friends for tea at home was one form of Chinese entertaining, but the real social life of China was found in the teahouses. Nothing better **exemplifies** the **gregarious** character of the Chinese than the teahouses. **Omnipresent**, vast numbers of teahouses lined the streets and parks of villages, towns, and cities. which they are always more than the restuarants. **Fortune** remarked, "As usual in all the Chinese towns which I have visited, there were vast numbers of tea and eating houses for they were all crowded with hundreds of natives, who, for a few cash can obtain a healthy and **substantial** meal."

The countryside was also dotted with teahouses, picture perfect in the **verdant** landscape with graceful **lilting eaves. Solitary** teahouses tended by monks or **hermits** could be chanced upon in even the most isolated sites on remote mountains. No matter where they were located, a cup of tea always prepare ready to welcome a stranger.

One entered the teahouse and chose any available chair at one of the lacquer tea tables. In winter it was better to seat near the stove, in summer near a window or door. Almost as soon as one had been seated a waiter **materialized** from nowhere to ask the traditional question, "What kind of tea would you like, Sir?" During the *Qing* Dynasty one could choose from an almost infinite variety of teas, requesting either a favorite name-tea or the house-tea. The waiter would place a *zhong* before the customer, put in a quantity of tea leaves, and fill it with boiling water. In general, tea was drunk "pure and genuine" (without milk or sugar) but

Unit 7 Essentials in Tea Drinking

in some regions it was customary to add sugar, and in other regions, milk. The waiter would refill the *zhong* with boiling water two or three times or until the strength and taste had been drawn out of the tea leaves.

In the larger teahouses musicians might play the **pipa**, **erhu**, **guzheng** or **guqin** as for background music. Singers were occasionally hired. Telling story, play, and **marionette** shows were other popular forms of teahouse entertainment included in the very reasonable price of two cash per *zhong* of tea. Most people, however, went to the teahouses just to talk, rest, warm by fire, read, **meditate**, and play cards or **majong**.

Lao She said "teahouses were frequented by people from all walks of life and every possible characters and **persuasion**. Teahouses were indeed a **microcosm** of Chinese society as a whole," where **opium** addicts, **swindlers**, card sharks, currency dealers, "come-on hostesses" and poets all rubbed shoulders. Order reigned among this hodge-podge of humanity because the cardinal rule in every teahouse was hospitality. Harsh words or anger over tea were universally condemned and never forgotten.

Teahouse foods, infinite in variety, stressing quality rather than quantity, were generally steamed and served in multi-layer bamboo steamers. Chinese restaurants in the West, which are modeled after Chinese tea-houses, are gradually adding the marvelous teahouse foods of China's imperial past to their menus. Usually these appear as appetizers known as the Cantonese *dim sum*, meaning literally to "dot the heart", or in Mandarin *dien xin*, the "heart-touchers",—expressions that give an idea how savory teahouse foods can be. Dumplings with meat stuffing, fried spring rolls are among the many teahouse specialities. In addition there was an almost endless variety of fried crisps eaten with numerous delicious dips. In general, noodles replace rice as the staple of teahouse meals, but people stopping in the teahouse for breakfast ate plain soft rice *congee* and tasty seasoned *congees* could be had throughout the day. People with sweet teeth were well served by exquisite, inventive sweets and desserts in the teahouses.

Teahouses naturally prepared dishes using tea. The most famous teahouse specialty dating as far back as the Song Dynasty and found in all Hangzhou teahouses was the marvelous dish of small freshwater shrimp from the West Lake cooked in the locally grow "Dragon Wells" green tea.

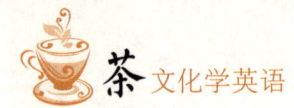

The last great period of teahouse glory was in the 1920s and 1930s. Europeans living in China preferred their restricted clubs while Chinese were unwelcome to the noisy teahouses frequented by the natives. Thus the Europeans missed the exuberant teahouse heyday that followed the Qing Dynasty's fall. Peek for a moment into China's lively teahouses and feel their special atmosphere described by Lao She:

"One could hear the most absurd stories…come into contact with the strangest views…hear the latest opera tune or the best way to prepare opium. In the teahouses one might also see rare art objects newly acquired by some patron-a jade fan pendant recently unearthed or a three-color glazed snuff bottle. Yes the teahouse was indeed an important place; it could even be reckoned a kind of cultural center." (*The Teahouse*)

Sadly, this was the last homage to the traditional teahouse. During the brutal Japanese occupation of China during World War II, the teahouses were forced to close one after another as a thousand years of teahouse life was suddenly snuffed out. Surviving teahouses had suffered irrevocably and their war wounds were glaring for all to see: "Everything from the building to the furniture was dull and shabby. Teahouse owners were obliged to take in lodgers to make ends meet."

Refined teahouse foods became a fond memory, and lucky were the teahouses that could still offer salted melon seeds or peanuts. Credit formerly extended automatically to any client requesting it had gone and henceforth everyone, even steady customers, had to pay on the spot. Inflation was so bad that the cost of living sometimes doubled in a day; it became a standing joke that teahouse patrons had to pay in advance because the price of tea went up so fast its price increased as one drank it. "Tea money" no longer kept teahouse owners in tea and many teahouses were closed in despair, their owners reduced to peddling hot tea in the streets after selling the teahouse that had been in their family for generations.

The decades after 1949 were bleaker still, and the teahouse that had once flourished in such great numbers had practically vanished. Only in the late 1970s did a few authorized teahouses begin to show a timid comeback. Selected ruined teahouses were restored with care and reopened on a trial basis. China's most famous teahouse in Shanghai built in the thirteenth century and now restored to pristine conditions is a major tourist attraction. Music, classic ballads, and teahouse dramas are again infusing life and drawing crowds to the revitalized teahouses. teahouse dramas have been presented in large European and U.S. cities in international cultural exchange programs. From the dismal brink of extinction teahouses have bounced back with surprising never and once again show signs of regaining their former preeminence in China's social life.

New words and expressions
生词和短语

eave [i:v] *n.* 檐,屋檐
hermit [ˈhɜːmɪt] *n.* 隐士
zhong *n.* 盅
pipa *n.* 琵琶
erhu *n.* 二胡
guzheng *n.* 古筝
guqin *n.* 古琴
mahjong [mɑːˈdʒɒŋ] *n.* 麻将
opium [ˈəʊpɪəm] *n.* 鸦片
swindler [ˈswɪndlə(r)] *n.* 骗子
marionette [ˌmærɪəˈnet] *n.* 牵线木偶
exemplify [ɪɡˈzemplɪfaɪ] *vt.* 例示;作为……的例子
gregarious [ɡrɪˈɡeərɪəs] *adj.* 群居性的;丛生的;合群的
omnipresent [ˌɒmnɪˈpreznt] *adj.* 无所不在的
Fortune [ˈfɔːtʃuːnh] 《财富》杂志
substantial [səbˈstænʃl] *adj.* 多的;大的;大量的;丰盛的
verdant [ˈvɜːdnt] *adj.* (指植物、田野)青翠的,嫩绿的;长满绿色植物的
lilting [ˈlɪltɪŋ] *adj.* (音调)抑扬顿挫的;(音乐)旋律轻快的
solitary [ˈsɒlətri] *adj.* 单独的,独自的;单个的,唯一的;荒凉的;偏僻的
materialized [məˈtɪərɪəlaɪz] *vi.* 突然出现;成形;实现
meditate [ˈmedɪteɪt] *vi.* 沉思,深思熟虑;*vt.* 计划;打算
persuasion [pəˈsweɪʒn] *n.* 说服,劝说;说服力;信念;信仰
microcosm [ˈmaɪkrəʊkɒzəm] *n.* 小宇宙;微化空间

Comprehension
理 解

Give answers to the following questions in your own words and complete sentence as far as possible.

1. What kind of place was the teahouse in old China?
2. What would be usually served in teahouses besides the tea?

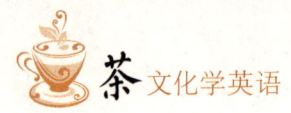

3. What did Laoshe describe about teahouses in his book?
4. Why did teahouses almost vanish in China after 1930s?
5. How do you think of the future of teahouses in China?

Notes on the text 课文注释

Laoshe: He is a great Chinese modern novelist, playwright and essayist, whose name originally Shu Qingchun. He was born in a family of Man ethnic nationality and converted to Christianity in 1922. He ever worked in England during 1924－1929 as well as in the US during 1946－1949. He is the first to be entitled as "People's Artist" after 1949. "Teahouse", written in 1957, is one of his great plays, which is a panorama of old Beijing life style, especially the teahouse culture. 老舍，原名舒庆春，是中国现代伟大的小说家、戏剧家和散文家。满族，1922年受洗礼加入基督教。曾分别于1924—1929年和1946—1949年赴英国和美国讲学。1949年新中国成立后，老舍第一个被授予"人民艺术家"称号。完成于1957年的话剧《茶馆》是其代表作之一，也是一幅描写旧中国老北京生活，尤其是茶馆文化的全景图。

Translation 参考译文

中国茶馆

接受好友的邀请到家中品茶是中国人的一种娱乐方式，但真正的社会生活却是在茶馆。没有比茶馆更能反映中国人的合群性的地方。在街道、村庄、城镇的公园都随处可见大量的茶馆，通常比饭馆还要多。《财富》杂志评论说："在我到过的中国城市中，通常都有大量的茶馆和饭馆，几百人拥挤其中，花很少的钱就能吃上营养而丰盛的一餐。"

在乡村也零星分散着一些茶馆，景致优美，青翠中透出线条优雅流畅的屋檐。即使在最偏远的山区也间或会看到一些孤寂的茶舍，由修行的和尚或隐士照管。但不论它们坐落何处，主人总是会备一杯好茶欢迎来客。

进入茶馆可以择一安静的茶桌坐下。冬季最好在火炉旁，夏季则可临窗或靠门。人一坐下，就会冒出某个茶房："先生，您喜欢喝什么茶？"在清代，可以选择很多的茶，点喜欢的名茶或茶馆备好的茶。茶房会在客人面前放一个茶盅，加入一些茶叶，然后冲入沸水。一般都是饮清茶，但一些地方也习惯加入糖或牛奶。茶房会在茶盅中续水2～3次或者一直续水至茶淡无味。

一些大茶馆会有琵琶、二胡、古筝或古琴等弹奏作为背景音乐。偶尔也有唱歌的。若喝2元一盅的茶，还可享受说书、唱戏和木偶戏等其他娱乐活动。然而，大多数人去茶馆不过是去聊天、休闲、取暖、看书、打盹、打牌或打麻将。

老舍曾说："茶馆是三教九流会面之处，可以容纳各色人物。一个大茶馆就是一个中国的小社会。"吸鸦片的、骗钱的、玩牌的、放债的、卖笑的和卖文的，鱼龙混杂。大杂烩中又有一种人人都遵守的秩序，那就是和气和好客。喝茶时粗言怒容是受人唾弃的行为。

茶馆中的佐食花样繁多，量少而考究，多是放在一层层的竹屉里蒸出来，再成屉地上给茶客。西方国家中的中国餐馆多是模仿中国茶馆的模式，其菜单也在逐步加进那些奇妙的中国传统的茶馆佐食。通常这些佐食皆为开胃品，广东话称为"早茶"，官话称"点心"，意为贴心、称心之物，可见茶馆佐食之味美。肉馅水饺和春卷是许多茶馆的特色风味。而且还有蘸酱吃的数不胜数的油炸薯片。茶馆的主食一般为面条而非米饭，但是到茶馆吃早饭的人可以吃到粽子，若是正逢时令，粽子整天都可吃到。各种精美新奇的甜点可以让爱吃甜食的人在茶馆尽情享受。

茶馆当然会用茶来配制各种菜肴。远在宋朝时，杭州各个茶馆中就有用当地龙井茶配制的西湖小龙虾，极负盛名。

20世纪20至30年代是茶馆最后的辉煌时期。那时，生活在中国的欧洲人却不喜欢中国人云集的吵吵嚷嚷的茶馆，宁愿待在中国人不能入内的一些俱乐部中。因此，欧洲人错过了中国茶馆在清王朝灭亡后充满活力的黄金岁月。从老舍笔下对中国茶馆的生动描写可以窥见一斑：

"在这里，可以听到最荒唐的新闻……奇怪的意见也在这里可以听到……这里还可以听到某京戏演员新近创造了什么腔儿，和煎熬鸦片烟最好的方法。这里也可以看到某人新得到的奇珍——个出土的玉扇坠儿或三彩的鼻烟壶。这真是个重要的地方，简直可以算作文化交流的场所。"（《茶馆》）

遗憾的是，这成了对传统茶馆的最后献礼。在残酷的第二次世界大战中，日本入侵中国，茶馆被迫关闭，延续了千年的茶馆文化戛然而止。幸存的茶馆

也遭受了无可挽回的损失，战争创伤触目惊心："从馆子到家什，一切都破破烂烂，茶馆老板不得不靠招揽房客来糊口度日。"

精致的茶馆点心成了美好的回忆，茶馆能供应瓜子和花生就算万幸了。昔日里只要愿意人人都可赊账的传统一去不复返了，现在即使常客也要当场现金付款。通货膨胀使物价逐日翻番，下面的现象成了疯传的笑话：茶客不得不提前预付茶钱，否则一杯茶未喝完茶价已涨。"茶钱"已不能维持茶馆生意，许多茶馆关门大吉，卖掉数代祖传的茶馆后，许多老板沦落街头，卖起了白开水。

新中国成立后的数十年间，茶馆生意仍然一片凋敝，曾经遍及全国的茶馆年难见踪影。直到 70 年代后期才有少量的国营茶馆开始试探着回归市场。那些被毁的高级茶馆开始精心修复，并开始试着营业。在上海，建立于公元 14 世纪的中国最著名的茶社现在已经恢复原貌，成了重要的旅游景点。音乐、戏曲和茶馆表演再次融入生活，吸引大众来到茶馆。茶馆表演甚至在国际文化交流中已被展示到欧洲和美国的大城市。从濒临绝迹的边缘重获活力，有迹象表明茶馆将会再一次成为中国人社会生活的中心。

Lesson 26
Tea Wares

Tea wares consist of tools serving for drinking, boiling, **scrunching**, burning and drying, cleaning, storing, and for other assistance. In a narrow sense, people mention drinking service only, such as: teapots, cups, tea bowls and trays, etc.

1. Descriptions of Chinese Tea Wares

Tea wares have been used for a long time in China and the tea drinking became more popular and public since *Tang* Dynasty. In the palaces and noble families, tea wares made of metals were served, and for civilians porcelain wares were commonly used. Tang scholars preferred blue/ white. porcelain as the material of tea cups from Shaoxing, Zhejiang province. This kind of green porcelain looks like jade with elegant design and exquisite decoration. Since the true color of tea was set off completely and beautifully in this dainty cup ('ou' in Chinese), it was listed as number one in Lu Yu's *The Classic of Tea*. Concerning about the function, the size and design of the cup well suited to the tea drinking habit of that time allowing for cooking tea powder with **green onion**, **ginger**, dates, **tangerine** peels and **peppermint**, then drinking the whole liquor as the same as the soup.

The preference for green porcelain or white porcelain was suddenly changed to black glazed teacups in the Song Dynasty. Moreover, tea bowls became common with the shape of an upturned bell. They were glazed in black, dark-brown, grey, blue/white and white colors.

Then blue/white porcelain tea wares predominated in the Yuan Dynasty and white glazed tea wares became popular in the Ming Dynasty. Tea wares which are made of porcelains and earthen clay were very much in **vogue** during the middle of Ming Dynasty. **Gilded** multicolored porcelain produced in Guangzhou, Guangdong Province and the bodyless **lacquer** wares of Fujian Province emerged in the Qing Dynasty. Due to the popularity of tea drinking, various kinds of tea wares continued to develop, for example, wares made of earthen clay, porcelains, copper, **tin**, jade, agata, lacquer, glass and **ceramic**, etc. All make a rich and colorful variety of tea wares in the history of tea—drinking in China. Among various kinds of tea wares, porcelain wares made in Jingdezhen, Jiangxi Province ranked first and brown earthen wares made in Yixing, Jiangsu Province took the top place for a long time. Tea-wares were not only highly valued in the domestic market but also exported and well received by foreign countries.

On the basis of grey porcelain of the Ming Dynasty, the multi-colored porcelains appeared. The products were known for their fine and thin wall and exquisite forms as well as their colorful and vivid drawings. They were also highly valued at home and abroad. Thanks to the porcelains exported, China won its name as "Country of Porcelains". Production of white glazed porcelain tea-wares was thriving in Jingdezhen in the Qing Dynasty. Two new products—"**enamel**" and "**translucent** colors" to be decorated on the glaze of porcelains were innovated and the multi-colored enamel porcelain tea-wares had reached to their perfection for their thin body wall, crystal pure white and classic styles. They were used only in the royal palaces and could hardly be found in the houses of ordinary people at that time.

2. How to Select Tea Wares

Chinese people use different kinds of tea wares with different kinds of tea. Green tea goes with white porcelain or celadon without a cover while scented tea with celadon or blue and white porcelain with a cover. Black tea goes well with purple clay ware with white inside glaze, or with white porcelain or warm colored wares or coffee wares. And Oolong tea is also excellent in purple clay ware. In other words, the harmonious combination of function, material, and color of tea ware is very essential to taste the essence of tea.

3. Appraisal Standards of the Boccaro Teapot

Generally, an excellent boccaro product should meet four requirements, that is to say, pure and superior material, harmonious shape and structure, skillful technique and convenience for use. For the image and structure of the boccaro teapots, we need to judge whether the nozzle, handle, lid, button and foot thereof are well connected with the body, whether scaling relations among the parts above are harmonious and whether they are beautiful or not. As for these aspects, three factors, "Jing, Qi and Shen", should be considered in the appraisal of the boccaro teapots. "Jing" refers to harmony of the shape and the fineness of the producing technique thereof; "Qi" represents the meaning and beauty of the teapots; while "Shen" denotes the spiritual charm of the teapots, available for us to taste and enjoy. Only those which perform well in these three factors may be deemed as excellent products.

Continuous playing of the boccaro teapots is capable to give us great confort, so the feeling of the surface is very important, even more important than the color. The boccaro teapot is also praised for its diversified shapes. As a part of the tea culture, the boccaro teapot pursues the artistic conception of "not seeking fame and wealth, but being free from secular bondages". We can only be dependent on our own feeling in judging the quality of a boccaro teapot. In the production of the boccaro teapots, the concept of Equi-Shape and Equi-Trend, that is, the equilibrium in the shaping theory, is used. Of course, we should not stick to the fixed patterns, for the teapots are made by manual techniques and the natural style should also be presented concurrently. The high fame of the boccaro teapot largely owes to its functions, so we should not ignore its functional beauty. In the appreciation of the inscription of the boccaro teapots, we can identify their producers and the authors of the inscribed poems and words, and enjoy the poems, paintings, calligraphies, and imprinting themselves, among others. Thus we can say, the decorating art of the boccaro teapots is a part of the Chinese traditional art, apparently featuring the integration of poem, calligraphy, painting and imprinting.

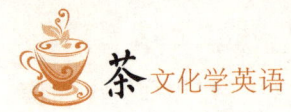

New words and expressions 生词和短语

scrunch [skrʌntʃ] v. 碾，压
ginger [ˈdʒɪndʒə(r)] n. 姜
peppermint [ˈpepəmɪnt] n.（植）薄荷
gild [gɪld] v. 修饰；粉饰
tin [tɪn] n. 锡
enamel [ɪˈnæml] n. 瓷釉

green onion [griːn ˈʌnjən] n. 葱
tangerine [ˌtændʒəˈriːn] n. 橘子
vogue [vəʊg] n. 流行；风行；时髦
lacquer [ˈlækə(r)] n. 亮漆；漆；漆器
ceramic [səˈræmɪk] adj. 陶器的
translucent [trænsˈluːsnt] adj. 半透明

Comprehension 理解

Give answers to the following questions in your own words and complete sentences as far as possible.

1. What kind of teapot did scholars prefer in Tang Dynasty?
2. In which dynasty did white glazed tea wares become popular?
3. Why should we choose different tea wares to go with different teas?
4. How to tell aboccaro teapot to be a good one or a bad one?
5. What relationship lies in between the tea wares and the painting art?

Notes on the text 课文注释

Boccaro Teapot: It is a kind of hand-made earthen clay teapot. It is made of a kind of boccaro earth which is usually hidden in a deep mining rock. Such boccaro earth is mainly produced in Yixing, Zhejiang province, so the Boccaro Teaport is traditionally called Yixing Boccaro Teapot. The chief characters of Boccaro Teapot are to keep the tea fragrance pure and avoid being stained with water or fire. And the wall of the teapot is capable to attract the fragrance of tea, in the long run, without tea inside the Boccaro Teapot can make the simple hotwater fragrant. 紫砂壶，是一种手工制作的陶土茶壶。制作原料为深藏矿物岩中的紫砂泥，原产地在江苏宜兴，又名宜兴紫砂壶。紫砂壶的特点是不夺茶香气又无熟汤味，壶壁吸附茶香，日久即使空壶中注入沸水也有茶香。

茶 具

茶具包括与饮茶、煮水、加热、清洁、贮藏以及其他的相关物品，但一般仅指泡饮茶叶用的茶壶、茶杯、茶碗和茶盘等。

1. 茶具材质

中国茶具历史悠久，饮茶风尚始于唐代，皇宫贵族多用金属茶具，而民间却以陶瓷茶碗为主。唐代文人偏好产于浙江绍兴的青瓷，这种青瓷看起来像玉，并有着优美的造型和华丽的装饰。茶汤在这种小瓯中映衬得非常漂亮，所以，这种茶具在陆羽的《茶经》中名列第一。关于茶具的功能，其大小和造型要很好地适合那个时代的饮茶习惯，允许茶粉与葱、姜、橘子皮和薄荷一起煮，然后将茶汤像喝汤一样全部喝下去。

人们对青瓷或白瓷的喜爱到了宋代突然有了改变，黑盏更受人们的青睐，口敞底小是茶盏常见的形态，并且有黑釉、酱釉、青釉、青白釉及白釉等多种样式。

元代青白釉茶具较多。明代盛行白茶盏，中期以后又以瓷壶和紫砂壶为风尚。到了清代出现了广州锦瓷、福州脱胎漆器等茶具。因为饮茶的普及，茶具也花样翻新，有陶器、瓷器、铜器、锡器、玉器、漆器、玻璃和搪陶等，琳琅满目，丰富多彩。在众多茶具中，尤以江西景德镇的瓷器和江苏宜兴的紫砂茶具为最好，这些茶具在国内外都享有盛誉。

在明代青瓷的基础上，出现了各种彩瓷。它们因其细腻、胎薄、造型优美以及多彩鲜活的绘画而闻名，在国内外都有很好的声誉。由于瓷器的出口，使中国获得了"瓷器之国"的美誉，清代景德镇盛产白釉茶具。"珐琅彩"和"粉彩"两种新彩料是清代的创新，同时，各种珐琅彩瓷器因其胎轻壁薄、釉白光亮和纹饰典雅而达到了完美的境界。这些精美的瓷器仅限于皇家使用，寻常百姓家难得一见。

2. 茶具选配

中国人使用各种不同的茶具泡饮不同类型的茶。绿茶多用白瓷或青瓷茶具冲泡，而花茶则用青瓷或青花瓷茶具。红茶以紫色土的白色瓷器为主，乌龙茶要用极好的紫色粘土制品。茶叶与茶具在材料和颜色方面要协调，使茶叶的品质充分发挥出来。

3. 紫砂壶的审评标准

一件优美的紫砂作品，大致应该具备四个相关条件：纯正上好的砂料，协调的造型结构，精湛的制作技巧和优良的使用功能，即好料、好形、好工和好用。所谓形象结构，是指壶的嘴、把、盖、纽、脚等与壶身整体衔接的状况与比例关系，是否协调，是否有美感。关于这方面要考虑"精、气、神"三个要素。"精"是指形制的协调程度和制作工艺的精细程度；"气"即气质风度，是壶的内涵气息与本质的美感度；"神"即神韵，一种能令人意会，体验出精神的韵味。一件紫砂只有这几个方面高度和谐、浑然一体，才能算得上是真正的好作品。

紫砂壶尤其需要不断把玩，让手感到舒适，达到心灵愉悦的目的。所以紫砂质表面的感觉比泥色更重要；紫砂壶之形，是存世各类器皿中最丰富的，素有"方非一式，圆不一相"之美誉。因为紫砂壶属整个茶文化的一部分，所以它追求的意境也应该是"淡泊平和，超世脱俗"。检验一把紫砂壶造型的优劣，全凭个人的感觉，制作壶时讲"等样""等势"，就是造型学讲的"均衡"。当然，我们也不能仅仅拘泥于固定的形式，也应将紫砂壶的手工技艺和自然风格同时表现出来。紫砂壶有这么高的知名度，一个重要的原因就是它的功能，我们不应忽视它这方面的功能。鉴赏紫砂壶款的意思有两层：一是鉴别壶的作者是谁，或题诗镌铭的作者是谁；另一层意思是欣赏题词的内容、镌刻的书画，还有印款（金石篆刻）等。紫砂壶的装饰艺术是中国传统艺术的一部分，它具有中国传统艺术"诗、书、画、印"四位一体的显著特点。

Lesson 27
How to Make a Good Cup of Tea

To prepare a good cup of tea, you need fine tea, good water and suitable tea sets. Each of these three elements is **indispensable**. And it is more important that you need some knowledge about appraising quality of tea and water, and also acquire skills to control the amount of tea, water temperature and the time of **brewing** according to different types of tea.

1. Appraising Quality of Tea

The good quality of dry tea is the most crucial element in making a good cup of tea. It can be observed with eyes and smelled with nose, simply to say: it is a way to judge the color, the fragrance, and the uniformity of the dry tea.

Different kinds of tea have different colors. Green tea should have a light green color, oolong a darker green or even brown color, black tea black. Regardless of the color, good tea leaves should have a **lustrous** quality; they will not look dull or hazy. The uniformity of the color often indicates the quality control in processing. If oolong tea has yellowish or brownish colors mixed with the green, it might indicate poor quality control during the drying or rolling process.

If the tea is fresh and well stored, it should retain its fragrance. This means that the moisture content should be less than five percent. If you twist the leaves with your thumb and index finger, they should turn to powder. If they don't, it often indicates that they are not fresh or are not well stored, and the water level has exceeded the ideal level. This means that much of the fragrance has probably already dissipated.

Good quality tea should have very little in the way of twigs or dust. The ultimate way of evaluating the quality of tea, though, is by tasting the brew, noting the quality of color, aroma and richness of the taste.

2. Appraising Quality of Water

A cup of tea is a tiny of tea, and a whole lot of water. Knowing what is in the water you use is critical to producing a great-tasting cup. Traditionally, a great deal of attention was paid to water quality. There are many traditional tales of people bringing good water from hundreds of miles away. In the *The classis of Tea*, Lu Yu spent a good deal of space commenting on the different qualities of water from various mountains and streams. He said that the best is the pure water obtained from the deep mountains, next from the upper stream of the rivers and the third from the wells.

The fresh mountain spring water is ideal, since it is living and vibrant. In the old days, people would often store boiled water in large clay containers, which had the effect of **revitalizing** the boiled water. In modern times, good filtered tap water can do a decent job in making good tea. The important thing is to remove the taste of **chlorine**. The amount of oxygen in the water can also be a factor in the final cup. Water that has been set overnight in a boiler will make a flat, lifeless cup of tea; hence, you should always fill your kettle with freshly drawn water.

The last factor is the amount of TDS(total dissolved solids), that is to say the amount of minerals in the water. It seems that 35~50 TDS would be the most widely agreed-upon number for great tea. A total lack of dissolved minerals makes for weak aromatic and flavor components, so distilled water should be avoided. An over-abundance can muddy the liquor and can cause lighter floral notes to get lost.

3. The Choice of Tea Vessels

Traditionally, people paid a great deal of attention to the tea wares and other utensils which were made in different forms, from different materials and to fit different functions of tea brewing. In China, Yixing tea ware was used in making Gongfu tea; in Japan, specific kinds of tea wares were used for the formal tea ceremony. Tea ware has been developed into an independent art.

Some people prefer to use glass tea ware so they can see the tea leaves unfold and expand clearly. With white **ceramic**, the color of the brewed tea can be enjoyed in its contrast with the purity of the white; this is often used with white, green and yellow tea. With Yixing tea ware, the scent of the tea **permeates** the tea ware, so that after years of using, the tea ware itself has a delicate, lasting fragrance; this is most often used with oolong tea, in order to greatly send off its complex aroma and flavor.

Of course, some tea ware can be used for any kind of tea, and serve any purpose. All you need is two equal-sized glass tea pots: one to serve as the tea pot, and one to serve as the decanter. In addition, you need a filter. The core method is to brew the tea in the pot, and then to pour it (through the strainer) into the decanter. This means that all the cups of tea that are poured will be of the same strength-and also that the tea will not be steeped too long.

4. Skills and Procedures

The ratio of tea to water, the temperature of the water, and the steeping time, are also important in making a good cup of tea.

A standard cup of tea is like a cup of coffee, 5.5 liquid ounces. So, the first step in correctly brewing a great cup of tea is to know the liquid capacity of your preferred teapot. The **capacity** of your brewing vessel determines how much tea you should use. The general rule of thumb is to use 2 grams of tea leaves for each cup of water. That is to say, if your tea takes one and one half teaspoons to make 2 grams, and you are using an 11-ounce tea pot, then you will need three teaspoons of tea to produce a pot.

As to the temperature of water, it is agreed that the boiling is not always the best. There are three stages when water is boiling. At the first stage, the bubbles look like crab eyes; at the second, the bubbles look like fish eyes; finally, they look like surging waves. The water boiling between the crab-eye stage and the fish-eye stage is the best for preparing tea. We should use big fire to make water boil quickly. If the water for making tea is too hot, tea leaves will be spoiled and tea liquor will turn to dark yellow very quickly.

The produced tea is in 3 distinct styles in three distinct styles: black, oolong and green. Each of these styles has different water temperature guidelines for steeping. For black teas, water should absolutely be brought to a rolling boil (100℃) before it is poured. For oolong teas, the water temperature should be slightly cooler (90℃~95℃), depending on the degree of oxidation in the particular oolong. Green teas require cooler water still (never over 80℃) and you should carry the water to the tea instead of the tea to the water. A common reason that tea tastes too bitter is that the temperature is too high, and the water absorbed too much catechin. The trick is to bring the water to boiling, and then to let it cool down to the right temperature.

As far as the steeping time is concerned, it is quite flexible. For green tea, it is enough to steep from three to five minutes, and when the color becomes pale green, the tea is ready, which can last 3~5 steeping times. A good Oolong tea may be steeped eight or more, maybe the first steeping should be for about one and a half minutes and in successive steeping, the time is increased by about half a minute per steeping. And a good Pu'er tea can be infused up to twenty times. The steeping time is from 20 to 30 seconds for the first few infusions, and from 2 up to 5 minutes for following infusions.

By the way, when drinking Oolong and Pu'er, an extra decanter is needed. Tea brewing is not directly poured to the cup, instead it is first completely poured off into the decanter, then accordingly poured into each cup to try to make the flavor in each one remain the same. When you pour tea into the guests' tea cups one by one and this act has a special name, that is, "the fabled Lord Guan making an inspection of the city". You drip the leftover tea respectively into the cups drop by drop and this act is called "The fabled General Han Xin mustering troops for inspection". Drinking a good cup of tea can also remind you of many Chinese traditional stories. Now a cup of tea is ready, just enjoy.

Unit 7 Essentials in Tea Drinking

New words and expressions
生词和短语

indispensable [ˌɪndɪˈspensəb(ə)l] *adj.* 不可缺少的，绝对必要的
 brew [bruː] *v.* 酿造；酝酿；酿酒；被冲泡
 lustrous [ˈlʌstrəs] *adj.* 有光泽的；光辉的
 capacity [kəˈpæsəti] *n.* 容量；容积；能力
 revitalize [riːˈvaɪtəlaɪz] *v.* 复活；恢复生气
 chlorine [ˈklɔːriːn] *n.* 氯
 ceramic [sɪˈræmɪk] *adj.* 陶瓷的，陶制的 *n.* 陶瓷，陶瓷制品
 permeate [ˈpɜːmieɪt] *v.* 渗透；透过；弥漫；透入

Comprehension
理 解

Give answers to the following questions in your own words and complete sentence as far as possible.

1. What are the main factors for making a good tea?

2. What are the "the fabled General Han Xin mustering troops for inspection" and "the fabled Lord Guan making an inspection of the city"?

3. How to tell if the tea is fresh or well-stored?

4. What is the main reason of the bitter taste of tea?

Notes on the text
课文注释

1. Gongfu tea：功夫茶是汉族民间传统的品茶风尚，其烹煎之法应是源于陆羽的《茶经》。功夫茶历来讲究"品饮功夫"。正因其是讲究品饮功夫的一种饮茶方式，故称为"功夫茶"。

2. Yixing tea ware：宜兴茶具，即紫砂茶具，它耐寒耐热，泡茶无熟汤味，能保真香，且传热缓慢，不易烫手，用它泡茶，也不会爆裂。

如何泡好一杯茶

一杯好茶需要好茶叶、好水和好茶具,三者缺一不可。更重要的是你得知道如何鉴别茶和水的品质,掌握茶和水的配比以及不同的茶所适宜的最佳水温和冲泡时间。

1. 选茶

茶的质量是最重要的。你必须用肉眼观察,用鼻子闻,简单说就是:察其色,闻其味,再用手捻,看叶子卷的紧密与否。

茶不同,颜色就不同。绿茶应呈淡绿色,乌龙茶则呈深绿色或褐色,红茶应呈现黑色。不论颜色如何,好的茶叶应该质地饱满,不应晦暗不清。颜色的均匀与否说明加工过程的精细程度。如果乌龙茶呈现黄色或棕色与绿色的混合色,说明其干燥或揉搓过程不够精细。

如果茶很新鲜或储存良好,它应该芳香依旧。这意味着水分含量应小于5%。如果用拇指或食指碾碎茶叶,它们应该呈粉末状。若非如此,通常说明该茶并非新茶或储存不当,并且水分含量已经高于理想水平,这意味着很多芳香已经挥发掉了。

质量好的茶应该几乎不掺杂细枝或粉尘。然而,评价茶质量的最终方法是通过品茶,从色泽、香气和口感上来评定茶的品质。

2. 选水

一杯茶中茶少水多,因此,了解你所使用的水对泡一杯好茶至关重要。传统做法是人们较多关注水质。人们从数百里外取水泡茶,这种传统故事很多。在《茶经》里,陆羽用大篇幅探讨了不同水质,从山泉水到溪水。他说最好的水来自深山,其次是来自河流上游的溪水,再次是井水。

新汲取的山泉水是最理想的,因为它鲜活明净。古时,人们通常将开水储存在较大的黏土容器里,因为它能保持水的鲜活。现在,经过精细过滤的自来水也可以完成冲泡一杯好茶的任务,但重要的一点是要去除氯的味道。水中氧气含量同样是一个重要因素。器皿中放置了一夜的水,会使茶平淡无味,因此,你需要经常向水壶添加刚提取的新鲜水。

最后一个因素是水中溶解的固形物，也就是水中的矿物质含量。似乎公认的可以泡制一杯好茶的水，其中的溶解固体总量是35%～50%。完全不含可溶解矿物质的水会影响茶的芳香和口感，因此要避免使用蒸馏水。当然，固形物含量过多则会使茶水混浊且会散失些许清香。

3. 选择茶具

传统上，人们十分重视用于冲泡茶叶的各式各样、质地不同、功能各异的茶具及其他器皿。在中国，宜兴茶具用于冲泡工夫茶；在日本，正式的茶道使用特制的茶具。茶具已发展为一门独立的艺术。

有些人独爱玻璃茶具，因为透过它们可以清晰地看到茶叶慢慢打开、伸展。若用白瓷茶具，茶叶的颜色与白色交相辉映，令人赏心悦目，这种茶具通常用于冲泡白茶、绿茶和黄茶。使用宜兴茶具，茶香会渗入茶具中，经久使用后，茶具本身将会带有一种细腻、持久的芳香。这种茶具通常用来冲泡乌龙茶，这样可以极大地将其独特复杂的香气和口感散发出来。

当然，有些茶具适用于任何一种茶并满足任何需求。你所需要的是两个大小相等的玻璃茶壶：一个用于做茶煲，另一个用来做滗水器。此外，你还需一个过滤器。主要做法是首先在茶煲里冲泡茶，然后将其倒入滗水器。这会让倒出来的茶具有同样的力度，且茶不宜浸泡太久。

4. 技巧与过程

茶与水的比例，水温和浸泡时间对冲泡一杯好茶同样重要。

一杯标准的茶如同一杯咖啡，需要5.5盎司（约150毫升）液体。因此，正确冲泡一杯好茶的第一步是熟知你所选用茶壶的液体容量。冲泡容器的容量决定你所使用的茶量。一般的经验做法是每杯水使用2克茶叶，即如果你的茶匙是一勺半等于2克，那么如果你需要使用11盎司（约300毫升）的茶壶，你就得加入三勺茶叶。

关于水温，普遍认为不宜使用沸水。水的沸腾有三个阶段：第一阶段，气泡看起来像螃蟹的眼睛；第二阶段，气泡如同鱼眼；最后阶段，气泡如同汹涌的海浪。泡茶的沸水最好介于螃蟹眼阶段和鱼眼阶段之间。应使用大火迅速煮沸。如果泡茶的水过热，会损坏茶叶，让茶水迅速变为深黄色。

加工后的茶叶主要有三种：红茶、乌龙茶和绿茶，每种茶需要在不同水温要

求下冲泡。对于红茶,温度要达100℃。对于乌龙茶,水温要稍低(90℃~95℃),这取决于特定乌龙茶的氧化度。绿茶需要更低温度的水(不超过80℃),需要将水添加到茶中,而非将茶添入水中。茶味道太苦的一个常见原因是温度过高,水吸收了大量的儿茶酚,秘诀在于让水沸腾,然后冷却至恰当温度。

关于冲泡的时间,则比较灵活。对于绿茶,只需浸泡3~5分钟,当颜色变为淡绿色时,茶便好了,可以持续3~5分钟。一杯好的乌龙茶冲泡时间要超过8分钟,连续冲泡,每次冲泡时间增加半分钟。一杯好的普洱茶注入水要达20次,最初几次注水冲泡时间为20~30秒,以后每次冲泡时间变为2~5分钟。

顺便说一下,在喝乌龙茶和普洱茶时,还需一个滗水器。泡好的茶并非直接倒入杯中,而是首先要完全倒进滗水器,然后相应地倒进每一个杯子中,保持每个杯子中茶的味道相同。当你一杯接一杯地为客人倒茶时,被雅成为"关公巡城",把茶壶中最后残留的茶汤分别一一滴入杯中,就被称为"韩信点兵"。品一杯好茶可以让你记住许多中国传统故事。现在,好茶已就绪,请品尝。

Unit 8
Tea Ceremony

Lesson 28
Chinese Tea Art

Four thousand years ago, a legendary person named Shennong tasted hundreds of grasses, and finally discovered the magical plant-tea, which could detoxify 72 kinds of poisons. From then on, tea has been playing an important role in people's daily life and has occupied a warm spot in Chinese people's affection. Moreover, tea has involved in every aspect of social life in China and **imperceptibly** mixed together with music, poem, painting, **calligraphy** and other arts as a whole, which forms the special traditional Chinese tea culture. As one branch, the tea art came into being in Tang Dynasty. It **embodies** the **distillation** of the drinking tea customs in different regions. Also, the tea art can show you the excellent tea-brewing skills, the delicate tea sets and the harmonious environment for drinking tea.

1. The Elegant and Classical Gongfu Tea

Gongfu Tea ceremony, which prevails in Southern Fujian, Chaozhou-Shantou region and Taiwan province, requires the particular skills, **exquisite** tea sets and quaint **etiquette**. It integrates the spirit of tea art into people's natural and harmonious actions, and strives for a rhyming beauty. In Chinese opinion, drinking Gongfu Tea is not just to quench one's thirst, but mainly to experience the pleasure and atmosphere of drinking and to enjoy the relaxation and comfort.

Now we will show you how to make Gongfu Tea. It needs to pay much attention to the choice of tea, water and tea set, and needs slow tasting. The procedures are quite particular including more than ten steps. However, if you have a relaxed and leisurely mood, you will definitely find the pleasure inside the ceremony.

Next, the tea art ladies will show you step by step.

The 1st step is called "Bei Ju Hou Yong", which means to prepare the tea set and list them properly according to the brewing process. The teapot we choose is Yixing purple clay teapot, also called Mengchen Pot in ancient time. The exquisite small cups are also purple clay products made in Yixing. The teapot and cups form a perfect pair, which is called "Ruochen Ou" in the past.

The 2nd step is "Jian Shang Cha Ming", meaning to appreciate the dry tea. A host in China who is good at building a tea tasting atmosphere, will particularly show his guests and friends the tea he is going to brew. This will help them know the quality of tea and reveal the host's good wills. The tea you are now seeing is Tieguanyin, which is the best type of Oolong tea in Southern Fujian Province and has been renowned for its excellence for a long time. It contains quite a strong body and shows the color of emerald green.

The 3rd step "Qing Quan Chu Fei", means to prepare hot water. Good cooking water is definitely needed to make good oolong tea so that its excellent aroma and taste can be revealed incisively and vividly.

The 4th step is called "Meng Chen Lin Lin", which means the warming of teapot. One of the aims of warming is to clean the teapot and remove the unwanted smell. In addition, with the teapot being warm, the intrinsic qualities of tea can be released properly.

The 5th step is "Wu Long Ru Gong", in Chinese which says "dark dragon goes into its palace", that's to say, to put the tea into teapot. The quantity depends on its quality. If the tea is too much, the leaves will be hard to stretch out; if too little, the taste will not be strong enough. Generally, the amount of tea should occupy 1/3 or 1/2 of the teapot.

The 6th step is called "Wen Run Wu Long" or "Bo Cha Xi Chen", which stands for the pre-brewing of the tea. Pour hot water into the teapot and scrap the spume on the water, and then quickly pour the water out of the teapot. This step can remove the impurities of tea, make it purer and stretched preliminarily.

The 7th step is "Xuan Hu Gao Chong". It means to pour a suitable amount of hot water into the teapot soon after last step when tea leaves are warm and humid. The water should be poured from high, which can make the tea sway in the teapot properly. When pouring, it is better to pour up and down 3 times slowly, implicating the Chinese saying "**phoenix** nods its head for three times". Tasting tea is one way of enjoyment and relaxation; being not too fast or slow can correspond to the "middle way" in Chinese culture, which means to be moderate while living.

The 8th step iscalled "Tui Pao Chou Mei", which means to scrap the spume of the tea with the teapot lid. It is just like spring breeze caressing one's cheeks.

The 9th step is "Chong Xi Xian Yan", and that means to wash the body of teapot with boiling water. It helps to heat the teapot and make the same temperatures inside and outside it.

The 10th step is "Ruo chen Chu Yu", which is to warm up the tea cups and maintain their temperatures. It can make the tea much more fragrant and tastier. The principle is the same as last step. When warming up the cups, you should act as quickly as possible with elegant skills and avoid colliding cups with each other because the quiet environments of tasting tea are quite different from the noisy drinking of wine.

The 11th step is called "You Shan Wan Shui", whose Chinese meaning is to travel around in leisure. Here it refers to the process of drying teapot so that the water in the bottom will not wet the table or drip into cups and affect the quality and taste of tea.

The 12th step, "Guan Gong Xun Cheng", means to pour tea infusion to tea cups which are lined on the table. Firstly, the tea cups should be lined up side by side; then raise the tea pot high and pour tea infusion into every cup back and forth. In this way the fragrance will not run off and tea infusion in each cup can be the same. The act of pouring should be steady and graceful, leaving the impression of resembling waves of water or drifting clouds.

The 13th step is "Han Xin Dian Bing". It means to put the left extraction in the teapot, which is also the essence of the tea into each cup separately until nothing else left. Both Guan Gong and Han Xin are two famous generals in ancient China.

The 14th step is "San Long Hu Ding". It means to use your thumb, first and middle fingers to hold a cup of tea and move it into a plate.

Now the ladies have made a pot of Gongfu Tea for our guests, please enjoy.

The 15th step is "Jian Shang Tang Se", which means to appreciate the color of tea infusion. Good Oolong tea can show a clear golden color in cups.

The 16th step is "Xi Wen You Xiang", which means to smell the aroma of the tea. Put the cup near nose and move it slowly around and smell it devotedly. Good Tieguanyin has the natural strong aroma of orchids, which is also called "Yin Yun", meaning melody, all along.

The 17th step is "Xi Pin Jia Ming", the taste of tea. A cup of tea should be drunk through several sips and swallowed slowly. At the beginning, the taste might be a little bitter, soon after, you will feel flower fragrance existing long time in your mouth. As long as you pay attention to tasting, you can realize the pleasure in it.

The last step, "Chong Shang Yu Yun", means to appreciate the tea again. After tasting the tea infusion, you can put the empty cup around your nose and smell the left fragrance lingering in the bottom of the cup.

Tasting tea is an elegant kind of art. In the eyes of those people who like tea, every tea set is a living. Imagine you are in a quiet room sitting among flowers and trees, with ancient and modern poems and paintings hanging on walls and beautiful folk music playing on, the quiet and enjoyable feeling will surround you. Holding a cup of famous tasty tea, and experiencing the joy in a graceful room, you'll find the wonderful enjoyment as if floating in the air with two wings and returning to purity and nature.

2. A Theme Tea Party of Five Rings and Wishes

Distinguished guests, ladies and gentlemen:

Good afternoon!

Tea is not only a type of beverage, but also an eternal carrier of culture and emotional exchanges between Chinese nation and peoples of the world. To hold Olympic Games in the hometown of tea will surely have enhanced the reputation of tea in China. In order to help everyone find a real traditional Chinese tea culture, to taste our national tea, and to promote a closer linking of tea and people's happy life, to let more friends know tea and love tea, tonight, we will specially present a tea art performance to celebrate 2008 Chinese Olympic Games to all the guests.

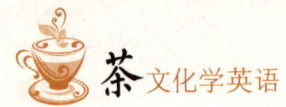

"Five Rings and Wishes Tea Art" is performed by five tea art masters dressed in five different colors, interpreting five types of tea with five different brewing techniques. What's more, five different colors of the tea just as five rings in the Olympic Games, yellow, green, blue, black and red, symbolize different meanings.

Chinese people believe in "Yuan", which means the destiny that ties people together, and Chinese tea arts have an amazing coincidence with the Olympic game this year. Five-ring flag has five rings with five different colors and with the sixth white color, coincidentally matches the traditional chinese six kinds of tea. And the pursuit of the Olympic spirit of unity and friendship is so initiated with the essential element of Chinese tea ceremony: harmony.

Now, I am highly honored to introduce for our leaders and guests the five types of tea which can symbolize the five colors of Olympics: yellow, green, blue, black, and red brewed by five tea art masters.

Yellow ring is made of yellow tea which is named by its yellow liquid and yellow leaves, mainly produced in Zhejiang, Sichuan, Hunan and Hubei province. Among them, "Junshan silver pin" is produced from the Junshan island of Yueyang in Hunan's Dongting Hill as the most representative one, ranking in Chinese Ten Famous Teas. "Junshan silver pin" as a single bud production, appreciate the tea buds as the highlights in the drinking course. The specialty of this tea lies in the beauty of the buds. At the beginning of the brewing, the tea buds just float at the surface of the water, after a while, sink down, and the tea tops give out bubbles just as pearls in a lark's mouth. Then every bud will upright in the cup, like bamboo shoot unearthed; or forest such as guns and knives, and then down to the bottom of the cup, or floating upright again, so from top to bottom ups and downs. It is called "Three ups, three downs" just as human life full of happiness and sorrows, delight and bitterness. The buds' delicate appearance, pure flavor and sweet taste make everyone refreshed in mind.

Green ring is made of green tea. It fully maintains the chlorophyll and Vitamin C because it is not fermented. When we are drinking green tea, we often appreciate the color, aroma, shape of the dry tea. As to its shape, they are strip, flat and spiral; to color, they are as green as jade or blackish green. And its aroma has delicate fragrance and smells like boiled chestnut. In brewing, the tea can be observed to have a slow stretch in the water, ups and downs. This dynamic change of the tea is known as the "tea dance." After a while, the aroma with the rising fog floating above the surface gives people a relaxed and happy feeling. Under the sun to see the tea liquid in the cup, tiny buds swimming in the water, glittering and sparkling. You will find a tender and sweet taste when drinking the tea.

Blue ring or Qing ring is made from oolong tea. Qing is also an Oriental color. Xunzi in "Exhortation to study" said "Qing chu yu lan er sheng yu lan"(The color Qing comes from the color Lan, but more lovely than the Lan.), which means a pupil can surpass his master or teacher in learning. And here"Qing"is the Chinese saying for the color of the oolong tea. Oolong tea is s semi-fermented tea which not only has the flower smell and the pure scent as the green tea, but also has the mellowed sweet aroma as the black tea. Her beautiful poise is on everyone's lips, such as, "Seven to stay Yuxiang bubble". It is integrated of Chinese tea culture with the tea skills closely. Such as the "holding teacup," "Guan Gong makes his rounds," "Hanxin counting soldiers," "Movable to three springs." Fully applying the tongues function, let tea rolling back and forth at both ends of the tongue. Let every part of the tongue feel the full taste of tea. Cheek and teeth also slowly appreciate the feeling.

Black ring is made from dark tea. Dark tea is mainly used to make food supply for frontier minorities, also known as tea along the border. We can trace its source to the Eastern Han Dynasty period with a history of 2000 years. When such Aged tea is brewed, one should be slow to appreciate the formation of the mellow in the process of drinking. Because of their unique effectiveness of lipid-lowering diet, Dark tea is referred to as "slim tea", "aerobics tea."

Red ring is made from black tea. Her charm not only lies in the black auburn of the color, thick sweet aroma, great taste, red-yellow infusion, infused leaves and tender bright, but also in her moderate temperament which can be of mutual integration with various spices. Therefore, you can drink the black tea only or mix it with others. To appreciate its fragrance, flavor and color, one should drink slowly, carefully, truly enjoy the pleasure of drinking.

"Good hill, good water. Buddhist smiles with no bother; hurry to come, hurry to go, drink some tea to the West or East."

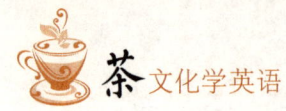

Today, I have the great honor on behalf of all the performers who present this Five Rings and Wishes Tea Art with the best wishes to you, and we wish you a happy family and good luck everyday! Best wishes to our motherland too!

New words and expressions 生词和短语

exquisite [ɪkˈskwɪzɪt] *adj.* 优雅的
etiquette [ˈetɪket] *n.* 礼节
imperceptibly [ˌɪmpəˈseptəblɪ] *adv.* 细微地；觉察不到地
calligraphy [kəˈlɪgrəfɪ] *n.* 书法
embodiment [ɪmˈbɒdɪmənt] *n.* 体现；具体化；化身
distillation [ˌdɪstɪˈleɪʃn] *n.* 精华
phoenix [ˈfiːnɪks] *n.* 凤凰

Comprehension 理解

Give answers to the following questions in your own words and complete sentence as far as possible.

1. List what you know about Gongfu Tea. (at least four points)

2. What are the procedures of making Gongfu Tea? Which one do you like best? Why?

3. Oolong tea can be considered the most fascinating of all kinds of tea, because _____.

4. What is the "yuan"(destiny) between Chinese tea and the Olympics?

5. What are the five colors in tea stand for respectively? Explain them in your own words.

Notes on the text 课文注释

1. Mengchen teapot：茶室四宝之一，紫砂茶壶称作"孟臣罐"，孟臣罐即泡茶的茶壶。

2. Ruochen tea cups：若琛瓯，一种薄瓷小杯，薄如纸，白似雪，小巧玲珑，酷似半个乒乓球和微型饭碗。

3. Chaoshan furnace：潮汕炉是烧开水用的火炉，广东潮州、汕头出产的风炉，有陶质的、有白铁皮的，故名潮汕炉，茶艺用。

Translation 参考译文

中国茶艺

四千年前，神话人物神农遍尝百草，然后发现了能解72种毒的神奇植物——茶。从此，茶在中国人的日常生活中占据了重要地位，深受人们喜爱。随后，茶渗入到社会各个方面，与音乐、诗歌、绘画、书法及其他艺术无形中融为一体，形成了传承至今的中国茶文化。茶艺作为茶文化的一个分支，最早出现于唐朝，融合了不同地区喝茶的精髓，展示了高超的沏茶技法、精美的茶具以及适合喝茶的和谐环境。

1. 古朴典雅的功夫茶

盛行于闽南、潮汕、台湾等地的功夫茶冲泡法，有着独特的技艺、精巧的茶具、奇趣的礼节，它融茶艺精神于自然和谐的动作之中，讲究一种自然的韵律美感。喝功夫茶并不是为了解渴，主要在于品味其茶趣与气氛，讲究细品茶味，慢闻其香，尽怡情养性之趣。

现在为大家表演功夫茶冲泡法，泡饮功夫茶，讲究好茶好水、好茶具和细品尝，功夫茶的冲泡步骤讲究，有十多步，但若您能保持一份闲逸的心情，那么您一定也会觉得乐在其中。

下面将由茶艺小姐为大家一一表演。

第一步：备具候用。将泡茶用具备好，并依沏泡时的需要合理布局，我们所用的茶壶为宜兴紫砂壶，古称"孟臣罐"，所用的小茶杯也为宜兴紫砂制品，玲珑典雅，与孟臣罐珠联璧合，古称"若琛瓯"。

第二步：鉴赏佳茗。讲究品茗气氛的主人，冲泡前会让宾客好友鉴赏一番茶叶，这样既让客人了解了茶叶的品质，又表现了主人的诚意。大家现在看到的铁观音是闽南乌龙茶中的极品，久负盛名，其身骨重实，色泽砂绿翠润。

第三步：清泉初沸。冲泡一壶好的乌龙茶，必须要有好水相配，才能将其

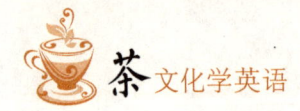

色香韵味淋漓尽致地表现出来。

第四步：孟臣淋霖。也就是常说的温壶，温壶的目的之一是清洁茶具，去除异味，此外，壶身温热，也可使茶叶的色、香、味的本质随着热度适宜地表现出来。

第五步：乌龙入宫。将茶叶从茶则中置入壶内，其分量随其品质而定，过多，则茶叶难于伸展，过少，则劲道不足，一般茶叶应以置入茶壶的 1/3 或 1/2 为佳。

第六步：温润乌龙。又叫拨茶洗尘，将茶置入茶壶后，注入沸水，并刮去泡沫，随即将茶汤倾入茶池中，称之为温润泡，这样可去掉茶叶的杂质异味，使之更加纯净，同时，使茶叶初步伸展。

第七步：悬壶高冲。即茶叶的冲泡，茶叶一经温润后，茶汁呼之欲出，继而将适量的开水高冲入壶内，冲至与壶口相平。高冲以利于激荡茶水，冲泡的速度不宜太急，宜三起三落，即"凤凰吐水三点头"。品茗是件赏心乐事，不急不缓，才合乎中庸之道。

第八步：推泡抽眉。又名春风拂面，茶叶经高冲后，壶口会有一些泡沫，用壶盖推掉壶口泡沫后将盖盖好。

第九步：重洗仙颜。用沸水从壶顶向下冲洗，也称之为冲壶，其作用是给壶盖、壶身加温，使壶身内外温度相同，上下交融。

第十步：若琛出浴。即温杯，保持茶杯的温度，可使茶的香气浓烈、滋味醇美，它的原理与温壶相同，可分为传里温杯和传外温杯两种，温杯时动作需利落、娴熟、温雅，减少杯间的碰撞，因为品茗与饮酒的环境是大不相同的。品茗的清雅气氛也与饮酒时的觥筹交错截然不同。

第十一步：游山玩水。即干壶，干壶是为了擦干壶底，不致使壶底的水滴湿桌面或顺流到杯中，影响茶的品质与风味。

第十二步：关公巡城。将茶杯紧凑排列，然后将茶壶提起，使茶汤依序巡回多次低斟，以避免香气逸失，同时保证茶汤均匀。倒茶时的水速要均细、稳健、不急不缓，如行云流水，有着无限的飘逸。

第十三步：韩信点兵。壶中最后所剩的茶汁是茶的精华所在，要依次点入杯中，力求不留剩茶。

第十四步：三龙护鼎。用大拇指和食指轻轻扶住杯缘，中指顶住杯底，将茶杯提起放入茶盘中。

现在，茶艺小姐已为大家冲泡好了一壶功夫茶，请来宾和她们一起品尝。

第十五步：鉴赏汤色。即观汤色之匀准，好的乌龙茶汤色清澈金黄，呈油茶色。

第十六步：喜闻幽香。将茶杯置于鼻端前后或左右徐徐移动，嗅闻茶香，好的铁观音具有天然的兰花香，且香气馥郁，素有"音韵"之誉。

第十七步：细品佳茗。一杯茶汤分几口啜饮，徐徐咽下，品一杯好的功夫茶，刚开始会略有苦感，继而满口生香，久久不散，令人回味无穷，只要有心品之，即能悟到茶中之乐。

第十八步：重赏余韵。茶汤饮完后，将空茶杯置于鼻前，再次嗅闻凝附于杯底的余香。

品茶是一种高雅的艺术享受，在茶人的眼里每一件茶具都是有生命的，在花木丛郁的雅室里，古今诗画面壁高挂，民族音乐悠扬轻颂，景德紫砂，玉洁冰心，茶香飘逸，胜似兰芷，身居幽室，捧一杯香茗在手，则有两翼徐徐生风，返璞归真之感。

2. "五福茶乡情"主题茶艺

各位领导、各位来宾、女士们、先生们：

大家好！

茶不仅是饮品，更是中华民族与世界各国人民文化和情感交流的永恒载体。茶叶故乡办奥运、奥运增进茶更香。为了让大家更真切地感受到中国传统茶文化，更深刻地了解中国的国饮，并把她更进一步推广和普及到人们的生活中，让更多的朋友识茶、懂茶、爱茶，今晚我们为大家带来的是《五福茶乡情》这套特为迎2008年奥运而作的茶艺节目。现在为来宾献上这道茶艺！

《五福茶乡情》是由五位茶艺师身着五种不同颜色的服装，一齐演绎五种不同茶类的冲泡技巧，五种不同茶类又分别代表奥运五环黄、绿、蓝、黑、红的颜色。

中华民族讲究个"缘"字，而中国茶与奥林匹克有着惊人的巧合。五环旗上的五环加上白底六种颜色，恰巧与中国传统的六大茶类相吻合。而奥林匹克

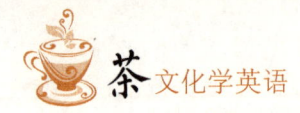

精神追求的"团结友好"与中国茶道所倡导的"和"又是如此异曲同工的"妙合"。

接下来我荣幸地为各位领导、来宾们一一介绍茶艺师们将为大家演绎的代表五环标志的黄、绿、蓝、黑、红等五道茶艺。

黄环（黄茶）：因其黄叶黄汤而得名。主产地在浙江、四川、湖南、湖北。其中以产于湖南岳阳洞庭湖中君山岛上的"君山银叶"最具代表性，被列为中国十大名茶。"君山银叶"为单芽制作，在品饮过程中突出对杯中茶芽的欣赏，是一种以赏芽为主的特种茶。刚冲泡时茶芽横卧水面，继而吸水徐徐下沉；芽尖产生气泡，犹如雀舌含珠。继而个个直立杯中，似春笋出土，如刀枪林立；接着沉入杯底后，再次直立浮升，如此上下沉浮，有"三落三起"之美称，犹如人生。她清秀袭人、口感醇和、鲜爽甘甜，品尝后，别有一番滋味在心头。

绿环（绿茶）：因其不经发酵，充分保持茶叶中的叶绿素、维生素C。品饮名优绿茶，先赏干茶的形、色、香。绿茶造型各异，或条状，或扁平，或螺旋形，或若针状。其色泽翠绿或墨绿，香气为板栗香或清香。冲泡时，可观察茶在水中缓慢舒展，上下沉浮。这种富于变幻的动态，茶人称其为"茶舞"。冲泡后，汤面冉冉上升的雾气中夹杂着缕缕茶香，犹如云蒸霞蔚。使人心旷神怡。隔杯对着阳光透视茶汤，还可见到微细茸毫在水中游荡、闪闪发光。从中可品出嫩茶香气，沁人肺腑。

蓝环（青茶）：青，东方之色也。荀子《劝学篇》里说"青出于蓝而胜于蓝"道出青与蓝之关系。青茶，又名乌龙茶，属半发酵茶，它既具绿茶的清香和花香，又具红茶醇厚回甘的滋味。世人都在传诵她美丽的丰姿。如"青蒂绿腹青蜓头""青褐油润呈宝光""蛤蟆背""岩韵""观音韵""绿叶红镶边、三红七绿""七泡留余香"等。青茶茶艺技巧与中国文化融合得最为密切。如："三龙护鼎""关公巡城""韩信点兵""三品方知其味，三春才能动心"等。充分调动"舌"的功能，让茶汤在舌的两端来回滚动，让舌的各个部位充分感受茶汤的滋味，慢慢体味颊齿留香的感觉。

黑环（黑茶）：主要用来制成紧压茶供应边疆少数民族饮用，又称边销茶。它的生产可追溯到东汉时期，距今已有2000多年的历史。若是品赏陈年茶，应在品饮的过程中细细体味其形成的"陈香"，其味醇、甘滑。因其独特的降脂减肥功效，被人们称为"窈窕茶""健美茶"。

　　红环（红茶）：她的迷人之处，不但在于色泽黑褐油润、香气浓郁带甜、滋味浓厚、汤色红艳透黄、叶底嫩匀红亮，而且还在于她性情温和、能和各种调味品相互融合，相映生辉。因此，红茶的饮用，既可清饮，也可调饮。若要真正领略它的"香、味、色"必须在"品"字上下功夫，缓缓斟饮，细细品缀，徐徐体味，超然自得"吃"出茶的真味来，真正享受到这种福分。

　　"山好好，水好好，空门一笑无烦恼；来匆匆，去匆匆，饮茶几杯各西东。"

　　今天，我代表所有演出人员以这套《五环茶艺》为大家和奥运带来最真切的祝福，祝您：合家欢乐、心想事成！也祝我们的祖国奥运年更加繁荣昌盛！

Lesson 29
Japanese Tea Ceremony

1. Introduction

Japanese tea ceremony(*Cha-o-yu*) is one of the Japan's most traditional arts. In a simple, but delicate tea house, the host or hostess (*teisyu*) makes fine aromatic tea and entertain their guests. Both the giver and receiver are expected to follow the rules of the ceremony, which have been developed and refined over hundreds of years.

Tea ceremony has its own special aspects. Taste and flavor is the first priority as serving, and drinking a bowl of fine aromatic tea is the core of tea ceremony. Sweets or sometimes meals accompany the ceremony.

Tea ceremony is often called a multiple art. **Exquisite** traditional arts and crafts such as tea-bowls, hanging scrolls, flowers, tea-room and garden are all essential parts of the ceremony. During the ceremony, reflecting the seasons, these **implements** are thoughtfully selected and utilized to show the host or hostess's mind. *O-temae*, the procedure for making tea in the company of guests, is often so elegant that make the first time viewer will doubtlessly be deeply moved.

Besides the external grace, it is important to recognize the internal aspects of the ceremony, partly because tea ceremony comes from the background of Zen Buddhism and **Samurai** manners. Through exchanges of hospitality and appreciation, the host or hostess and guests can share a quiet, heartwarming, peaceful time and reach a state of spiritual enlightenment so called *Wa-Kei-Sei-Jaku* and *Ichigo-ichie*. Since the complexity and forms of the ceremony are so **sophisticated**, some people feel troublesome and keep away from tea ceremony.

Nonetheless, the internal aspects and manners of tea ceremony are typical and provide the foundation of the Japanese life-style. Indeed, tea ceremony has integrated both spiritual and material aspects of Japanese culture, which is often called a symbol of Japan.

2. Tea Room

In *Chaji*, the formal ceremony, small tea-room is used. The entrance for guests, called *nijiri-guchi* is so narrow that you have to crawl to pass through it. This is said to represent that a tea-room is a space to share the same enjoyment regardless of the social classes.

In all types of ceremony, the tea-room is decorated with a hanging scroll and flowers. They often represent the theme of the ceremony, so the guests can appreciate them.

3. Tea Utensils

(1) Hearth (*Ro*) and kettle (*Kama*): They are used in boiling water. The hearth set on tatami-mats from March to October is called *Furo*.

(2) Water container (*Mizusashi*): Water in *mizusashi* is used to wash tea bowl and chasen (bamboo whisk), or poured into Kama to make hot water.

(3) Chashaku: A spoon, often make from bamboo, use for shovel up *Matcha*.

(4) Tea container (*Natsume*): tea container. "Natsume" is named after jujube because of its shape.

(5) Chasen: Bamboo whisk to beat the mixture of *Matcha* and hot water in a tea bowl.

(6) Hishaku: Ladle, often make of bamboo or wood.

(7) Chakin: Moist napkin make by linen or cotton to wipe the bowl.

(8) Kensui: Slop bowl to discard water used for washing.

(9) Guest's Belongings: When attending an ooyose-chakai, some preparations are necessary. It is recommended that you bring afolding fan, sweet cutter and pocket paper.

4. A Closer Look at Tea Ceremony

The formal style of tea ceremony is called *chaji*. It has a number of stages. The guests are served a meal, called *cha-kaiseki*, and then the sweets and finally

two different kinds of tea. One type of tea is rather thin, called *usu-cha*, and the other is stronger and is referred to as *koi-cha*.

The ceremony is conducted in a **solemn** and **ritualistic** manner, costing about 4 hours. *Chaji* is actually unfamiliar to the majority of people, because it is "by invitation" and participants are required to be familiar with the manners and customs of the ceremony.

1) The seating order of guests

Shokyaku, the main and most important guest, is often the eldest or the most experienced guest, since *Shokyaku* can represent all the guests in many scenes. It is recommended to a beginner to take the sheet at the middle of the guests (*Jikyaku*). Thus a beginner can learn how to take sweets or how to drink tea by watching the former.

2) *Sorei* (host/hostess and guests bow together)

The host or hostess appears at the *sado-guchi*, the preparation—room door, and then bows. At the same time, all the guests also bow. Then the host or hostess brings tea-utensils into the tea—room and begins to clean them up.

3) *Hanto* serves the sweets

Hanto, an assistant to the host, comes from the *mizuya* (preparing room) and serve the sweets in the bowl with a pair of chopsticks to *shokyaku*. When there are so many guests, some more bowls are used to distribute. Sometimes the sweets are distributed individually on small plates. The guests also bow the *hanto* before they receive the bowl.

4) Guests take the sweets

Receiving a bowl of sweets from the higher guest, the guest bows to the next, takes a sweet onto the pocket paper with chopsticks, and wipes the tip of chopsticks with a corner of the pocket paper. Then the guest replaces the chopsticks on the bowl, and places it between the next guest and himself/ herself, bows to the next guest (meaning "please"), and then begins to eat. The guest should keep used pocket paper.

5) The host/hostess makes tea

After cleaning up the utensils, the host or hostess begins to make tea. He/she puts two scoops of *matcha*, and pours hot water into the bowl with ladles, then host or hostess stirs the tea into froth up with *chasen* (bamboo whisk), and *hanto* serves it to the guests.

6) The guests partake of tea

The guest bows to the host or hostess, then puts the bowl on the left palm, and raises it slightly with thanks, turning it in a clockwise direction, to show the respect to the host or hostess. And then the guest drinks the tea. After finishing, the guest wipes the lip of the bowl with fingers at the place the guest drank, then wipe the fingers with pocket paper. And turn the bowl counter clockwise, twice, and back to face him/herself. Finally, the guest put the bowl in front of him self/herself and give thanks host or hostess. Later, the *hanto* comes to collect the bowl.

After confirming that all other guests have taken the tea, *syokyaku* says to the host or hostess, "Thank you very much for serving tea. please put the utensils back". Then the host or hostess begins to clean up and puts back the utensils.

New words and expressions
生词和短语

exquisite [ˈekskwIzIt] adj. 精致的
implement [ˈImplIm(ə)nt] n. 工具；器械
sophisticated [səˈfistikitid] adj. 复杂的；久尽世故的
samurai 日 [ˈsæmuraI] [史]（日本封建时代的）武士
solemn [ˈsɔləm] adj. 庄严的；隆重的
ritualistic [ˌritʃuəˈlIstIk] adj. 仪式的；惯例的

Comprehension
理 解

Give answers to the following questions in your own words and complete sentence as far as possible.

1. Why tea ceremony is called a multiple art in Japan?
2. Please describe the internal aspects of the ceremony.
3. Please describe the decorations in Japanese tea rooms.
4. What should a young guest do in a tea ceremony?
5. Please retell the ritualistic manners in a tea ceremony.

Notes on the text 课文注释

Samurai manners：武士道起源于日本镰仓幕府，后经江户时代吸收儒家和佛家的思想而形成。最初倡导忠诚、信义、廉耻、尚武、名誉，是日本文化精神的核心。

Translation 参考译文

日本茶道

1. 简介

日本茶道是日本最传统的艺术之一。在一个简洁却精致的茶室中，男主人或女主人为客人冲泡和敬奉上等的香茶。无论是主人还是客人都要遵循茶道的规矩，而这些规矩是在几百年中逐渐形成并且不断完善的。

茶道有许多有趣的事情，泡茶时要将茶的滋味和香气放在首位进行关注，而品尝一碗香茶则是茶道中的核心内容。茶道中伴有甜点或者主食。

茶道通常被认为是一种综合艺术。高雅的茶道传统艺术和工艺品如茶碗、挂轴、插花、茶室和茶庭都是茶道重要的组成部分。在应季而举行的茶道仪式上，这些用品都是经过精心挑选的，以此充分反映男女主人的意趣。"御点前（日语）"是指在客人的陪同下进行泡茶，这一仪式十分典雅以致使初次参与的客人看后无不深受感动。

尽管茶道外在形式高贵典雅，但是更为重要的是内容，这部分与茶道起源于禅宗思想及武士行为方式有关。通过主人与客人互示友好和敬意，主客双方可以共享这个宁静温馨的时光，并且到达一种精神上的澄明状态，称之为"和、敬、清、寂"和"一期一会"。由于茶道形式及内容极其复杂以致有些人对其避而远之。

尽管如此，茶道的内涵及形式都十分独特，是日本人生活方式的根基。事实上，日本茶道将日本的精神文化与物质文化连为一个整体，通常被认为是日本文化的标志。

2. 茶室

正式的茶道往往在小的茶室中进行。客人进入茶室的入口被称为"躏口"，躏口非常窄，客人必须爬行进入。据说，这代表着在茶室这个空间之内，无论客人的高低贵贱，可以共享同样的乐趣。

在所有的茶事中，茶室都装饰有挂轴和插花。它们通常代表着茶道的主题，以备客人们鉴赏。

3. 茶具

（1）火炉和茶釜：他们是被用来烧水的。3~10月，常被放置在榻榻米垫子上的火炉被称为风炉。

（2）清水罐：清水罐中的水用来清洗茶碗和茶筅（竹制搅拌器），或倒入茶釜中烧开。

（3）茶勺：通常为竹制小勺，用以铲起抹茶。

（4）茶罐（枣形罐）：用以盛放茶叶。由于形状似枣而得名。

（5）茶筅：竹制搅拌器，用以在茶碗中搅匀抹茶与热水。

（6）水勺：长柄勺，通常为竹制品或木制品。

（7）茶巾：由亚麻或棉布做成的湿巾，用以擦拭茶碗。

（8）污水罐：盛放清洗茶叶后的废弃水。

（9）客人应备齐的物品：参加茶会做些准备是必要的。推荐随身带上折扇、餐刀（甜品切割器具）和怀纸。

4. 茶道细节

正式的茶道仪式被称为茶事，分许多阶段。客人首先享用正餐，名为"怀石料理"，然后是甜品，最后是两种不同的茶。一种滋味淡泊，名叫淡茶，另一种滋味浓强，称之为"浓茶"。

茶道仪式庄严而有序地进行，大约持续四个小时。大多数人不熟悉茶事，因为这种奉茶仪式的参加者一般都是特别邀请的，要求熟悉整个仪式的流程及习俗。

（1）宾客就座：主宾是最重要的客人，通常为最年长或德高望重之人，因为主宾可以在许多仪式中代表所有客人。最好是让初学者坐在宾客中间，这样，初学者就可以通过观察前者学习如何吃甜品和如何喝茶了。

（2）行礼（男主人/女主人与宾客互相鞠躬）：男女主人站在备茶室门口向客

人鞠躬。与此同时，所有的宾客对主人回敬。然后，将茶具带到茶室，进行清洁。

（3）助手呈送甜品：主人的助手从水屋（备茶室）出来，负责将盛在碗中的甜品和一双筷子呈给主宾。如果客人太多，可用多个碗分送甜品，有时甜品也可盛放在小碟子中分送。客人在接过盛放甜品的碗前也向助手鞠躬。

（4）宾客品尝甜品：从年长的客人手中接过甜品时，客人需先鞠躬。客人将甜品用筷子放入怀纸中，再用怀纸的一角擦拭筷子的顶端。然后将筷子重新放回碗上，并将碗放在自己与下一个宾客之间，鞠躬（意为"请"）后，方可享用甜品。客人需保留用过的怀纸。

（5）主人沏茶：清洁完茶具后，主人开始沏茶。舀两勺抹茶，并用水勺在碗中倒入热水。然后，主人用茶筅（竹制搅拌器）搅动茶水至起沫，最后由助手呈上。

（6）宾客品茶：客人向主人鞠躬后，将茶碗放在左手掌上，满怀感激之情将茶碗稍稍抬起并顺时针旋转，表示对主人的敬意。然后便可喝茶。喝完茶后，客人用手指在喝茶时触碰的碗沿上擦拭，再用怀纸拭净手指。然后将茶碗逆时针旋转两下，将茶碗后部面对自己。最后将茶碗放在自己的前面，并向主人表示感谢。片刻之后，助手会过来将碗收走。

在确认所有的宾客都已喝过茶后，主宾需对主人说："感谢您的款待，请将茶具收回。"然后，主人便可收拾茶具将其放回原处。

Lesson 30
Etiquette in Tea Ceremony

1. Chinese Tea Ceremonies

The art of drinking and serving tea is an important and special event in China. It's time to relax and enjoy the taste and the smell of tea.

The Chinese tea ceremony is all about the tea. The smells and tastes are the most important parts of the ceremony, so the rules for making and pouring tea are not always the same.

In most areas of China, tea is made in small clay teapots. The pot is **rinsed** with boiling water and then the tea leaves are added to the pot by using chopsticks or a bamboo scoop. The tea leaves are rinsed in hot water in the pot first, and then pour out of the spume, then, hot water is added again to the leaves to make the tea.

The temperature of the water is important. It needs to be hot but not too hot, otherwise it will spoil the taste. The art of preparing and making tea is called Cha Dao.

In less than a minute, the tea maker pours the tea into small narrow cups, but he doesn't pour one cup at a time. Instead, the cups are arranged in a circle and the maker pours the tea one by one.

He fills the cups just over half way. The Chinese believe that the rest part represent friendship and affection.

The maker passes a cup to each guest and invites him or her to smell the tea first. You should thank him by tapping on the table three times with your fingers.

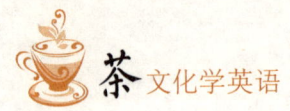

Next, each guest pours their tea into a drinking cup and smells the frangance of the empty narrow cup. Finally they drink the tea.

It is the most polite way to empty the cup in three swallows.

2. Japanese Tea Ceremonies

Tea is one of the most popular drinks in Japan and a tea ceremony is a very important and special event. It's time to relax and enjoy the loveliness in it. There are two types of tea ceremony-the Chanoyu, sometimes called the Matcha, and the Sencha. The word 'chanoyu' means 'hot water for tea'.

The Chanoyu ceremony takes place in a wooden or bamboo teahouse called a Chashitsu. The room is usually for four guests. The garden around the teahouse is very simple with lots of green plants rather than flowers, a small rock garden, and a stream. A path winds its way through the garden leading to the teahouse. If you are invited to a Chanoyu tea ceremony, there are certain rules to follow.

First you must wait at the entrance to the garden until you are calm and ready to enter. The Teishu or tea master welcomes you when you are in the garden. He or she brings fresh water for you to drink and to wash your hands. Now you follow the Teishu along the path to the teahouse.

Inside the teahouse, the Teishu makes the tea using **powdered** green tea called 'matcha'. The tea is mixed with boiled water using a bamboo **whisk** and served in small bowls.

Guests sit on the floor around a low table. When the Teishu gives you your tea, bow, take your bowl with your left hand, and then hold it with your right hand. Place the bowl in front of you and turn it to the right so that you don't drink from the side that was facing you. Usually the Teishu gives you a sweet cake or a mochi to eat because the tea is bitter.

When you finish your tea, turn the bowl to the left and place it on the table in front of you, you must drink it all! You turn the bowl to show the Teishu respect: it means that the edge of the cup he gave you was the best, but you are not good enough to drink from that side. Sometimes the guests share one bowl that they pass around.

The Sencha ceremony is more relaxing than the Chanoyu ceremony. The rules for serving the tea are traditional, but the occasion is more easy-going for the tea drinkers.

Most people in Japan don't have their own teahouse, but they often join a "tea club" where they go every week to take part in the tea ceremony.

3. Korean Tea Ceremonies

Tea is one of the most popular drinks in Korea. Tea ceremonies were first held in Korea more than a thousand years ago.

They are still recognized today as special occasions by Buddhist monks and ordinary people.

The ceremonies in Korea are similar to those held in Japan and China, but they are not as formal as the ceremonies in Japan. Korean Buddhists monks spend many hours meditating and thinking about their religion and their life. They use the tea ceremony to help them **meditate**.

Ordinary people also feel that tea ceremonies are spiritual because they are closely associated with their religion. "Tea," they say, "is a healthy, enjoyable and **stimulating** drink, full of good qualities. It reduces loneliness and calms your heart; it is a comfort in everyday life".

There are tea rooms in most cities and even small towns in Korea where friends can gather and drink tea together.

Many Koreans today still have tea ceremonies for important occasions including birthdays and anniversaries.

4. Russian Tea Ceremonies

Tea is the most favorable drink in Russia. It is made and served in teapots or samovars—a Russian tea kettle.

In some areas they use three teapots that sit on the top of each other to keep the tea warm. Often the teapots are decorated with pictures from Russian folk stories and sometimes, they are made in the shape of something so that they look like a person or an animal.

Three teapots are used when you want to make two different kinds of tea at the same time.

The middle pot usually holds strong black tea, the smallest pot on the top holds herbal or mint tea, and the large pot on the bottom holds hot water. The teas can be mixed with each other and **diluted** with hot water as you pour out each cup. Everyone can mix the type of tea they like.

People drink tea by using cups, but more often Russians use a podstakanniki

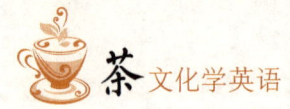

—a special glass in a silver holder.

Russian people usually drink tea after meals rather than with a meal, but when tea is made by using a samovar, it means it is ready to be used all day long. A samovar is shaped like an urn and there is a special place for a small teapot to sit on the top.

Water is heated in the samovar and a strong dark tea is made using lots of tea leaves in the teapot on top. The strong tea is called zavarka. The tea is so strong that it has to be diluted with water from the samovar before you can drink it.

You mix a drop of tea with hot water taken from the tap or spout on the front of the samovar. As the water is used, you need to refill the samovar and every few hours you have to make a fresh pot of black tea.

Samovars are usually made from metal. Some samovars are small and only hold about three litres of water but some can hold up to 30 litres. You can see them at home, in offices and in restaurants.

New words and expressions
生词和短语

rinse [rɪns] v. 冲洗
powdered [ˈpaʊdəd] adj. 变成粉末的；涂粉的
whisk [wɪsk] n. 搅拌器
meditate [ˈmedɪteɪt] v. 考虑；计划
stimulating [ˈstɪmjuleɪtɪŋ] adj. 刺激的
dilute [daɪˈl(j)uːt] v. 稀释

Comprehension
理 解

Give answers to the following questions in your own words and complete sentences as far as possible.

1. In China, what must the guests do when they receive the tea cup in Cha Dao?

2. In Japan, what does it mean by turning the bowl to the Teishu after finishing your tea?

3. According to the passage, why tea and tea ceremony so popular to the or-

dinary people in Korea?

4. Why are there 3 different kettles during the process of making tea in Russia?

5. What can you get from the difference of tea ceremonies between the Eastern and Western countries?

茶 礼

1. 中国茶艺

在中国，品茶和奉茶是一项重要而特殊的仪式。现在，我们可以放松一下，尽情享受茶叶诱人的味道和清新的香气。

中国茶道主要关注茶叶本身。茶叶的香气与味道是仪式上最重要的组成部分，因此沏茶与倒茶便显得不是那么重要。

在中国的大部分地区，人们用陶土制成的茶壶沏茶。先用沸水烫壶，再用筷子或竹勺将茶叶放入壶中，用热水洗茶后，再用热水冲泡。

在这一过程中，水温十分重要。茶叶需用热水冲泡，但水温过高又会破坏茶叶的味道。因而，备茶和沏茶堪称一门艺术，被称为茶道。

沏茶者利用不到一分钟的时间将茶水倒入闻香杯中，但并不是一次性将它倒满，而是将茶盏围成一个圈，然后依次倒入。

沏茶者只将茶水倒入七分满，因为中国人认为剩余的茶盏空间代表着友谊与爱慕。

沏茶者将闻香杯依次递给客人，并首先邀请他们闻茶。此时，客人应当用手指叩桌三下表示感谢。接下来，客人将茶水倒入自己的品茗杯中并闻嗅茶叶余留在闻香杯中的香气。

在饮茶中，最礼貌的做法是分三口喝完茶水。

2. 日本茶道

在日本，茶叶是最流行的饮料之一，品茶仪式也是一项十分重要而特殊的活动。现在，是时候放松一下来欣赏你身边这个简单而不乏可爱的仪式了。日本有两种茶叙仪式，一种为茶汤，有时亦被称为抹茶，另一种则为煎茶。"cha-

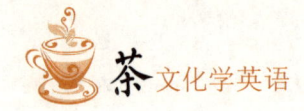

noyu"意为沏茶用的热水。

茶汤仪式一般在木制或竹制的茶室中举行，房间通常可容纳四名客人。茶室周围的花园十分简单，种植着许多绿色植物，但没有花卉，一个小型奇石园中，小溪潺潺流过。一条蜿蜒的小路穿过花园通向茶室。如果你要去参加茶之汤茶叙仪式，就必须遵守一些规则。

在进入茶室前，要先静下心来，除去一切凡尘杂念，做好进入的准备。进入花园后，主人会提供清水供你漱口和洗手，以此表示对你的欢迎。之后便可跟随主人沿着小路进入茶室。

在茶室中，主人用抹茶（绿色粉末状）做茶叶，混入开水后，用竹签搅拌，再倒入茶碗中。

客人围坐在低矮的茶桌旁。当主人将茶递给你时，你应该先鞠躬，用左手接过茶碗，然后用右手托住。再将茶碗置于你的正前方，手托着将茶碗置于身体右侧，从而使自己喝茶的时候不会正面冲着主人。由于茶水稍苦，主人通常也会提供一些蛋糕或糯米团。

喝完茶水后，将茶碗向左旋转，放在茶桌上，注意要把茶水喝得一干二净。旋转茶碗是为了表示对主人的尊敬：它意味着主人交给你的那一侧茶碗是最尊贵的，而你自己却不够资格来从那一侧饮茶。有时，客人们会每人一口轮流品饮一碗茶。

相对于茶汤仪式，煎茶仪式的奉茶规则虽然传统，但对饮者来说，这个场合却能让人轻松许多。

在日本，大部分人都没有属于自己的茶室，但他们通常会加入品茶俱乐部，每周参加奉茶仪式。

3. 韩国茶礼

茶是韩国最流行的饮品之一。韩国最早的奉茶仪式始于一千多年前。

现如今，佛教人士及普通大众仍将奉茶仪式视为极为特殊的活动。

韩国的奉茶仪式与日本和中国的奉茶仪式相似，但却不及日本的正式。韩国的佛教人士花费大量的时间思考宗教与人生，而奉茶仪式可以为他们提供进行冥想的条件。

普通大众也认为奉茶仪式活动场所是与宗教事务紧密相关的精神圣地。他们说："茶具有多项品质，可以使人身体健康，保持愉悦的心情，并能使人精神振奋。此外，还可以减少孤独感，让人心情平静；可以说，茶是每日生活的必备品。"

韩国大部分的城市及小镇都有茶馆，在这里，朋友们可以相聚饮茶。

如今，许多韩国人仍在重要的场合举行奉茶仪式，包括特殊的生日聚会或纪念日。

4. 俄罗斯的茶叙仪式

茶或许算是俄罗斯最受欢迎的饮品了。通常人们用普通茶壶或专门的俄式茶壶冲泡茶叶。

在部分地区，人们将三个茶壶摞在一起以保持水温。通常情况下，茶壶装饰有俄罗斯民间故事的插图，有时将三个茶壶叠放在一起时，其形状可以形成一个人物造型或动物造型。

要同时沏出两种不同种类的茶水需要三个茶壶。中间的茶壶通常盛放浓红茶，顶上最小的盛放药草茶和薄荷茶，底下最大的壶则盛放热水。茶水倒出时，可以将其互相混合，并用热水稀释。每个人可以根据自己的喜好进行调配。

人们通常用茶杯喝茶，但俄罗斯人经常使用的是一种放在银制杯托中的玻璃杯。

在俄罗斯，人们通常在饭后而不是餐中饮茶，但如果用俄式大茶壶沏茶以供一天的饮用，则可另当别论。俄式大茶壶形似茶瓮，其顶端可放置小茶壶。俄式大茶壶用来加温，而顶端的小茶壶则用来泡浓茶，此茶名为扎瓦卡。在饮用之前，需将其用大茶壶中的热水稀释以防过于浓烈。将茶水与从大茶壶中取出的热水融合。待其中的热水用尽后需将其重新注满，并且每隔几小时就需重新冲泡一壶浓茶。

俄式茶壶大多用金属制成。有些俄式茶壶比较小，只能盛装三升水，但有些则能盛下三十多升。俄式大茶壶随处可见。

Lesson 31
Spirit of Tea

Chinese nation has formed her special tea spirit after thousands of years of accumulation and development. Chinese people psooess the character of nature and modest which is the same with drinking tea. Unlike Japanese, Chinese are not strict with ceremonious and religious colors. However, Chinese **tea ceremony** does have its unique characters, is different from the daily taste of tea. The highest state of drinking tea in China is a process in which the philosophy, ethnics, morality are involved and we can cultivate ourselves, mold our characters, think about the life, practice meditation and get the psychological enjoyment and refreshment in personality.

The spirit of tea ceremony is various, among which the most representative and authoritative one is brought forward by Lin Zhi, a well-known "**aficionado** of Wuyi Mountain tea". In his theory, harmony ("He" in Chinese), peace ("Jing" in Chinese), joy ("Yi" in Chinese) and authenticity ("Zhen" in Chinese) represent the core of Chinese tea spirit.

1. Harmony: the Core and the Soul of Philosophy of Chinese Tea Ceremony

In China, the notion of harmony is shared by Confucianism, Buddhism and Daoism as the philosophical ideal. The harmony that the tea ceremony seeks originates from *The Book of Changes*, with Chinese title "Zhouyi". In that book, it is stressed that everything in the world is composed of Yin and Yang, the two opposite principles in nature. When Yin and Yang are balanced, everything all around the world goes well. Further, in the **masterpiece** *The Classic of Tea*, Lu Yu pointed out that the stove which is casted by steel belongs to "gold"; when it is placed on the ground, another character "earth" appears; then coal in the stove belongs to "wood" and the burning process of coal belongs to "fire"; and finally the tea soup stewed belongs to "water". The process of stewing tea is the mutual promotion and restraint between the five elements, through which the harmonious integrity is gained. It shows that the theory of five elements ("Wuxing theory" in Chinese) together with others and builds up the foundation of the philosophy for tea ceremony.

Confucianism extracted the *Golden Mean* from the philosophy of harmony. In the eye of Confucians, harmony means to be moderate and proper, that is to say, harmony means everything is well positioned. The explanation of Confucianism reveals itself best in the tea-related activities. The beauty of mean can be expressed in various ways: in the process of making tea, four kinds of taste including sour, sweet, bitter and astringent should reach a compromise, the speed of making tea and the quantity of tea should be moderate; in entertaining the guests, serving the tea to the distinguished and the seniors, and strong tea represents strong hospitality, which are the civil rituals; in tasting tea, one can know its fragrance only after tasting of high-quality tea and then praise it in the mind.

2. Peace: Indispensable in Practicing the Tea Ceremony

Chinese tea ceremony is a way of cultivating and pursuing the real self. Chinese ceremony creates a kind of muted atmosphere and a clear mind from the ceremonious process. When the faint scent of tea infiltrates into every corner of our hearts and souls, our souls will be transparent in the muteness, your spirit will be elevated, and people will be integral to the nature and reach the unity of the universe and mankind.

3. Joy: the Feeling of soul in the Process of the Practices of Ceremony

Joy is pleasure and happiness. Chinese tea ceremony is both suitable with the refined and the daily life, which goes without concrete and fixed rituals. Chinese tea ceremony **highlights** the arbitrary state of Daoism. Historically, the nobilities stressed the rarity of tea which tended to show off their authorities and wealth and became affiliated to the grace. Elites and artists emphasized the charm and aroma of Chinese tea ceremony, expressed their emotions in their artistic works and made friends with each other. Buddhism highlights the function of tea, whose intention is to preserve their health and lengthen their life. The common people prefer the taste of the tea, which can get rid of the smell of seafood and greasy; relieve the irritable and thirst and then enjoy the life. Whichever group we belong to, we can get the physiological pleasure and psychological suitableness from the tea-related activities. The character of joy makes tea welcomed by a wide large number of people.

4. Authenticity: What Chinese Tea Ceremony Ultimately Seeks

Authenticity not only includes the genuine quality, the genuine smell and taste; it also in cludes the best environment, the calligraphy and the paintings should be the authentic works of the celebrities; what's more the appliances for use also should be the genuine bamboo, the genuine wood, the genuine pottery and the genuine ceramics. More important, the hospitality towards the guests should be genuine, which includes the real emotion and sincerity and the free mind. Every process of tea-related activity should be genuine.

There are three levels for genuine Chinese tea ceremony, in which the first level is the genuine way to do the things, It means to seek the real feeling of genuine from the activities of tea, so achieve the goal of cultivating and sensing the life; the second level is the genuine affection, it means to prompt the development of the bonds among tea friends, so accomplish the state of the real confidentiality; the third level is the genuine nature, it means to relax oneself.

Reading Material
阅读材料

The Significance of the Spirit of Tea

The modern society depends on high-tech and information to produce more social wealth, which can make an ever-prosperous life. During their process of industrialization, some countries in East Asia absorbed the advanced technology and expertise, but the dispirited cultural value and customs eroded the society and resulted in moral crisis and money worship and extremism. The experience of social development testify that modernization should not be the sole objective, the modern society also need the suitable spiritual civilization, so we need to utilize the spiritual resources in traditional culture. The cultural and reasonable factors contained by tea culture in history have played and are still playing the positive roles in modern society. Tea culture is the elegant culture which the celebrities are keen in participation. Besides, tea culture also belongs to all walks of people.

1. The spirit of tea is morality-centered, which emphasizes on the collective value of people and opposes to selfishess, and claims that friendship is more important than interests, stresses the communication between people and advocates the respect towards the people and the cultivation of moralities, all of which will help to balance the minds and solve the confusions of modern generation and raise the literacy level for all.

2. The spirit of tea can help us tackle the challenges of lives. Under the circumstances of severe social and marketing competition, we suffer high pressure facing the nervous daily work, dinners and complicated relationship in work. With the involvement of tea culture, we can relax the spirits and the bodies.

3. The culture of tea has played an important role in raising the level of people's lives and prospering the cultural lives. The culture of tea owns some characters of knowledge, interest and benefit, which is a kind of pleasure of beauty.

4. The culture of tea is beneficial to the construction of civil society. In today's China, the tide of merchandises floods into the society and we are all more desirable towards the material goods, and the ever-faster life pace and severe competition, which make modern people unbalanced in minds and exposed to a serious relationship. The culture of tea is the quiet and healthy one which can ease the tightened soul and balance the slanted minds. The spirit of tea ceremony which takes harmony as center, advocating the principle of peaceful lifestyle which treats each other politely and devotes to others and makes a better mutual understanding to establish a new type of relationship which is favorable to all of us.

5. The culture of tea promotes the society more open and fosters the cultural communication. The frequent communication of tea culture all over the world makes the tea beyond the boundary and then become the spiritual wealth shared by all.

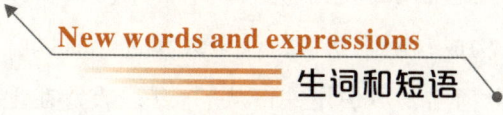

New words and expressions
生词和短语

tea ceremony 茶道

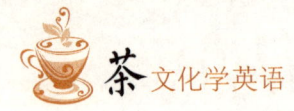

highlight [ˈhaɪlaɪt] v. 强调；以……为重点
aficionado [əˌfɪʃəˈnɑːdəʊ] n. 爱好者
masterpiece [ˈmɑːstəpiːs] n. 名作；杰作

Comprehension 理解

Give answers to the following questions in your own words and complete sentences as far as possible.

1. Illustrate the four characters of the spirit of tea ceremony.
2. What is the harmony in Chinese philosophy?
3. How to get authenticity in tea ceremony?
4. List out the social functions of tea.
5. Illustrate the psychological functions of tea.

Translation 参考译文

茶之精神

几千年的积淀与发展使中华民族形成了符合自己国民特性的茶文化精神。中国人的民族特性是崇尚自然，朴实谦和，不重形式。饮茶也是这样，不像日本茶道具有严格的仪式和浓厚的宗教色彩。但茶道毕竟不同于一般的饮茶，中国饮茶的最高境界——茶道，指在茶事活动中融入哲理、伦理、道德，通过品茗来修身养性、陶冶情操、品味人生、参禅悟道，达到精神上的享受和人格上的洗礼。

中国茶道精神有很多，但比较权威的是由"武夷山茶痴"林治先生提出的"和、静、怡、真"，人们把它作为中国茶道四谛。

1. "和"是中国茶道哲学思想的核心，是茶道的灵魂

"和"是儒、佛、道三教共同的哲学理念。茶道追求的"和"源于《周易》，《周易》强调，世间万物皆由阴阳两要素构成，阴阳协调，保全大和之元气以普利万物才是人间真道。陆羽在《茶经》中指出，风炉用铁铸从"金"；放置在地上从"土"；炉中烧的木炭从"木"；木炭燃烧从"火"；风炉上煮的茶汤从

"水"。煮茶的过程就是金、木、水、火、土五行相生相克并达到和谐统一的过程。可见五行调和等理念是茶道哲学的基础。

儒家从"和"的哲学理念中推出"中庸之道"的中和思想。在儒家眼里和是中，和是度，和是宜，和是当，和是一切恰到好处。儒家对和的诠释，在茶事活动中表现得淋漓尽致。在泡茶时，表现为"酸甜苦涩调太和，掌握迟速量适中"的中庸之美，在待客时表现为"奉茶为礼尊长者，备茶浓意表浓情"的明礼之伦。在饮茶过程中表现为"饮罢佳茗方知深，赞叹此乃草中英"的谦和之理。

2. "静"是中国茶道修习的不二法门

中国茶道是修身养性，追寻自我之道。中国茶道正是通过茶道创造一种宁静的氛围和一个空灵的心境，当茶的清香静静地浸润你的心田和肺腑的每一个角落的时候，你的心灵便在虚静中显得空明，你的精神便在虚静中升华净化，你将在虚静中与大自然融涵玄会，达到"天人合一"的境界。

3. "怡"是中国茶道修习实践中的心灵感受

"怡"者，和悦、愉快之道。中国茶道是雅俗共赏之道，它体现于平时的日常生活之中，它不讲形式，不拘一格。突出体现了道家"自恣以适己"的随意性。历史上王公贵族讲茶道，他们重在"茶之珍"，意在炫耀权势，夸示富贵，附庸风雅。文人学士讲茶道重在"茶之韵"，托物寄怀，激扬文思，交朋结友。佛家讲茶道重在"茶之功"，意在品茗养生，报生尽年，羽化成仙。普通老百姓讲茶道重在"茶之味"，意在去腥除腻，涤烦解渴，享受人生。无论什么人都可以在茶事活动中取得生理上的快感和精神上的畅适。中国茶道的这种怡悦性，使得它有极广泛的群众基础。

4. "真"是中国茶道的终极追求

中国茶道所讲究的"真"，不仅包括茶应是真茶、真香、真味；环境最好是真山真水；挂的字画最好是名家名人的真迹；用的器具最好是真竹、真木、真陶、真瓷，还包含了对人要真心；敬客要真情；说话要真诚；心境要真闲。茶事活动的每一个环节都要求真。

中国茶道追求的"真"有三重含义：追求道之真，即通过茶事活动追求"道"的真切体悟，达到修身养性，品味人生之目的。追求情之真，即通过品茗诉怀，使茶友之间的真情得以发展，达到茶人之间互见真心的境界。追求性之

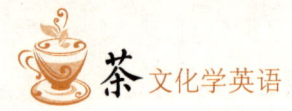 文化学英语

真，即在品茗过程中，真正放松自己。

阅读材料

茶道精神的作用

现代社会依靠高科技和信息，创造的物质财富将越来越多，生活也将更加富裕。东亚一些国家在推行工业化过程中，在吸收西方的优秀科技和工艺技术的同时，西方颓废的文化价值观、风俗习惯也侵蚀到社会，随之产生道德危机，拜金主义和极端个人主义等盛行。社会发展的经验表明，现代化不是唯一目标，现代化社会需要与之相适应的精神文明，需要发掘优秀传统文化的精神资源。茶文化所具有的历史性、时代性及其他合理因素，在现代社会中正在发挥积极作用。茶文化是高雅文化，社会名流和知名人士乐意参加。茶文化也是大众文化，民众广为参与。茶文化覆盖全民，影响到整个社会，表现在以下几个方面。

1. 茶文化以德为中心，重视人的群体价值，倡导无私奉献，反对见利忘义和唯利是图。主张义重于利，注重协调人与人之间的相互关系，提倡对人尊敬，重视修身养德，有利于人的心态平衡，解决现代人的精神困惑，提高人的文化素质。

2. 茶文化是应对人生挑战的益友。在激烈的社会竞争、市场竞争下，紧张的工作、应酬，复杂的人际关系给人们带来了巨大的压力。学习茶文化，可以使精神和身心放松一番，以应对人生的挑战。

3. 提高人们的生活质量，丰富人们的文化生活。茶文化具有知识性、趣味性和康乐性，是一种美的享受。

4. 有利于社会文明建设。在当今的现实生活中，商品大潮汹涌、物欲膨胀、生活节奏加快、竞争激烈导致人心浮躁、心理易于失衡、人际关系趋于紧张。而茶文化是雅静、健康的文化，它能使人们绷紧的心灵之弦得以放松，倾斜的心理得以平衡。以"和"为核心的茶道精神，提倡和诚处世、以礼待人、对人多奉献一点爱心和理解的平和心态，倡导建立和睦相处、相互尊重、互相关心的新型人际关系。

5. 推进国际文化交流。国际茶文化的频繁交流使茶文化成为人类文明的共同精神财富。

参考文献

[1] C. R. Harler. The Culture and Marketing of Tea [M]. London: Oxford University Press, 1964.

[2] J. L. Dun. ed. The Essence of Chinese Civilization [M]. New York: Van Nostrand, 1967.

[3] John C. Evans. Tea in China [M]. New York: Greenwood Press, 1992.

[4] Kakuzo Okakura. The Book of Tea [M]. Tokyo: Kenkyusha, 2008.

[5] Lao She. Teahouse [M]. Translated by John Howard—Gibbon. Beijing: Foreign Languages Press, 1980.

[6] Lin Yutang. The Importance of Living [M]. New York: John Day Company, 1937.

[7] Lu Yu. The Classic of Tea [M]. Translated by Francis Ross Carpenter. Boston: Little, Brown and Company, 1974.

[8] Robert Fortune. A Journey to the Tea Countries of China [M]. London: John Murray, 1852.

[9] Tang Xianzu. Peony Pavilion (Mudan Ting) [M]. Translated by Cyril Birch. Bloomington: Indiana University Press, 1980.

[10] Tei Yamanishi. Food Reviews International: Special Issue on Tea. 1995, 11 (3).

[11] Thomas Eden. ed. Tea [M]. London: Longman, 1976.

[12] Victor R. Mair & Erling Hoh. The True History of Tea [M]. London: Thames & Hudson Ltd., 2009.

[13] Wang Ling. Chinese Tea Culture [M]. Beijing: Foreign Languages Press, 2000.

[14] Wendy Rasmussen, Ric Rhinehart. Tea Basic: A Quick and Easy Guide. John Wiley & Sons, Inc. 1999.

[15] William H. Ukers. The Romance of Tea [M]. New York: The Tea and Coffee Trade Journal Co., 1936.

[16] William Watson. Ancient China [M]. London: British Broadcasting Company, 1974.

后　记

《茶文化学英语》自 2010 年春季开始搜集资料,迄今为止历时 6 年,现终将付梓印刷,即将与读者见面,内心有激动也有惶恐,既期待这本中英文对照版教材能够丰富和完善我国高校茶学专业的课程建设和教材建设,也恐自己学有不逮,不能很好地完成这项使命。无论如何,本次茶学专业教师和英语系教师通力合作,共同编写这本中英文对照版《茶文化学英语》教材至少是个很好的尝试,两位主编各自都获得了宝贵的合作经验,并对各自的学科领域有了更好的理解和认识。在编辑本教材时,两位主编分工明确,为保证专业知识的准确性,有关茶科学的章节均由第一主编直接编写英文资料,再由第二主编翻译为中文,其余人文知识类课文则先由第一主编写中文资料,再由第二主编翻译为英文。所有课文的词汇、注释和阅读理解环节的问题均由第二主编先进行设定,然后交由第一主编进行审定,最后,两位主编一起对各章节的安排和内容进行通读和修订,确保各章节之间内容上的连贯性和科学性。

在本书的编写过程中,山东农业大学茶学系的向勤锃、黄晓琴老师搜集了部分英文素材,外国语学院外国语言学与应用语言学方向的硕士研究生汤小丽、赵彩彩、荆延刚、丁群和朱迪艳等同学参与了部分翻译、注释、词汇标注和校对工作,在此一并致谢。

最后,本书要特别感谢世界图书出版西安有限公司的相关领导及责任编辑,他们高度敬业的态度和严谨踏实的专业精神最终保证了本书的顺利问世。希望本书的出版能为广大茶文化爱好者和研究者以及英语学习者提供一份通俗易懂的资料。

张丽霞　朱法荣
2015 年 9 月